September 10, 2006
Eve of Chai Elul, 5766

Thank you so much for your benevolent and generous support and valiant efforts on behalf of Chabad – Gan Israel's Scholarship Programs,

This evening, dedicated to the living legacy of The Lubavitcher Rebbe, we commemorate the auspicious day of Chai Elul — the eighteenth day of the month of Elul — the birthday of the saintly Baal Shem Tov as well as the birthday of the Alter Rebbe, the founder of Chabad Chassidus.

We proudly present you with a wonderful book, entitled "The Great Mission: The Life and Story of Rabbi Yisrael Baal Shem Tov", a collection of stories of Rabbi Yisrael Baal Shem Tov. His Torah teachings, life lessons and documented accounts of the wonders and miracles which he performed, make The Great Mission more than a biography, but a helpful companion to all those wishing to understand the roots of Chasidic philosophy.

May the great merits of your benevolence stand you and your loved ones in good stead for many years to come. In the name of all of the poor and under-privileged children you have so graciously assisted, we humbly thank you.

Please accept our prayerful wishes to you and to all of your loved ones for a Ksiva Va'Chasima Tova, a happy and a healthy New Year – and may we merit to hear only good tidings from Israel and indeed the world over, culminating with the coming of Moshiach Tzidkeinu, Amen.

On behalf of all the Rabbis and Staff, we remain,

Rabbi Joshua B. Gordon
Rabbi Mordechai Einbinder

THE GREAT MISSION

The life and story of
RABBI YISRAEL BAAL SHEM TOV

Compiled by
Rabbi Eli Friedman

Translated by
Rabbi Elchonon Lesches

KEHOT PUBLICATION SOCIETY
770 Eastern Parkway / Brooklyn, NY 11213

THE GREAT MISSION
THE LIFE & STORY OF
RABBI YISRAEL BAAL SHEM TOV

Published and Copyrighted © 2004
Revised Edition 2005
by
KEHOT PUBLICATION SOCIETY
770 Eastern Parkway • Brooklyn, New York 11213
(718) 774-4000 • FAX (718) 774-2718

Order Department:
291 Kingston Avenue • Brooklyn, New York 11213
(718) 778-0226 • FAX (718) 778-4148
www.kehotonline.com

ISBN 0-8266-0681-4

Manufactured in the United States of America

Contents

CONTENTS

Translator's Foreword

IT WAS A DISMAL POINT in Jewish history. The infamous years of *tach v'tat* (1648-1649) had wrought havoc and despair among East European Jewry. Chmielnicki and his horde of bloodthirsty Cossacks brought widespread decimation to every Jewish community. Pillage, murder and unspeakable torture ravaged the land as the Cossacks drenched the very soil with Jewish blood.

Things were hardly better on the spiritual plane. Due to harsh economic conditions, scores of working Jews remained unlettered, many even unable to mouth the simplest texts. The learned shunned the ignorant and condemned their illiteracy. In the eyes of the scholarly world, this mass of unlearned Jewry remained an eternal embarrassment, an aberration to Torah-true life.

And then, as collective Jewry teetered on the verge of physical and spiritual collapse, G-d forbid, a unique individual by the name of Rabbi Yisrael Baal Shem Tov emerged to lead thousands, energizing them anew in their service of the Creator. He revealed the innate spiritual worth of every soul—regardless of background or stature—and declared G-d's inestimable love for each and every individual Jew. Similarly, he highlighted the immense spiritual gain achieved through the sincere prayers and *Tehillim* uttered by these unlearned folk. Thus, the light of spirituality now shone for simple Jews as well.

The Baal Shem Tov imbued the mitzvah of *Ahavat Yisrael* with fresh meaning, teaching that all Jews deserve the unconditional love of their brethren—thereby forever changing the universal perception of this mitzvah. Due to his influence, this cornerstone of Jewish life was extended to even total strangers and unlearned folk.

Another fundamental teaching centered on Divine Providence—G-d's constant and specific supervision over every detail of His handiwork, which, the Baal Shem Tov taught, pertains to every element of Creation. This cardinal principle enjoined man to learn something from every occurrence in this world, to infer a lesson with practical application in the daily service of G-d.

These and his many other teachings restored the spirits of a flagging nation, injecting enthusiasm and life into his thousands of followers. The Baal Shem Tov lightened man's continuous struggle, empowering him to reveal the inherent qualities needed to overcome spiritual hindrances. Indeed, the enduring light of the Baal Shem Tov continues to illuminate our world.

Rabbi Eli Friedman of Safed, Israel, has done the monumental work of sifting and sorting through a veritable mountain of talks and letters to find, within the teachings of Chabad Chasidus, material pertaining to the Baal Shem Tov. It is an honor to translate these awe-inspiring stories, words that seem to possess a power of their own to move and effect inner change. Much like opening the case of a brilliant diamond, this book reveals to the English-speaking audience the dazzling radiance created by the Baal Shem Tov and his teachings, as recorded by the leaders of Chabad.

Just as a writer cannot create without writing tools, a book cannot be formed without a host of helping hands: First and foremost, I humbly express my gratitude to Hashem for the opportunity to present this collection of stories. I also thank my wife, Gitty, for making this all possible through her support and encouragement. Deep acknowledgment and thanks are due to

the capable staff at Kehot Publication Society, headed by Rabbi
Yosef B. Friedman, for the initiative in making this publication
possible and giving the manuscript its final polish.

It was the Baal Shem Tov who heard Moshiach, the long-
awaited Redeemer, proclaim that the Redemption depended on
disseminating the teachings of Chasidus. Thus, our energies
remain devoted to completing this vital mission, as entrusted to
us by the Baal Shem Tov. It is hoped that the inspiring Chasidic
ideals found within this book serve as a stepping stone in the
path leading to the much-awaited time when the "Knowledge of
Divinity will fill the earth as waters cover the sea."

Rabbi Elchonon Lesches

10 Kislev 5765

EDITOR'S NOTE: The translation of the story entitled *The Great
Mission* has been adapted from the English edition of *Likkutei
Dibburim* vol. 4, pp. 97-121, trans. Uri Kaploun (Kehot, 1997).

A LIFE OF RADIANCE

Blessed Beginnings

Few could emulate the extraordinary measure of hospitality practiced by Rabbi Eliezer and his wife Sarah, an elderly couple who lived in the small village of Okup, nestled high among the Carpathian Mountains. Greatly learned and exceedingly righteous, Rabbi Eliezer exerted great effort in welcoming any guest who entered his home. He and his wife spent most of their meager income on generous acts of hospitality, and it was not unusual for the couple to host twenty, thirty guests around their Shabbat table. Though well advanced in years, the pious couple was not blessed with offspring, and they grieved silently, resigned to their childless lot.

One week, as the couple and their guests concluded the Shabbat meal, they suddenly heard a loud pounding at the door. A hush descended on the room as the guests looked at Rabbi Eliezer in bewilderment. "Who could that be?" they mused aloud. "Could someone have arrived on Shabbat, G-d forbid?"

Opening the door, Rabbi Eliezer was startled to see a stranger standing wearily on his doorstep. "Good Shabbat, my dear fellow Jew," said Rabbi Eliezer warmly, ignoring the protesting thoughts that rushed through his mind. "Have you eaten?"

"Not yet," responded the stranger tersely.

"Please come in," offered Rabbi Eliezer. "I have everything you need for the Shabbat meal."

Placing a goblet of wine before the stranger, Rabbi Eliezer hurried into the kitchen and returned bearing heaping platters of food, setting out a lavish meal as his guests looked on in horror. "Have you ever seen such a thing?" they whispered amongst themselves. "That fellow has undoubtedly desecrated the holy Shabbat. By arriving in our village on this sacred day, he clearly defied the Biblical prohibition of walking long distances beyond city limits. Yet, just look how respectfully Rabbi Eliezer treats him—as though this was a good Jew, befitting of such hospitality!"

"This is intolerable!" hissed one of the guests loudly. "Our Sages would be severely displeased to see Rabbi Eliezer's conduct. Our Patriarch Abraham was an incomparable host, but the Midrash (*Bereshit Rabbah* 49:4) relates that whenever his guests finished eating, Abraham prodded them to thank G-d for the meal. Whoever dared refuse was pressured to comply until, in the end, they finally conceded. Yet, in walks a desecrator of the Shabbat, and Rabbi Eliezer treats him with the greatest marks of respect! You could think he was serving royalty!"

These caustic comments pierced the gentle soul of Rabbi Eliezer. Excusing himself, he ran into a nearby room and burst into a fit of weeping. He, too, was shocked to see a wanderer enter his home on the holy Shabbat day. Doubt and confusion swirled in his heart, but Rabbi Eliezer restrained his feelings fiercely. "What's wrong with you, Eliezer?" he berated himself. "What kind of a host leaves his guest sitting alone at the table? Imagine how embarrassed he must feel!"

Returning to the dining room, Rabbi Eliezer served his guest with even more enthusiasm, mentally blocking out the glares of the other guests. That afternoon he served the newcomer a hearty *Seudah Shlishit* meal and, at the conclusion of Shabbat, Rabbi Eliezer hurried to prepare a comfortable bed for his guest. "I have a rule that whoever eats here on Shabbat must sleep over," he said to the newcomer. "I also insist on keeping my guests through Sunday morning; you are free to leave after midday."

The following afternoon, after enjoying a filling meal, the stranger rose to leave. Rabbi Eliezer accompanied him out of the house and into the street, escorting him for a small distance before bidding farewell. Just then the stranger turned to him, a strange fire shining in his eyes. "I am Elijah the Prophet," he revealed. "G-d sent me to test you on the Shabbat day, and you passed admirably. And now, I have good tidings to relay: It has been decreed in Heaven that, in merit of your unquestioning hospitality, you shall be blessed with a son!"

Rabbi Eliezer stood mutely, hardly believing his ears. His surroundings seemed to fade into oblivion as the stranger's words resonated through his being. "When your son turns two-and-a-half," continued the stranger, "tell him the following words: *'Fear no creature! Fear only G-d, the G-d of heaven and earth!'*"

Having concluded his mission, the stranger swiftly strode down the street and was soon hidden from sight. Both shaken and elated, Rabbi Eliezer returned home and related the incredible tidings to his wife. Indeed, the very next year, on the eighteenth day of Elul 5458 (1698), Sarah gave birth to a healthy boy whom the righteous couple named "Yisrael."

In the Forest

RIGHT FROM BIRTH, young Yisrael exhibited an uncanny, almost supernatural, form of development. At the age of three months, the young boy could already walk and talk like an adult! His parents soon realized that their wonder child was destined for greatness but, as time passed, Rabbi Eliezer sensed he would not merit to raise his only son. Struck by severe illness, Rabbi Eliezer was confined to bed, and summoned young Yisrael as he felt his strength waning. "Yisralik, my son, listen closely," said Rabbi Eliezer. "Remember these two things your entire life: *Fear no creature! Fear only G-d, the G-d of heaven and earth! Secondly, love every Jew dearly, no matter who and no matter where.*"

After these impassioned words, Rabbi Eliezer recited the *Shema*, closed his eyes, and departed this world. His grieving son had hardly come to terms with this terrible loss when, a year later, his mother passed away. The Jewish community of Okup took little Yisrael under its protective wing, trying their best to substitute for his righteous parents. They housed him with a hospitable family, fed and clothed him, and even enrolled him in *cheder*.

Unlike other children his age, Yisrael showed overwhelming attachment to the vast forests and open fields surrounding Okup. Hardly had *cheder* finished when little Yisrael could be seen heading for the soothing sounds of rustling leaves, chirping birds and gurgling streams. He often ventured deep, deep into the woods, far beyond marked trails. Once there, little Yisrael reviewed his studies aloud, his clear voice resonating through the woods.

At times, Yisrael became so engrossed in his studies that he slept overnight in the forest. Having absorbed his father's parting words with every fiber of his being, the young boy showed total disregard for the dangerous snakes and fearsome animals that inhabited the forest. Oblivious to dark and cold, Yisrael could hear his father's message reverberating in his ears: *Fear only G-d, the G-d of heaven and earth.*

Whenever he returned to the village, the Jewish residents shook their heads in dismay. They had accepted responsibility to care for the young boy, and dared not imagine what dangers he faced in the forest. "Just look at him coming now!" the women would wring their hands worriedly. "Another traipse in the forest! Why does he disappear for hours on end in that dangerous place?"

Yisrael ignored their well-meaning criticism. He knew they could never understand what drew him to the forest—the untouched majesty of nature, his craving for solitude and privacy, and the closeness he felt to the Creator. He continued his lonely excursions, drawing strength from the tranquility the forest.

One day, when Yisrael was all of seven years old, he was on one of his trips to the forest when he suddenly heard a voice coming from the deep recesses of the forest. Slowly, stealthily, he approached the source of the noise and beheld an amazing sight: there, in a clearing among the trees, stood a figure wrapped in *tallit* and *tefillin*, praying with extraordinary fervor. Yisrael had never heard such spiritual devotion in his life! The very words of prayer seemed to blaze with spiritual brilliance, radiating with energy.

Stepping gingerly, Yisrael found a hiding place between the trees where he could continue watching unnoticed. A feeling of warm admiration and awe ran through the young boy. "This must be one of the thirty-six hidden *tzaddikim* in whose merit the world is sustained," he thought in wonder. Yisrael continued watching as the stranger finished his prayers and began reciting *Tehillim*, deep feeling infusing his words. Afterwards, the stranger opened a worn volume and began studying aloud with incredible spiritual sweetness.

Many hours passed. The stranger rose and packed his *tallit*, *tefillin* and sacred books into a sack. Slinging the sack over his shoulder, the stranger picked up a walking staff and turned to leave when a flicker of movement caught his eye. Startled, he looked up to see a boy emerge from between the trees. "A young boy all alone in the forest!" he exclaimed. "What are you doing here? Aren't you afraid to stay here alone?"

"I love the fields and the forest," responded young Yisrael. "Here there are no liars, no arrogant people. I'm not afraid of the forest at all. Before his death, my father instructed me to fear nothing but G-d, the G-d of heaven and earth."

A glimmer rose in the stranger's eyes. "Are you, perchance, the son of the great *tzaddik* Rabbi Eliezer?"

"Yes, I am his son."

The stranger put down his walking staff and rummaged through his sack. "Here," he said, taking out the Talmudic tractate of *Pesachim*, "let's study together."

Surrounded by the silent trees, they sat and studied for some time, and when the stranger rose to leave little Yisrael instinctively joined him. The pair traveled great distances together, passing through towns and cities, villages and hamlets. Despite their tiring journey, they made certain to spend a few hours every day absorbed in study and prayer.

Three years passed in this fashion. One day, as they reached the outskirts of a small village, the stranger led Yisrael into a wooded area just outside the village. There, deep among the trees, stood a wooden hut. "Rabbi Meir lives here," said the stranger softly. "The village residents think he is merely a simple laborer but, in truth, he is a *tzaddik* and an accomplished Torah scholar. This is your destination. I will leave soon, but you must stay with Rabbi Meir."

The pair entered the hut and were greeted warmly by Rabbi Meir. As if by prearranged signal, Rabbi Meir took Yisrael by the hand and, together, the pair stood in the doorway, waving farewell to the mysterious stranger. Yisrael watched the stranger leave with grateful eyes, thankful for three years of pure spiritual bliss.

Guided by the righteous Rabbi Meir, little Yisrael grew in spiritual stature as he absorbed the unique lessons that filled his days. His teacher threw the portals of Torah wide open, revealing the many layers of interpretation found in every verse and subject. Despite his tender years, Yisrael grasped every concept Rabbi Meir presented, and the ensuing four years passed in progressive study.

With time, young Yisrael realized that Rabbi Meir belonged to a select circle of hidden *tzaddikim*, righteous saints disguised by the cloak of simple labor. Members of this group spent their lives visiting the many Jewish communities scattered throughout the land. Wherever they arrived, these hidden *tzaddikim* lodged in the local synagogue and sustained themselves on meager portions of food they had brought along, never asking for help or assistance. In their own unique way, these *tzaddikim* encouraged and uplifted the simple Jews they encountered, infusing their spiritual service with renewed energy.

Rabbi Adam Baal Shem of Ropshitz headed this elite group. At the tender age of eleven years old, Yisrael was deemed worthy to join these *tzaddikim* and the entire group welcomed the youth with respect normally reserved for those more advanced in years. Fully accepting his new responsibilities, Rabbi Yisrael took the wandering staff in hand and he, too, began traveling incognito, inspiring all those he met.

Ingenious Concepts

Despite THEIR TREMENDOUS age difference, the older *tzaddikim* quickly recognized the unique capabilities of the latest newcomer and deferred to him on matters of spiritual guidance. His insight, his clarity of thought and his novel outlook never ceased to amaze them. Indeed, Rabbi Yisrael soon presented the group with a number of ingenious concepts, revolutionary ideas that would change the very landscape of Judaism. After due consideration, the older *tzaddikim* unanimously accepted every one of his suggestions. The suggestions included:

Concern, not condemnation
Encourage *Tehillim* and Divine praise
Uplift the sincere and the simple
Bolster economic stability
Educational involvement

Concern, not Condemnation

Rabbi Yisrael, all of fourteen years old, addressed the circle of hidden *tzaddikim*. "I suggest we concentrate our efforts on showering concern and encouragement, encouraging simple Jews in their sincere service of G-d. I am sure that genuine regard will, in turn, strengthen their level of religious observance. Enough condemnation! Enough frightening the ignorant masses with grim portrayals of punishment and purgatory for their sins. Our first step should be to view even the simplest Jew in a different perspective: to discover and reveal the inherent good within every Jewish soul, simultaneously arousing Divine mercy for all their needs."

The hidden *tzaddikim* knew all too well what Rabbi Yisrael meant. East European Jewry was still reeling from the widespread decimation visited upon them by the Cossacks, headed by Bogdan Chmielnicki and his horde of bloodthirsty followers. The infamous years of 1648-1649 (known by the Hebrew years, "*tach v'tat*") brought havoc and despair to every Jewish community; not a city was spared. Pillage, murder and unspeakable torture ravaged every family as the Cossacks left behind countless orphans and shattered families. Tens of thousands of Jews were cut down in the prime of their life and entire communities were put to the sword.

Needless to say, these atrocities remained fresh in the minds of Jews throughout Eastern Europe. Itinerant preachers, "*maggidim*," eager to arouse the masses to repentance and remorse, often portrayed this horrific period as fair Divine punishment for the collective sins of European Jewry. To further illustrate their words, preachers skillfully depicted the frightening tortures meted out to sinners doomed to languish in purgatory. Though their intentions were noble, the learned preachers failed to convey their message of repentance appropriately, planting dread and horror, by way of speeches laced with rebuke and condemnation.

Instead of receiving encouragement, the simple Jews left these speeches with even more anguish, as they bemoaned their lowly spiritual state. The frightening tones of the *maggidim*; the gruesome depictions of torture and suffering; the words of sarcasm, anger and ridicule—only served to further demoralize the already depressed Jewish populace.

Well acquainted with this disturbing trend, the hidden *tzaddikim* were encouraged by the revolutionary approach of Rabbi

Yisrael. Rabbi Yisrael and his fellow *tzaddikim* immediately set out to implement this new resolution, toiling unceasingly to change the accepted mindset, by elevating and revealing the true worth of the unlearned, sincere Jew.

One hot summer day, Rabbi Yisrael arrived in a village populated by unlearned Jews. Despite their lack of scholarship, these simple laborers and farmers were sincere and devout people who loved G-d dearly. Early every morning, the villagers would fill the local synagogue where they recited the entire book of *Tehillim*. On Shabbat they would complete *Tehillim* twice: once before the morning prayers, once again in the late afternoon. Periodically, one of the few scholars in the village would feel a twinge of compassion and teach some *Chumash* or *Mishnayot* to the ignorant laborers.

As Rabbi Yisrael entered the village he noticed the long, drawn faces of the farmers and workers. It did not take long for Rabbi Yisrael to realize how terribly the village suffered from drought; rain had not blessed the land in many months. Produce sagged listlessly along parched fields; wild weeds clogged the dry water cisterns. Vegetables withered under the blazing sun. It seemed as though, after months of intense labor, the entire crop would be completely destroyed, and the community faced the imminent hunger with growing dread.

Pained at the suffering of his fellow Jews, Rabbi Yisrael resolved to quickly return with other hidden *tzaddikim*, to help storm the gates of Heaven for Divine mercy. Indeed, the very next day, Thursday, Rabbi Yisrael returned to the village with a group of hidden *tzaddikim* and immediately began beseeching G-d for mercy. Their earnest prayers bore fruit and soon the heavens darkened with rumbling clouds. A soaking downpour drenched the village, filling empty water cisterns and reviving the endangered crop.

Ecstatic with joy, the village residents spilled out into the streets, their faces radiating delight and happiness. The entire village—even small children—praised G-d for His abundant mercies as they cried out exclamations of relief. "Blessed is He who lives forever!" proclaimed one. "G-d's salvation comes in the blink of an eye!" rejoiced another.

"This calls for a special resolution!" declared the community leaders. After holding a special session to discuss various suggestions, they established the upcoming Shabbat as a "Shabbat of Thanksgiving." Addressing the crowd, the leaders instructed everyone to complete the book of *Tehillim* an additional time that Shabbat. "Everyone must participate in this special third recital!" they announced. "Only invalids, new mothers, and young children will be exempted. Furthermore, we hereby direct every household to bake a sweet pastry tomorrow and reserve it for distribution during the afternoon *Seudah Shlishit* meal. On Shabbat, when the pastry is divided between the children, be sure to retell G-d's miracles and wonders to the youngsters, so that they can comprehend the great miracle we experienced."

A ripple of excitement ran through the crowd. Not to be outdone, the womenfolk also decided to make that Shabbat special: instead of bringing the customary candle to brighten the synagogue, that Shabbat they resolved to each bring two candles.

Rabbi Yisrael and his fellow *tzaddikim* felt immense pleasure and delight as they witnessed this outpouring of sincere gratitude towards G-d. The cries of joy; the heartfelt praise and gratitude; the combined efforts for a more spiritual Shabbat—made a tremendous impact on Rabbi Yisrael's group, and they decided to stay longer in the village in order to see the celebrations firsthand.

Early Friday morning, a carriage carrying an eminent preacher clattered into the village and rode directly to the home of the community leader. The preacher alighted and thrust a sheaf of papers into the leader's hand. The papers declared him to be an expert preacher, capable of bringing an entire audience to tears within a few minutes, a skillful orator whose word alone had generated true penitents. "I must preach for the entire village this Shabbat!" he demanded. "Just look at my recommendations!"

The community leader—an unlearned yet refined Jew—shook his head in dismay. "We just declared this week a 'Shabbat of Thanksgiving,' he explained. "The time normally reserved for preaching is unavailable; we plan to recite the entire Book of *Tehillim* instead."

"What impudence!" raged the *maggid*. "How dare you tell a scholar like me that you have no time to hear my wisdom! Don't you realize you have desecrated the honor of the Torah itself? You have time to eat cake and sleep, but you don't have time to hear my words of Torah? Purgatory is too small for sinners like you!"

Pale with shock, the community leader began stammering in fright as he begged the preacher for forgiveness and understanding. "Let's both go to the *rav*," he suggested. "Perhaps he can find a resolution to our problem."

"Never!" declared the *maggid* angrily. "Since when must I lower myself and approach the *rav*? According to ancient custom, visiting preachers need only consult with the community leader, not the *rav*. The opposite is true: a regular *maggid* waits until the *rav* sends a distinguished delegation to invite him, but a scholar like myself—well, let the *rav* come to me!"

Embarrassed and hurt, the community leader ran off to consult with the *rav*. A modest and caring soul, the *rav* quickly assented to personally greet the *maggid*. "Certainly, certainly," he said aloud. "Respecting the Torah and its scholars is of paramount importance—particularly for wandering preachers who sacrifice so much just to arouse others to repentance, thereby achieving communal merit. I would be overjoyed to meet him."

The rabbi joined the community leader and, together, they returned to greet the *maggid*. Upon seeing this mark of respect, the *maggid* calmed down somewhat and began conversing in various Torah concepts, astounding the rabbi with his breadth of knowledge. "You are truly an accomplished scholar," said the rabbi, "and it will be our pleasure if you can preach for our community."

Vindicated, the *maggid* waited as the rabbi consulted with the community leader. "It is settled!" declared the rabbi shortly. "You will speak for us on Shabbat afternoon after *Seudah Shlishit*, until the conclusion of Shabbat." The news spread quickly: tomorrow the community would merit hearing the Torah thoughts of a respected preacher, whose words had proven to arouse feelings of repentance and contrition in his listeners.

That Shabbat was one of jubilation and thanksgiving. The streets themselves seemed to rejoice. The synagogue was aglow with twice as many candles than usual; the community recited additional *Tehillim* with extraordinary fervor; and all the local children enjoyed their tasty Shabbat pastries as they listened wide-eyed to an account of the recent miracle. For their part, Rabbi Yisrael and his colleagues were deeply impressed by the sincere show of gratitude, and felt justified in staying over for Shabbat.

Shabbat afternoon, after a joyous *Seudah Shlishit*, the community crammed into the local synagogue, waiting to hear the visiting *maggid* speak. The *maggid* approached the podium, turned to the congregation, and began his speech in an angry tone: "The *Mishnah* states, 'Seven kinds of punishment come to the world for seven kinds of transgressions'" (*Avot* 5:8). Translating his words into Yiddish, the *maggid* enumerated all seven forms of punishment. "Famine, panic and drought!" he thundered. "Destruction, pestilence, war and wild beasts!"

The *shul* erupted in a fit of wailing. Eager to continue, the *maggid* raised his voice over the weeping and began berating the congregation loudly, condemning them for failing to observe G-d's commandments with meticulous care. The wailing grew stronger. Fear and terror gripped every heart as the *maggid* depicted the inevitable Divine retribution hovering over the village. Tears streamed from the eyes of the community elders, the simple laborers, women and children. "Improve your sinful ways!" roared the *maggid*. "Otherwise, you are fated to suffer severe punishment. By incurring His wrath, G-d will strike with all sorts of unspeakable calamities, beginning with famine and hunger—just like what happened in *tach v'tat*."

This last comment threw the congregation into sheer panic. Women ran screaming from the synagogue, pulling their hysterical children behind them. Others fainted in the aisles. As the wailing and crying reached a crescendo, Rabbi Yisrael decided to act. The *maggid* had single-handedly turned a Shabbat of pure spiritual bliss into catastrophe. Leaping onto small table, Rabbi Yisrael turned to the *maggid* and shouted above the tumult. "Why do you condemn these Jews?" he demanded. "The *Midrash* describes how G-d asked Moshe our Master to rebuke Him! Instead of reprimanding us for failing to serve G-d properly, rebuke G-d—so to speak—for not showing His children more compassion! Listen to me! Now that we have truly merited to see His mercies, and G-d has blessed us with rain, we shall certainly serve Him appropriately."

The congregation looked at Rabbi Yisrael in admiration, feeling his truthful words pierce the atmosphere of doom and anguish. "True! True!" they roared in unison. *Kaddish* was quickly recited and the congregation began the evening prayer as feelings of joy and gratitude pervaded the synagogue once again.

In similar vein, the circle of hidden *tzaddikim* continued spreading Rabbi Yisrael's message of hope and encouragement. After fifteen years, in the year 5487 (1728), they noticed a significant change sweep through many communities: instead of despair and low self-worth, simple Jews had begun serving G-d with enthusiasm and vigor.

Before the eyes of the hidden *tzaddikim*, the elderly *tzaddik* Rabbi Meir singled out Rabbi Yisrael and placed his hands upon the young man's head. "May blessings be showered upon your head!" he exclaimed, "for your revolutionary approach of *Ahavat Yisrael*." In fact, the hidden *tzaddikim* renamed the Hebrew year when Rabbi Yisrael first introduced his innovation—the year of *tof-ayin-beit* (1712)—as an acronym for *tavo alav bracha* (May blessings come upon him [in merit of this new approach]).

With time, Rabbi Yisrael's stature grew among the circle of hidden *tzaddikim*, and he soon earned the title, *Rabbi Yisrael Baal Shem Tov* (Master of the Good Name).

15

Encourage Tehillim and Divine Praise

On his sixteenth birthday, the Baal Shem Tov wandered out into the wide, open fields to meditate on the significance of this special day. He had been lodging at a local inn in a nearby village, managed by Aaron Shlomo the innkeeper and his wife Zlata Rivka. The simplest of Jews, Aaron Shlomo was barely literate and had great trouble stumbling through the daily prayers. Yet, he and his wife were extremely G-d-fearing folk who praised G-d at every opportunity. "Blessed is He forever!" murmured the innkeeper constantly. His pious wife, too, could often be heard saying, "Blessed be His Holy Name."

Now, all alone in the vast expanse of land, the Baal Shem Tov recited *Tehillim* with great feeling, concentrating on the various mystical intentions associated with each verse. His mentor, the hidden *tzaddik* Rabbi Chaim, had imbued him with the deepest wisdom of the Kabbalah, and the Baal Shem Tov felt closely familiar with the esoteric dimension of Torah. Immersed in thought, the Baal Shem Tov soon became oblivious to his physical surroundings as his soul rose to more spiritual realms.

Suddenly the Baal Shem Tov saw Elijah the Prophet standing before him, a kind smile playing on the Prophet's lips. The Baal Shem Tov felt humbled: though he had merited such visions before—whether in the home of Rabbi Meir or during assemblies of the hidden *tzaddikim*—this was the first time he saw the Prophet alone. Yet the enigmatic smile puzzled him—was the Prophet mocking him?

Said the Prophet: "You invest so much effort and time in meditation, trying to attain lofty spiritual levels, while the heartfelt words uttered by Aaron Shlomo and his wife create a tremendous uproar in Heaven, far greater than the uproar caused by the esoteric meditations of great *tzaddikim*."

The Baal Shem Tov listened in amazement as Elijah the Prophet continued to describe the great spiritual pleasure and delight generated by sincere Divine praise. "When Jews bless G-d by saying 'Thank G-d,' 'Blessed be G-d' etc., this causes great satisfaction On High," revealed the Prophet. "This is particularly true when such praise is uttered by simple folk, whose sincerity and faith unite them constantly with the Creator."

The Baal Shem Tov later shared this revelation with the hidden *tzaddikim*, and suggested an additional approach. "It behooves us to inquire after the welfare of simple Jews," he explained. "This will cause them to praise G-d by answering, 'Thank G-d, I have ample livelihood,' or 'Thank G-d, my children are well.' Even when they are not faring well, our concern will cause them to arouse Divine mercy, by answering 'May the Healer of all flesh send me a complete recovery,' and similar supplications."

The hidden *tzaddikim* listened as the Baal Shem Tov finished presenting his revolutionary idea. "Simple Jews have inestimable power," he concluded. "Their sincere utterances of praise arouse far greater spiritual delight than anything we can achieve. G-d Himself, as it were, derives supreme satisfaction from these heartfelt blessings and prayers."

During his extensive wandering, the Baal Shem Tov spread this custom of thanking G-d among the simple masses, encouraging them to praise G-d verbally at every opportunity. The Baal Shem Tov traveled incognito, dressed in the rough cloth of peasant farmers, which helped him mingle freely with the simple and unlearned. One day, as he arrived in a village, he heard about a *porush*, an erudite scholar totally disassociated from any vestige of worldliness, who lived nearby. Secluded in a single room, the *porush* studied assiduously throughout his every waking hour, just as he had done each day for the past fifty years. "The *porush* is a righteous saint!" people whispered in awe. "He learns, standing, an entire morning, crowned in *tallit* and *tefillin*. Only in the afternoon, after *Minchah*, does he stop to taste some bread and water. His mere presence radiates holiness and virtue."

Upon hearing this impressive description, the Baal Shem Tov resolved to visit the *porush* personally. Entering the quiet room, he approached the *porush* and found him deeply absorbed in study. "How is your health?" asked the Baal Shem Tov. "Do you have enough for your needs?"

The *porush* continued his studies, purposely ignoring the disrespectful interruption. The Baal Shem Tov repeated his questions again and again, but the scholar refused to even acknowledge his presence. Soon the *porush* could no longer contain his anger: how dare a simple farmer disturb his studies! Pointing to the door, he gestured impatiently for the Baal Shem Tov to leave.

"Rabbi," said the Baal Shem Tov. "Why don't you allow G-d His rightful sustenance?"

The scholar looked incredulously at the stranger dressed in peasant garb. He had never heard an illiterate farmer say anything meaningful, much less make cryptic references about G-d and His needs! Sensing his bewilderment, the Baal Shem Tov hastened to explain: "Jews are sustained by G-d's abundant blessings. Yet, how is G-d sustained, so to speak? The Psalmist says, 'Yet You, Holy One, are enthroned upon the praises of Israel' (Psalms 22:4). Simply put, this means that our Creator enjoys, and is sustained by, the praises and songs we utter. This joy arouses greater Divine satisfaction which, in turn, channels health and sustenance to Jews and their families everywhere."

Uplift the Sincere and the Simple

At age eighteen, the Baal Shem Tov had already become one of the most respected members of the circle of hidden *tzaddikim*. Adding to his original innovations, the Baal Shem Tov proposed an extensive effort to uplift and encourage the unlettered. "These people deserve our special attention," he explained. "We should draw them closer, give them our undivided attention, and encourage their earnest recital of *Tehillim* and daily prayers. Doing so will arouse their innate feelings of hope, faith, and unswerving belief in G-d."

The circle of hidden *tzaddikim* nodded in assent, signifying their profound disapproval of the wide chasm that existed at that time between two classes of Jewry: the learned scholar and the simple, unlearned Jew. Torah scholars throughout the land had separated themselves from intermingling with the ignorant, forming an elitist class of their own that denigrated common Jews. The scholar avoided the laborer; the learned ridiculed the illiterate. Even mourners and those observing *yahrzeit* were barely allowed to lead the services for the "real" worshippers. Soon unlearned Jews were forced to found their own synagogues, just so they could have a place to pray. Considered inferior and boorish, simple Jews had a tremendously difficult time associating with their heritage, and sometimes wondered if they truly counted.

The Baal Shem Tov dedicated his heart and soul to uplifting these downtrodden souls. Disguising himself as a common laborer, the Baal Shem Tov was constantly found in the company of simple Jews and often addressed them from the center of the marketplace. A rapt audience gathered whenever he began speaking, listening in silent wonder to his uplifting messages of inspiration and encouragement.

Drawing on his incredible wealth of knowledge, the Baal Shem Tov captivated his listeners with Talmudic stories and teachings. A heartwarming moral accompanied every story; warmth and affection permeated his words. His voice rang clear and true, infusing strength and comfort. Listening to his message, simple Jews were filled with renewed hope and faith, realizing that they, too, played an important role in serving G-d. Interwoven between his stories, the Baal Shem Tov also encouraged his audience not to emulate the negative qualities of their gentile neighbors. Similarly, he influenced them to avoid gossip and empty chatter, slander and cursing.

The Baal Shem Tov showered particular attention upon the children of these simple Jews. He spent hours enjoying their company, teaching them to say the *Modeh ani*, the *Shema*, and the verses of *Torah tziva* and *Beyadcha afkid ruchi*. Distributing apples and nuts, the Baal Shem Tov encouraged them to recite the appropriate blessings before and after eating food, coaching those still unfamiliar with the words. Similarly, he taught them to answer "*Amen!*" with enthusiasm and verve. He would regularly place his holy hands on their hearts and say, "Be a warm Jew!"

Bolster Economic Stability

The widespread havoc caused by the murderous Cossacks displaced ancient communities throughout Europe. Fearing similar pogroms, many Jews fled the organized hate found in outlying small towns and villages, and sought shelter in larger, more civilized cities and towns. Unfortunately, the exploding population of Jews in these cities undermined existing sources of financial stability, as hundreds of new residents sought to eke out a living. Entire families literally starved in the streets. Given the circumstances, little chance of economic improvement seemed possible, and the Baal Shem Tov turned his attention to the widespread poverty of his brethren.

"We need to rebuild the Jewish nation," he addressed the hidden *tzaddikim*. "This terrible poverty has shattered the morale of our people; despair and depression are rampant. We need to calm their spirits and remove the shadow of fear, raising those crushed by abject poverty. Restoring the pride of our people is a worthy goal."

The hidden *tzaddikim* began visiting various cities throughout the country, influencing families to take up agricultural work in smaller villages and hamlets. "Men can support their families by toiling the land," they argued. "Women can work at weaving, raising animals, and cultivating vegetables." The *tzaddikim* even took measures to help specific families relocate, taking care to provide these families with financial independence. Far from preaching empty talk, many hidden *tzaddikim* themselves also became farmers and crop growers. They moved to smaller villages where they could work at tilling and cultivating the land.

During his extensive wanderings, the Baal Shem Tov asked pointed questions of his hosts, discovering which areas were governed by landowners friendly to Jews. Later, when he visited the larger cities, the Baal Shem Tov coaxed those he met to achieve financial independence by moving to these selfsame agricultural colonies and villages. "This particular landowner is very kind to

20

Jews," he would say. "The people living in such-and-such a village form a warm and friendly community." Through outlining the advantages of specific areas, he enabled many families to find safe, financially stable locations, where they could raise their families without worry.

The strenuous efforts of the Baal Shem Tov and his colleagues bore fruit: hundreds of families left the larger cities for financial independence found in smaller towns and colonies. Thanks to individual guidance and support offered by the hidden *tzaddikim*, impoverished families finally found a place where they could live in comfort and safety.

Educational Involvement

Aside from his involvement in all these areas, the widespread educational degeneration weighed heavily on the Baal Shem Tov's mind. Barely able to make ends meet, parents were simply unable to hire teachers and, after hours of exhausting labor, returned home too exhausted to educate their own children. An entire generation was growing up illiterate. Determined to change the face of Jewish education, the Baal Shem Tov raised the issue with the hidden *tzaddikim* and implored them to become actively involved in turning the tide of ignorance. "Teachers are urgently needed in many villages," he explained, "particularly in impoverished areas where the locals cannot afford to provide their children with a Torah-true education. Grown children cannot read the Hebrew alphabet! In case of need, we ourselves can serve as teachers."

Unlike his other innovations, the Baal Shem Tov needed large amounts of money to bring this suggestion into action. He therefore chose two hidden *tzaddikim*—Rabbi Aaron Dovid, a carpenter from Brody, and Rabbi Shalom Chaim, a tailor from Lvov—charging them with the noble mission of raising funds for this worthy project. Eager to attain their goal, the pair was extremely successful in finding adequate funds to facilitate the Baal Shem Tov's inspiration.

The Baal Shem Tov himself became a teacher's assistant in the town of Brody, in the year 1716. Every morning he rounded up all the local children from their respective homes and brought them to *cheder*, shielding them from vicious dogs who tried attacking them on the way. As they marched together to *cheder*, the Baal Shem Tov said *Birkot Hashachar* with the children, their clear voices ringing out as they sang *Torah tziva* and the *Shema*. During recess, the Baal Shem Tov played along with the children, relating stories of Moshe Rabbenu and *Matan Torah* to them. Afterwards, he walked them home as the children recited *Shema* and the verse of *Beyadcha afkid ruchi* together with him.

Years later, the Baal Shem Tov remarked to his disciples, "The time I spent as a teacher's helper were the best years of my life. I could feel the great Divine pleasure aroused by these sincere children. The angels in Heaven envied my charges, these 'young lambs' who could effect such great spiritual satisfaction."

The very nature of agricultural work demanded hours of strenuous labor in the fields, preventing many parents from forming close bonds with their children. Noticing this, the Baal Shem Tov did his utmost to improve parent-child relationships. His influence prevented the growing generation gap between elders and their offspring. The Baal Shem Tov once said: "When I worked as a teacher's helper, I exerted great effort to imbue the children with profound love for their parents. I achieved this by highlighting the positive qualities of their respective parents."

Besides influencing children, the Baal Shem Tov and the hidden *tzaddikim* worked hard toward furthering adult education. Many grown men had remained illiterate, for in their youth they worked alongside their parents in the fields, trying to alleviate the terrible poverty at home. Study was unfeasible. Their ignorance deepened over the years, and some could not even read fluently.

The hidden *tzaddikim* therefore set out to educate others, elevating the general level of scholarship. Rabbi Hirsh Leib, one of the hidden *tzaddikim*, was especially active in this field and his efforts were crowned with great success. Due to the Baal Shem

Tov's initiative, grown men learned to read Hebrew fluently, enabling them to study and pray on their own. After many years, the hidden *tzaddikim* effectively banished ignorance and shame from countless homes and succeeded in raising the communal standard of scholarship.

A Decade of Spiritual Gain

DURING THE YEARS THAT HE WORKED as a teacher's assistant in Brody, the Baal Shem Tov was hired to tutor a young orphan being raised in the home of Rabbi Avraham Gershon—an erudite scholar living in the nearby city of Kitov. The Baal Shem Tov taught the hapless orphan *Chumash* and, with time, became engaged to Leah Rochel, Rabbi Gershon's sister. The Baal Shem Tov's humble bearing and unlettered manner had completely deceived Rabbi Gershon, and the scholar was appalled to hear of his sister's engagement. He did everything possible to terminate their engagement and, later, their marriage, but his sister recognized the unique qualities of her husband and adamantly refused to reconsider. She bore the Baal Shem Tov two children—a son, whom they named Tzvi, and a daughter, whom they named Adel.

In ensuing years, Rabbi Gershon tormented the Baal Shem Tov, berating his brother-in-law for his shameful ignorance and boorish habits. "My poor sister did not deserve an ignoramus as a husband," he often remarked callously. In a letter penned to Rabbi Gershon, the Baal Shem Tov apologized profusely for his "unlettered" state. "I hear you are sorely grieved at my inability to learn," wrote the hidden *tzaddik*. "I ask you a simple question: Am I to blame for being orphaned from both parents at a young age? To please you, I pledge to rectify my ignorance. In my capacity as a teacher's helper, I will try to study some Torah for, thank G-d, I have already taught myself how to write...."

Years later, after being revealed as an incomparable Torah scholar and wonder-worker, the Baal Shem Tov once reminded his brother-in-law about this period of aggravation: "Today, the eve of Yom Kippur, is a day of forgiveness and atonement. Thus, I hereby affirm with my own handwriting that I have completely forgiven you for antagonizing and berating me during my years of wandering—a time when you were unaware of my true identity...."

One winter Friday afternoon, the Baal Shem Tov suddenly felt a wave of intense exhaustion overpower him, and he fell into a deep slumber. As he slept, he envisioned an elderly sage standing before him, light streaming from his face. "Do you recognize me, Yisralik?" asked the venerable stranger.

"No," responded the Baal Shem Tov. "I don't remember you at all."

"I have been sent from Heaven to teach you Torah," revealed the stranger. "You must leave the city every day, and head toward the mountains, where I will come to teach you the Torah's deepest secrets. There is, however, one stipulation: no one—not even your wife—may know of our study sessions. Complete secrecy is absolutely imperative."

"But what is your name?" cried the Baal Shem Tov.

"Why is my name important to you?" replied the stranger. "When the time comes, you will know my name."

Startled, the Baal Shem Tov awoke from his sleep and promptly dismissed the mysterious stranger. "Dreams are worthless," he thought quietly. "The verse explicitly states, 'Dreams speak naught'" (Zechariah 10:2).

With the approach of Shabbat, the Baal Shem Tov hurried to immerse in the *mikveh*. As was his custom, the Baal Shem Tov immersed with his eyes open—only this time he suddenly saw the venerable stranger standing in the water, gazing at him! The Baal Shem Tov rose out of the water and immediately felt a spirit of purity and sanctity envelop his soul. An inexplicable feeling of spiritual bliss filled his being, and the Baal Shem Tov sensed it was somehow connected to the righteous stranger.

That night, after the Friday night meal, the stranger appeared once again to the Baal Shem Tov in his sleep. "Yisralik, my son, don't brush off your dreams as meaningless," he said kindly. "I carry a true message; a vision laden with significance. I will prove it to you: On Sunday morning, leave the city and head for the mountains. I will meet you there, between the second and third mountain. Before you come, you must immerse four times in the *mikveh*."

The stranger disappeared and the Baal Shem Tov awoke instantly. No longer did he doubt the veracity of his visions; no longer did he question the stranger's sincerity. Most importantly, he felt assured that G-d had orchestrated these mysterious events, preparing limitless spiritual horizons for him. "I have merited this solely due to my saintly ancestors," he thought gratefully. "Their sincere prayers have caused this tremendous spiritual gain."

On Shabbat morning, as the Baal Shem Tov entered the synagogue, he felt all eyes turn on him. The congregation gazed at him in awe, as if seeing the simple teacher's assistant for the very first time, and the Baal Shem Tov realized that his supernal visitor had left a noticeable mark. The worshippers honored the Baal Shem Tov with the most coveted *aliyah* of *maftir*, an absolutely unprecedented move. That afternoon, during the *Seudah Shlishit* meal, Rabbi Gershon greeted him respectfully and inquired after his health. "You have changed," remarked Rabbi Gershon in astonishment. "I notice a tremendous transformation, as though you've become a different person!"

The Baal Shem Tov remained silent, anxiously awaiting his upcoming rendezvous with the mysterious stranger. The next morning, he arose early and immersed four times in the *mikveh*, exactly as instructed by the stranger. A thick, heavy snow had begun to fall, blanketing the region in white stillness, but the Baal Shem Tov would not be fazed. Bundled in a warm fur coat, he made his way slowly through the snow. Hearing an approaching noise, the Baal Shem Tov turned to see a non-Jewish peasant riding a snow sleigh toward him. "I felt bad for you trying to walk in this weather," explained the driver. "Come with me; I'm also traveling toward the mountains."

The Baal Shem Tov gratefully accepted the offer and climbed onto the sleigh, riding in silence as the horses neared the mountains. Upon arriving at the second mountain, the Baal Shem Tov climbed off the sleigh and trudged toward the valley that separated the second and third mountains. There, framed against the snow, he could see the stranger walking towards him. "Here!" said the stranger, pointing toward a cave hewn into the mountainside.

Entering the cave, the Baal Shem Tov was astonished to find it well-illuminated and furnished with a table and two chairs. The mysterious stranger withdrew a book from his coat, opened it to the first page, and placed it on the table. "Look inside," he instructed the Baal Shem Tov, "and begin reading aloud." Saying so, the stranger spread his hands out wide above the Baal Shem Tov's head, indicating his blessing.

Years later—when the Baal Shem Tov retold this incident to his disciples—he described his turbulent emotions at that time. "I am still forbidden to reveal the book's title," he said. "Immediately as I began reading, I felt as though the gates of wisdom were flung open before me, illuminating my eyes with new insight. It was as if an additional, lofty soul had vested itself within my being, enabling me to understand the deepest secrets of Creation. I felt as though I was experiencing the awe-inspiring revelation of G-dliness at Mount Sinai!"

After two hours, the stranger said, "Enough for today, my son. Tomorrow, G-d willing, you shall return and then we can continue. But remember—you must not breathe a word of this to any living soul."

"But what is your name?" pleaded the Baal Shem Tov.

The stranger shook his head impatiently. "It is not time," he said with finality. The pair left the cave and walked back across the snow in utter silence. Approaching the city, the stranger placed his hands on the Baal Shem Tov's head and blessed him, then turned and walked back toward the mountains. The Baal Shem Tov stared after him for a while, mentally deciding to continue these secret lessons. The things he read kindled a strange fire in his soul; his being pulsated with unusual intensity. Entering his humble hovel in Brody, the Baal Shem Tov kept silent about his whereabouts, and his pious wife respected his need for secrecy.

The Baal Shem Tov and the stranger continued learning every day for an entire year, hidden safely in their undiscovered cave. One summer day, as they returned to Brody, the stranger suddenly turned to the Baal Shem Tov and made a startling announcement. "The time has come to reveal my name," he disclosed. "I am Achiya Hashiloni."

Achiya Hashiloni! The mere name filled the Baal Shem Tov with awe. This lofty soul had been a disciple of King David and, later, the mentor of Elijah the Prophet. Unfettered by the constraints imposed by physical life, Achiya was present during the historical Exodus from Egypt; had merited to witness the Crossing of the Sea of Reeds; and saw the G-dly Revelation at Mount Sinai.

Achiya Hashiloni! He was the seventh in the unbroken chain of tradition stretching back to Mount Sinai—Moses, Joshua, Pinchas, Eli, Samuel the Prophet, King David, and Achiya Hashiloni. The name reverberated within him. He, the mortal Rabbi Yisrael, had somehow merited this sublime revelation every day during the past year! Terrified at the mere thought, the Baal Shem Tov swooned and fell to the ground. When he came to, the Baal Shem Tov rose and listened in deference to his celestial instructor. "You will leave Brody," instructed Achiya Hashiloni. "Move to a smaller village; we will continue our lessons there."

Aided by his brother-in-law Rabbi Gershon, the Baal Shem Tov moved to a village near Kitov, where he opened a modest inn. This enabled his wife to eke out a meager livelihood and support their family while the Baal Shem Tov spent his time in the mountains, learning assiduously under the tutelage of his unique mentor. Posing as a lime porter, he spent an entire week studying in the mountains, returning home only for Shabbat. In a letter dated from that period, the Baal Shem Tov described his primary place of residence: "I write from here, sitting under an apple tree, deep within the mountains that lie between Kitov and Kossov."

A decade passed, a decade of uplifting spiritual bliss and incredible gain. It took ten years for Achiya Hashiloni to teach his disciple the entire *Chumash*, from the first verse until the very last. Passing through the various layers of interpretation, teacher and student lingered most in the garden of the mystical dimension of Torah, exploring the deepest secrets of Creation, exactly as it is studied in *Gan Eden*.

End of an Era

WORDS CANNOT DESCRIBE the Baal Shem Tov's incredible bliss as he basked in the company of his esteemed mentor. He lived in a world of light and purity; learned the language of the animals and trees; studied the hidden secrets of Creation; and familiarized himself with the myriad chambers found in celestial worlds. Endowed with spiritual light, he gazed from one end of the world to the other, perceiving even the smallest details from great distances. The supernatural became the norm, as the physical restraints of time and space fell away.

His elation came to an abrupt end one day by a terse statement of his teacher, Achiya Hashiloni. "Our period of solitude is drawing to a close," he revealed. "Know then, Yisralik, that the time of your revelation draws near. Such is G-d's decree!"

Dread seized the Baal Shem Tov. Was he truly worthy to lead others, to serve as a communal guide and spiritual mentor? He balked at the notion of acquiring publicity and fame, preferring instead to continue living a life of solitude. Pushing his mentor's declaration out of his mind, the Baal Shem Tov continued studying alone in the mountains, relishing every moment.

One day, as the Baal Shem Tov sat absorbed in thought, an urgent cry pierced his silent surroundings. Turning, he saw a gentile shepherd gesticulating wildly toward him, as though trying to communicate a message. "My master, my master," he gasped, "finally I have found you! Please, come closer!"

The Baal Shem Tov walked toward the shepherd and the flock of sheep grazing quietly on the lush mountainside nearby. "I have something incredible to relate," declared the shepherd with great emotion. "A month ago, as I was tending my sheep on a mountainside not far from here, I suddenly spied a scholarly-looking individual pacing the valley down below. He kept walking back and forth, as if searching for something. Finally he stopped before a large stone, lifted it, and furtively placed a sheaf of papers under it.

"I became very curious," continued the shepherd. "What kind of precious treasure now lay under this stone? I made a mental mark of the exact location and, feigning disinterest, returned to my sheep. Later, after the stranger left, I descended the mountain and approached the stone. I hardly began lifting the stone when a stern voice rang out: 'Don't dare touch those papers!'

"Glancing up, I saw the stranger watching me from his vantage point; he had not left after all. He began walking toward me, shouting as he approached. Shaking with fear, I ran up the mountain, only to find him climbing up after me. I stood there in terror, not knowing what to expect, when the stranger reached me and said the following words: 'Those papers are very holy; they are destined for the rabbi who secludes himself in these mountains. Any other hand that dares touch them will wither and dry up. Remember, you have been warned!'

"After delivering his rebuke, the stranger continued with a request. 'During your wanderings, you might meet this holy rabbi. I beg you—if you do see him, tell him about the package waiting under this stone and show him its whereabouts.' He then gave me a sum of money as compensation for my troubles, and left as mysteriously as he had come. And now," concluded the shepherd, "I have finally found you! Come, I will show you the hidden papers."

Astounded, the Baal Shem Tov followed the shepherd dutifully down the mountain, crossing many valleys and hills until they reached a large stone. "Here!" cried the shepherd, "I have fulfilled my duty!"

The Baal Shem Tov lifted the stone and removed the sheaf of papers. "This is more payment for your services," he said, offering the shepherd the same sum that the stranger had given him. "But remember—don't tell a soul about this!"

Returning to the cave, the Baal Shem Tov inspected the papers closely and was shocked to find a personal letter addressed to him, penned by none other than the celebrated leader of the hidden *tzaddikim*—Rabbi Adam Baal Shem. According to the letter, the mysterious mailman had been Rabbi Adam's son, the *tzaddik* Rabbi Leib. Most of the writings held the deepest mystical secrets, coached in cryptic terms understood by select few, but the letter also related two remarkable stories pertaining to Rabbi Yisrael and his destined revelation.

The Two Stories

SECLUDED IN HIS CAVE, the Baal Shem Tov began reading the first story:

A Jew from Safed

In the ancient city of Safed, high atop the mountains, lived a simple Jew who barely understood the meaning of the Hebrew prayers. Despite his ignorance, he was exceedingly pious and meritorious, a sincere individual who performed good deeds veiled by the cloak of secrecy. One night in the year 5333 (1573), as he sat on the floor of his home bewailing the destruction of the Holy Temple, the Jew heard a knock at the door. "Who's there?" he called out.

"Elijah the Prophet!" came the response.

Awestruck, the simple Jew went to the door and with shaking hands opened it, ushering the celestial visitor into his humble home. Barely had Elijah entered the doorway when the house was filled with bright radiance, a shimmering joy that transformed every room. The babies awoke instantly, and began dancing in their cribs. "Sit, sit," proposed the simple Jew. "My master and teacher, please sit."

Elijah sat down on a rickety chair and turned to the simple Jew. "I have come to reveal a deep secret: the year of Moshiach's arrival. However, I am curious to know the reason why G-d has singled you out for this unique privilege. Pray tell, what extraordinary deed did you perform on the day of your Bar Mitzvah? In merit of this deed, the Heavenly Court ruled that you are deserving to hear this and many other awesome secrets."

"What I did, I did for G-d's honor," replied the simple Jew with sincerity. "Why should I reveal my deed to others? If, as you say, the transmission of esoteric secrets depends on revealing my deed—then I wholeheartedly forgo the honor. I was taught to do things for G-d's sake, should be hidden from publicity."

Hardly had the Jew finished speaking when Elijah disappeared, rebuffed by the adamant refusal of the simple Jew. The Heavenly Court was in an uproar. Such sincerity and devotion were completely unprecedented: never had anyone turned down the chance to study under the tutelage of Elijah the Prophet merely for the sake of concealing their good deeds. After extended debate, the Court decided to reward the Jew nonetheless. Elijah returned and taught the simple Jew Torah, revealing esoteric secrets hidden from all but the most saintly.

With time, the Jew became a truly righteous individual, until he attained a lofty spiritual level reserved for a handful of *tzaddikim* in every generation. Yet, despite his greatness, the Jew continued living unpretentiously, conducting his life in a simple fashion. Not a soul knew his true worth.

At the end of his life, the Jew from Safed departed this world, and his soul was immediately admitted into *Gan Eden*. Welcoming angels led the soul directly to the radiant chamber of the Patriarchs, the ultimate reward for a righteous life spent on earth. "Is this enough?" demanded the celestial angels. "This soul deserves special reward for concealing its greatness for so many years. No one even suspected his saintliness. All his deeds were performed solely for the sake of Heaven, without the slightest shadow of self-worth!"

After due consideration, the Heavenly Court decided to send this lofty soul back to earth. Having spent a life in the shadows of obscurity, this soul would now brighten the world with Divine light and warmth. Destined to touch the souls of countless thousands, the teachings and deeds of this soul would illuminate communities everywhere until the coming of Moshiach.

"This is your soul," concluded Rabbi Adam Baal Shem, addressing himself to the reader, Rabbi Yisrael. "Your revelation is irrevocable, fixed and predestined. Do not hesitate in your task to illuminate the world with a new path in the service of G-d, thereby bringing an awareness of G-d to all. You will bring a spirit of purity and holiness to the world, forging the way for the ultimate Redemption."

Encounter with Achiya Hashiloni

After finishing the first story, Rabbi Yisrael began reading the second narrative, an awe-inspiring account that had transpired to Rabbi Adam Baal Shem himself:

"One Shabbat morning," the story began, "as I sat in the synagogue listening to the Torah reading, I suddenly saw Achiya Hashiloni. 'Be prepared to leave at the conclusion of Shabbat,' he said. 'We are traveling to Lvov.'

"Right after I recited *Havdalah*, Achiya Hashiloni suddenly appeared at my house and beckoned me outside. 'Remain in your Shabbat garments,' he said. Hurriedly donning a coat, I rushed outside and found a horse and carriage waiting. The driver sat quietly up front, waiting for us to climb into the carriage.

"Barely had the carriage begun moving, when Achiya Hashiloni turned to me, his voice firm against the dark

night. "Sing the song '*Eliyahu Hanavi*,'" he said. I sang
alone, reciting the numerous stanzas from memory. As I
finished the song, I looked up, and to my utter amazement,
we had already arrived in Lvov. Somehow, we had tra-
versed a distance of seventy *parsas* (about 167 miles) in a
matter of minutes! I had heard of *kfitzat haderech*, the
miraculous shortening of the road, but this was the first
time I actually experienced such a phenomenon.

"Sensing my wonder, Achiya Hashiloni turned to me
kindly. 'Why are you so astounded, my child?' he asked.
'Have you any idea who our driver is? If you would only
know his identity, you would sit in awe and dread, just as
I have during our journey....

"I hardly had time to digest his words when the wagon
stopped before a nondescript house. Achiya Hashiloni
alighted and I followed him into the house. It stood
empty, as though awaiting our arrival. Achiya Hashiloni
began pacing the room, his face burning like a fiery brand.
Two hours passed in this fashion: I stood there motionless,
watching my teacher walk back and forth, his face shining
with an unearthly light, when the door suddenly opened
and a tall, elderly person entered the room. 'Welcome,
Rabbi Eliezer!' cried Achiya Hashiloni in delight. 'How
fortunate you are to have borne a child unique to both this
and all the celestial worlds! Please be seated!'

"Awestruck, I realized that our guest was none other
than your father, the righteous Rabbi Eliezer. 'Our holy
master knows that I come from a world where there is no
sitting or standing,' replied Rabbi Eliezer.

"'Nevertheless, I insist,' said Achiya Hashiloni. 'It is
important not to alter accepted customs. Even the angels
who visited our Patriarch Abraham were careful to sit and
eat in his presence.'

"Rabbi Eliezer acceded and sat on a chair. Achiya
Hashiloni turned to him and asked, "Why did you summon me? What is your request?"

"'It is the matter of my son,' he replied quietly. 'Hardly a day goes by that he does not implore me to speak up on his behalf, to intercede before you and rescind his forced revelation.'

"'Impossible!' said Achiya Hashiloni. He continued in an impassioned voice, convincing us of the urgency of his demand. "Tell Rabbi Yisrael in my name that he *must* reveal his true greatness, for such has been decreed in the Heavenly Court! Otherwise, he has—G-d forbid—no reason to continue living on this material world. His soul descended with the explicit understanding that it would become revealed and spread the wellsprings of his teachings outward.'

"Achiya Hashiloni pointed toward me. 'Adam now knows the particulars of our situation,' he said. "In due time, I will allow him to reveal our present meeting. Your son Yisrael will admit that I am correct! Moreover, I instruct Adam to tell your son that, until he proceeds to reveal his greatness, he will no longer see me again!'

"Rabbi Eliezer vanished from the room and I stood there in shock, hardly believing my eyes. 'It is time to eat *Melava Malka*," said Achiya Hashiloni to me. "Come eat something; then I will send you back home. There are additional matters I must attend to in Lvov.'

"But I am frightened to travel alone at night!" I protested.

"'Do not fear anyone!' responded my teacher. 'Fear only G-d and his servants—the Torah scholars who learn His word.'

"I ate something and Achiya Hashiloni escorted me outside, and there was the wagon and the holy driver. After hearing my esteemed teacher confer the Priestly Blessing on me, I climbed into the wagon and soon we were off. Our surroundings rushed by in a blur, and twenty minutes later, the wagon stood outside my home! It was exactly one o'clock in the morning.

"Two days passed uneventfully when suddenly Achiya Hashiloni appeared before me again. He looked worried, unsure of future developments. 'I am concerned that Rabbi Yisrael will refuse to reveal himself,' he confided. 'Since I already told his father that I will not see him again until he abandons his seclusion, it depends on you now to convince Rabbi Yisrael. You alone can persuade him!'"

"I immediately began searching for your whereabouts," continued Rabbi Adam in his letter, "but all my efforts were for naught. I simply could not locate you anywhere. After some time, Achiya Hashiloni appeared to me again, deep distress evident in his eyes. 'Adam, I see that in Heaven, you are being prevented from meeting with Rabbi Yisrael. The reason for this is known to G-d alone, Who cannot be understood by mortals. I have a solution: Transcribe all the pertinent information on paper and have your son deliver the letter. He will already find the means to ensure that the letter reaches its intended destination.'

"Heeding my master's advice, I transcribed everything on paper, entrusting the manuscript to my son. He searched far and wide for you, traveling great distances to complete his mission, but he returned empty-handed. Greatly grieved at our failure, we had no choice but to wait for Achiya Hashiloni once more, hoping he could narrow our search somewhat. Indeed, hardly had a few days passed when I saw Achiya Hashiloni again. 'Rabbi Yisrael has chosen seclusion in the mountains,' he disclosed. 'You can find him near Kitov. Send your son to hide the papers somewhere among the mountains and, G-d willing, Rabbi Yisrael will find them.'

"In conclusion, I offer a fervent prayer to G-d that, indeed, you will quickly find these writings," wrote Rabbi Adam Baal Shem in his letter. "I pray you will hearken to our esteemed teacher and fulfill his request, thereby spreading Divinity throughout the world and hastening the ultimate Redemption."

Rabbi Yisrael set the letter down and began pacing the cave in great agitation. Though the letter had made an indelible impression on him, he could hardly bear the thought of revealing his true worth. Soon other letters arrived from Rabbi Adam Baal Shem, delivered in the same manner as the first. "If you refuse to reveal yourself," he wrote, "you tip the Scales of Judgment adversely for the entire world, bringing punishment and destruction."

And, in another letter, "Why are you refusing to reveal yourself? I sense that your objection is delaying the Redemption. Sacrifice your will for the good of the Jewish Nation!" As time passed, Rabbi Adam began demanding Rabbi Yisrael's revelation even more, threatening to sever their existing bond. "If you continue to repudiate me," he warned, "I demand you burn all the letters you received from me in the past year."

Finally Rabbi Yisrael relented to the wishes of Achiya Hashiloni and Rabbi Adam Baal Shem, effectively paving the way for his revelation. In deep humility, he continued bemoaning his fate, insisting he was unworthy for such weighty responsibility. His many letters of that period underscored a single concern: his reluctance to become a leader.

"Fright has set my hair on end," Rabbi Yisrael wrote to his brother-in-law, Rabbi Gershon of Kitov. "I am appalled at the very notion of accepting this awesome responsibility of revealing my self to everyone. Who am I to take on such a lofty mission? There are, undoubtedly, others far more deserving than myself! But, dear brother-in-law, I have no choice in the matter. Such is decreed by G-d and I must accept it, particularly since my beloved teacher—Achiya Hashiloni—supports the decree and has refused to see me again until I fulfill his bidding. I have therefore accepted to follow the directive of G-d's Word, as verbalized through the mouth of my esteemed teacher. Many will rise to attack and antagonize me, but I trust in G-d alone."

And, in a letter to the hidden *tzaddik* Rabbi Mordechai, the

Baal Shem Tov wrote the following: "It appears I will be forced to reveal my self after all. This causes me tremendous anguish: why am I better than other righteous *tzaddikim* older than me? Moreover, I know my revelation will cause a great uproar, awaking strife and strenuous opposition as numerous antagonists try to obliterate me. True, my heart is confident in G-d's abundant mercies, but what do I need this terrible hardship for? My life is so good—I study Torah in seclusion, sheltered from the follies of our lowly world, but now a period of suffering awaits me...."

"My soul mourns deeply," he wrote in another letter to Rabbi Mordechai. "By what merit are you allowed to continue living in seclusion while I must reveal myself? Did we not both drink from the same source of blessed water? Here I am, alone in exile, my soul mired in impurity, yet I was chosen to guide others. Though many are holier and better than myself, I am expected to cleanse them before G-d!

"True, all this has come at the express request of my teacher, Achiya Hashiloni, who conferred his explicit blessing in accordance with the demands of the Heavenly Court. Despite this, I still feel inferior and unworthy. My only consolation is that any position—even the lowliest manager of water wells—is decreed by Heaven. Hence, if Heaven has decreed that I possess adequate merit to lead others, certainly I will fill this role with talent and skill."

In yet another letter addressed to his former mentor—the hidden *tzaddik* Rabbi Chaim—the Baal Shem Tov demands: "Why is my lot so bitter? Do I deserve to suffer so?" And, in a letter to his son Rabbi Tzvi, the Baal Shem Tov wrote: "Though the Heavens have forced my hand, since the bitter day [of my revelation] I cry every day, bewailing my terrible misfortune...."

On the eighteenth day of Elul 5494 (1734), coinciding with his thirty-sixth birthday, the Baal Shem Tov became revealed as an incomparable Torah scholar and wonder-worker, thoroughly proficient in the deepest secrets of Creation. "When we had completed studying the final words of Torah," he wrote, "I turned thirty-six and was revealed."

Since that blessed date, his brilliant light continues to illuminate the world and its inhabitants, an enduring and pure light that blazes forth toward the ultimate Redemption.

The Twofold Approach

A NEW PERIOD HAD BEGUN. Immediately following his revelation, the Baal Shem Tov began revitalizing Jewish communities throughout Eastern Europe, breathing new life into scholar and laborer alike. His approach was twofold, one that addressed both the material and spiritual concerns of his brethren.

In that period, many Jews in the region earned their livelihood by dealing with local landowners—dukes and noblemen who leased parts of their vast estates to generate some income. Countless Jews rented flour mills, inns, motels, liquor stores, and some bought the rights to manage forests and rivers. Woe to the hapless Jew who could not meet his monthly rent! Landowners often subjected violators to cruel punishment, using torture and imprisonment to penalize and frighten their tenants.

The Baal Shem Tov used his influence to lighten the oppressive load facing these overburdened Jews. He lent them large sums of money, enabling them to secure jobs and support their families. In times of distress, he personally traveled to intercede with callous landowners, persuading them to exercise compassion and show patience with their impoverished tenants. In emergency situations, when hearing of a family languishing in jail, the Baal Shem Tov raised enough ransom money to pay all outstanding debts and secure their immediate release. The Baal

Shem Tov established a special charity for ransom money, which he used to fund these life-saving missions. Among his letters are many references to this vital work:

"I hereby enclose the sum of one-thousand gold coins to Anthon Schiertizki, the noble master of the village Ternopka, in order that he release all captives upon receipt of this letter. Within the next month, I will complete all remaining payments owed to his honor...."

In another letter: "I have graciously received from the noble master and duke, Anthony son of Theodore of Latshov, the sum of one-hundred gold coins, toward redeeming the captives jailed in the holy congregation of Tultshin. Please G-d, I hope to absolve their debt within two weeks. In merit of your contribution, I pray that G-d heal you from all illness, thus sanctifying His Great Name...."

And, in a letter to Rabbi Noach, a philanthropist from Sidilkov, "I confirm receipt of your letter and advise you to divide your estates—after a full and wholesome life—in the following manner: Each of your sons should have equal share in your mill. Your large house should be converted into a synagogue, in accordance with the will of the city elders. As for your fortune—reserve three-hundred to fund Talmud Torah schools, another three-hundred for the worthy activities of the *Chevra Kaddisha*, and four-hundred towards my fund that redeems imprisoned captives."

To his son, Rabbi Tzvi, the Baal Shem Tov wrote the following: "The deliverer of this letter brings with him three-hundred coins. Go to Count Anthony, give him the entire sum, and relay this message in Polish: 'My father commands you to release the captives. Should you refuse, your end will be bitter.' I trust in G-d that this will have the desired effect...."

And in another letter to his son: "I urgently need one-thousand coins for my work in redeeming captives, extended as a loan over the coming month. Please G-d, place great effort in fulfilling my request; the money is imperative so I can release those bound in prison!"

43

And, in a letter addressed to Rabbi Nachman of Horodenka, the Baal Shem Tov makes a desperate plea: "We are in a critical time now. In the past month alone, I have spent over three-hundred coins on redeeming captives. G-d alone can achieve salvation...."

Neither did the spiritual environment of the times escape his influence. As outlined in earlier chapters, the Baal Shem Tov placed tremendous emphasis on raising the stature of simple, unlearned Jews, imbuing them with renewed life and vitality. Through his revolutionary work, many unlettered Jews began a life of literacy and study. In addition, the Baal Shem Tov revealed the esoteric dimension of Torah to learned scholars, enlightening them with the pure light of Chasidus. Transformed by his clarity of thought and novel teachings, scholars looked at their spiritual accomplishments differently, realizing how much their service of G-d still lacked. By influencing both the unlettered and the learned, the Baal Shem Tov effectively raised spiritual standards everywhere.

To further his work, the Baal Shem Tov personally traveled throughout the country, visiting numerous large cities, smaller towns, and almost forgotten villages. A perusal of his letters enumerates no less than twenty-one separate locations.[1] He visited every major study center, including the famous Torah academies at Brisk, Minsk, Slutsk, Smargon, Halusk and Pinsk, captivating numerous students with his unparalleled erudition.

---

1. Anipoli, Barashid, Latzov, Koritz, Kraminitz, Krasna, Lechewitz, Littin, Ludmir, Lvov, Ostila, Ostrow, Polonnoye, Potik, Rekittna, Sidilkov, Slavita, the village of Ternopka, Tultshin, Ushpeitzin and Yassi (Moldova).

The Inner Circle

W ITHIN SIX YEARS, the Baal Shem Tov had drawn sixty[1] select
disciples into his inner circle. His leadership was firm, confident
and systematic. His very presence demanded obedience. His disciples, all accomplished scholars and saintly individuals, aroused
reverence and respect wherever they went. Some possessed *ruach
hakodesh*, and had even merited seeing Elijah the Prophet.
Having attained lofty spiritual levels, select students could even
communicate directly with Heaven, relaying questions and
receiving explicit answers.

---

1. Though the Baal Shem Tov had sixty select disciples, the names of only
twenty-four are found scattered among his letters: 1) Rabbi Boruch of Kaminka;
2) Rabbi Dovid Lahkes; 3) Rabbi Dovid Furkas; 4) Rabbi Dovid of Mikolayev;
5) Rabbi Dovid of Kolomia; 6) Rabbi DovBer (later to succeed the Baal Shem
Tov, becoming known as the *Maggid* of Mezritch); 7) Rabbi Zev Wolf Kitzes;
8) Rabbi Yehuda Leib Pyastinner; 9) Rabbi Yaakov Yosef of Polonnoye;
10) Rabbi Yitzchak of Drohobitz; 11) Rabbi Yeshaya of Yanov; 12) Rabbi
Chaim Hakohen Rapaport, rabbi of Lvov and author of many scholarly works,
(including *Shaalot u'Teshuvot Rabbi Chaim Hakohen*); 13) Rabbi Chaim of
Krasna; 14) Rabbi Meir Margolis, the rabbi of Ostrow (author of *Shaalot
u'Teshuvot Meir Netivim*); 15) Rabbi Menachem Mendel of Be'er; 16) Rabbi
Menachem Mendel of Premishlan; 17) Rabbi Moshe of Kitov; 18) Rabbi
Moshe of Daalin; 19) Rabbi Nachman of Horodenka; 20) Rabbi Nachman of
Kossov; 21) Rabbi Pinchas of Koritz; 22) Rabbi Tzvi Hirsh, the Baal Shem
Tov's personal scribe; 23) Rabbi Shmuel of Kaminka; 24) Rabbi Shimshon of
Anipoli.

On auspicious occasions, the Baal Shem Tov would eat together with his circle of select disciples, while all others could merely stand and watch. Only those thoroughly proficient in the Kabbalistic works of the holy Arizal could grace his table. "Six years have already passed since my revelation," the Baal Shem Tov wrote in a letter. "Thank G-d, erudite, righteous scholars have flocked to me, thirstily absorbing my teachings as they ascend the mountain of G-d."

Displaying phenomenal aptitude for organization, the Baal Shem Tov quickly formed centers across the county. Some were established in the vicinity of his disciples, while others were managed by certain disciples sent specifically to those locations. His disciples disseminated the Baal Shem Tov's teachings faith-fully, fulfilling their worthy mission with energy and unlimited enthusiasm. Each was a leader, establishing a center of light and warmth in their particular place, as chosen by the Baal Shem Tov.

Aside from their regular duties, these disciples wandered from town to town, spreading word of the Baal Shem Tov's greatness. They related stories describing the numerous miracles wrought by this famous wonder-worker—how he cured the terminally ill, healed the barren, and opened the Heavenly gates of blessing for all in need. "His supernatural powers match those of the Talmudic Sages," asserted his disciples. "In our day, they are unequivocally unique."

Scarcely content with relating riveting stories, his disciples placed careful emphasis on spreading the novel teachings of the Baal Shem Tov, imbuing others with his illuminating words. The spiritual path of service forged by the Baal Shem Tov blazed across the country, gaining loyal adherents in countless Jewish communities.

The Baal Shem Tov established a special fund to support his disciples, the hidden *tzaddikim*, who had chosen to take the wan-dering stick in hand, not resting until they could illuminate oth-ers with the fire of Chasidus. "All the hidden *tzaddikim*—may their light shine forth!—receive ample sustenance from my fund," wrote the Baal Shem Tov. "Each and all receive an allotted portion, calculated according to their individual needs."

In a letter to Rabbi Nachman of Horodenka, the Baal Shem Tov wrote, "My messenger hereby gives you three-hundred gold coins to support the hidden *tzaddikim*. Swear you will not spend even a single penny of this sum in order to support me."

The Baal Shem Tov cared deeply about the hidden *tzaddikim* living in the Holy Land, and he raised money for them as well. "You have graciously consented to donate two-thousand ducats annually," he wrote to a donor. "Now that—by the grace of G-d—I have been appointed to head also the charity supporting hidden *tzaddikim* in the Holy Land, I beseech you to donate toward this worthy cause as well. Your additional donation will sustain the righteous, the 'pillars of the world,' who live in the Holy Land (may it be rebuilt speedily in our times)."

And, in a letter written by Rabbi Pinchas of Koritz—one of the Baal Shem Tov's select disciples—to Rabbi Tzvi, the Rebbe's son, we find: "I have personally raised one-thousand gold coins in Polish currency, to sustain and support hidden *tzaddikim* exiled in the Diaspora."

The dedicated work of his selfless disciples quickly bore fruit, and the Baal Shem Tov's influence swept rapidly through the country, gaining devoted adherents in all communities. His revolutionary approach of love and warmth toward any Jew—even the simplest ignoramus—won the hearts of Jews throughout Poland and Lithuania. In 5514 (1754), scarcely twenty years after his revelation, the Baal Shem Tov's followers numbered in the tens of thousands. Hundreds were erudite Torah scholars and righteous *tzaddikim* who strove to spread the teachings of Chasidus ever outward. As dedicated emissaries of the Baal Shem Tov, they wandered from city to town, infusing Jewish communities with renewed enthusiasm and vitality in their observance of Torah and *mitzvot*.

Winds of Opposition

THE NOVEL APPROACH of the Baal Shem Tov and his widespread popularity alarmed many Torah scholars, particularly those living in Lithuania. Leading scholars of the region—especially those from the Torah center of Vilna—rose to oppose the teachings of Chasidus. Misled by purposeful distortions of the Baal Shem Tov's teachings, his antagonists branded his message as sacrilegious and sent him explicit warnings to desist. In 5517 (1757), they convened an urgent assembly in the city of Shklov, passing a resolution that placed the Baal Shem Tov and his movement under the ban of excommunication.

In response, the Baal Shem Tov's disciples penned their shock and outrage: "United by all those who recognize truth, and together with the larger Jewish Nation who believe in G-d and His servants—the righteous *tzaddikim*, the sincere and the upright—we hereby negate the ban of excommunication passed in Shklov on the nineteenth of Tammuz 5517 (1757), against our leader and master, teacher of the Diaspora, the Baal Shem Tov (may he live long and blessed years). The ban placed upon him, upon us, and upon all Jews following his path, is completely baseless, founded totally on slander and lies. It does not contain the power to excommunicate or ostracize—Heaven protect us all!—but contains only nonsensical folly and evil design. The ban is groundless and without meaning, completely nullified like the dust of the earth."

The Baal Shem Tov himself signed the above declaration, followed by thirteen of his disciples.[1] In a letter to his brother-in-law, Rabbi Gershon of Kitov, he decried the negative effects of the ban proclaimed by his opponents, "I hereby inform you of my revelation and the tremendous opposition I face. Verily, I cannot even walk out on the street safely any more...."

He also penned a special letter to the rabbis of Yassi: "I write this letter to protect my teachings and holy path of service against slander, and for the sake of peace. I swear by my life that this holy path of service contains not the slightest sacrilege, deviation or digression from the G-dly path. My teachings are founded on the esoteric dissertations of the mystic, Rabbi Moshe Cordovero (*Ramak*; 1522-1570). I trust that G-d will illuminate the eyes of my antagonists, helping them recognize my sincerity and truth."

The Baal Shem Tov forbade his followers from entering into debates with his opponents, or slandering them in return. "I come with words of caution to your esteemed honor," he wrote to his disciple Rabbi Yaakov Yosef, the rabbi of Polonnoye and author of the acclaimed *Toldot Yaakov Yosef*. "Do not speak harshly against our attackers and enemies; regardless, they will disperse before us like wind-driven chaff. As you are aware, when my soul ascended Heavenward in 5507, it was revealed to me that I would gain fame throughout the entire world. Hence, my dear student, remember that you gain tremendously through silence—as our Sages observe, 'A word is worth one coin, silence is worth two.' Even in my youth, before my revelation, I suffered persecution at the hands of many rabbis and *tzaddikim*. Even my

1. These were: 1) Rabbi Dovid Lahkes; 2) Rabbi Dovid Furkas; 3) Rabbi Dovid of Mikolayev; 4) Rabbi DovBer (later to succeed the Baal Shem Tov, becoming known as the *Maggid* of Mezritch); 5) Rabbi Zev Wolf Kitzes; 6) Rabbi Yehuda Leib Pyastinner; 7) Rabbi Yaakov Yosef of Polonnoye; 8) Rabbi Yitzchak of Drohobitz; 9) Rabbi Yeshaya of Yanov; 10) Rabbi Meir Margolis; 11) Rabbi Menachem Mendel of Be'er; 12) Rabbi Tzvi Hirsh, the Baal Shem Tov's scribe; 13) Rabbi Shimshon of Anipoli.

own brother-in-law—*may his saintly light shine!*—antagonized me. Yet, G-d hearkens and protects the persecuted...."

In another letter signed by the Baal Shem Tov, he expresses his firm resolution to ignore all hostilities of his attackers. "We, the undersigned, have resolved not to answer our antagonists—whether with kind words or the opposite. We forgive all those who hate us with complete forgiveness. May sins perish and not, G-d forbid, the sinners themselves...." Signatures of Rabbi DovBer (later the *Maggid* of Mezritch) and the *Toldot Yaakov Yosef* also appear on this letter.

At times the Baal Shem Tov was forced into debate and, on occasion, asked his disciples to assist in his defense of Chasidus. "If your health permits, travel at once to meet me here [in Sidilkov]," he wrote to Rabbi DovBer. "We are pressured to debate our enemies, and I need a scholarly giant who can support his claims with clear-cut proof from the Talmud. If, however, you are unable to come, at least ensure that the *rav* of Polonnoye should join me...."

In a correspondence with the rabbi of Shklov—a bastion of anti-Chasidic sentiment—the Baal Shem Tov resolutely defended his stance: "I am writing to remove the hate and lies perpetrated by our enemies, those bent on destroying G-d's vineyard, on silencing the sincere and G-d-fearing who have joined our path. Our enemies denounce us on baseless charges, including the accusation forwarded by their leader that decries the various mannerisms and movements we exhibit during prayer. Apparently he has forgotten the explicit statement found in *Kuzari*, who was questioned regarding this very issue. The *Kuzari's* answer—pure, golden words—are found in his book.

"Besides," continued the Baal Shem Tov, "these mannerisms are not done purposely, G-d forbid. I come merely to rectify and enliven the old, dry bones of our nation, infusing every religious aspect with life and vitality. Renewed energy brings bodily movement with it, unintentionally and on its own accord. Devotion and energized life brings freshness to the prayers, as is readily understood by any rational person. This is not an inculcated custom, as our inane enemies would have you believe."

"If, however, your esteemed honor wishes to respond with clear, logical statements, I am prepared to continue debating the merits of this issue. Illuminated by the blinding light of truth, you will then see clear justification for our path which, in turn, will prompt you to join our cause. This will bring sweetness and spiritual bliss to your study and service of the heart—i.e., prayer. I write this as a friend, one who prays for the entire Jewish Nation, and for my antagonists in particular, hoping that they attain complete repentance."

His path of service validated by Heaven, the Baal Shem Tov shared his air of assurance with his students, many whom experienced suffering at the hands of opposing forces. In a letter to his disciple, Rabbi Yaakov Yosef, the Baal Shem Tov wrote: "Though the Torah itself commands us to rule in accordance with the majority, this only applies when both parties are associated with Torah and purity. If the majority is inclined toward the opposite—are we enjoined to follow them just because they are the majority, Heaven forbid? I envision clearly—having been revealed to me by the Heavens themselves—that our small group is the one inclined toward the pure path of Torah!"

Final Days

SHORTLY BEFORE HIS PASSING, the Baal Shem Tov divined that his mission on earth was nearing its close. He celebrated the *Lag B'Omer* meal that year with extraordinary elation, hinting to his disciples that he had merely eighteen days remaining on this earth. "My light will shine until the coming of Moshiach!" he assured his distraught followers.

Eighteen days later—on Wednesday, the first day of Shavuot 5520 (1760)—at the age of sixty-one years, eight months and eighteen days, the Baal Shem Tov's pure soul ascended heavenward. Before his passing, he turned to his grieving disciples and instructed them to sing his favorite tune—the plaintive, soulsearching melody composed by his student, Rabbi Michel of Zlotchov. As they sang, the Baal Shem Tov declared the following: "I guarantee for all generations that whoever, whenever and wherever this song is sung, arousing G-d's mercy with feelings of repentance—I will hear this song in whichever Heavenly chamber I am found. I will sing along and arouse G-d's mercies, channeling Divine blessing upon the singer.

"I have the option of ascending to Heaven in a whirlwind, much like Elijah the Prophet," continued the Baal Shem Tov, "yet I forgo this honor, choosing instead to fulfill the Biblical verse, 'For you are dust, and shall return to dust'" (Genesis 3:19).

In fulfillment of express instructions found in his will, only ten persons remained in the room during the Baal Shem Tov's last moments of life. They were: Rabbi Leib Pyastinner, Rabbi Nachman of Horodenka, Rabbi Shimshon of Anipoli, Rabbi Boruch of Kaminka, Rabbi Zev Wolf Kitzes, Rabbi Dovid Lahkes, Rabbi Dovid Furkas, Rabbi Dovid of Mikolayev, Rabbi Kehot and Rabbi DovBer, the future *Maggid* of Mezritch.

After his passing, his followers comforted themselves with a letter written by the Baal Shem Tov less than two months earlier. "My dear ones, you will undoubtedly read this letter after my physical life," it began. "I know you all to be upright and sincere people who will fulfill my instructions to the letter. After securing your forgiveness, I hereby command:

(a) Whoever succeeds my leadership shall not live in [my village] Mezibush, by no means whatsoever,

(b) Respect whoever is chosen to replace my position with even more respect than was accorded to me for, in truth, I am aware that my successor is worthy of praise even among the righteous,

(c) Days of conflict are approaching, days when the young will shame their elders, G-d protect us all! My dear children, do not associate yourselves with these unscrupulous people. Truth forges a path, plainly revealing that G-d and His Law are true, and our path is true, without the slightest doubt or misgiving,

(d) The most important thing of all—for the sake of G-d, do not fight or squabble amongst yourselves! Peace alone shall reign supreme in our camp!"

Rabbi DovBer, the *Maggid* of Mezritch, disciple and successor of the Baal Shem Tov, later declared: "Were the Baal Shem Tov alive in the time of the Talmudic Sages, he would be considered a phenomenon."

THE FOUNDATIONS
OF CHASIDUS

Innovative Teachings

AMONG HIS INNOVATIVE TEACHINGS, the Baal Shem Tov advanced a number of ideas, fundamental basics that would energize and revitalize the spiritual lives of world Jewry. These were:

Sanctity of the words of Torah
Divine providence
Revealing spiritual qualities within the simplest Jews
Unconditional love toward fellow Jews

Sanctity of the Words of Torah

The Baal Shem Tov highlighted the holiness attained by simply reciting words of Torah and revealed the sanctity inherent within the actual words. "Were people to realize the sheer power of Torah," the Baal Shem Tov once observed, "it would be impossible to find a single Jew not thoroughly proficient in the entire *Chumash* and *Tehillim*!"

On another occasion, the Baal Shem Tov remarked: "Man is constantly overwhelmed by daily frustrations. While trying to earn a livelihood and provide for his family, man encounters many difficulties along the way. These frustrations can be compared to the great Deluge, a flood of problems that threaten to drown our spiritual ambitions. What is the solution to this dilemma? '[G-d said to Noah:] Enter the ark, you and your household'" (Genesis 7:1).

Playing on the Hebrew word *teiva*—which can mean either "ark" or "word"—the Baal Shem Tov interpreted this verse to underscore the unique quality of Torah and prayer. "Enter the *teiva*," he explained. "Come into the sacred words of Torah and prayer, thereby forming a protective barrier against the menacing waters of our physical world. Cleaving to holy words redeems 'you and your household,' channeling Divine salvation in all aspects.

"In this regard, the simplest Jew equals the greatest scholar. The unassuming sincerity and devotion of the unlearned enables them to attain a state of complete attachment with the words of *Tehillim* and prayer they utter. In this merit, they arouse Divine mercy and draw infinite blessing into our world, bringing ultimate salvation to all."

The following incident demonstrates the power of reciting *Tehillim* sincerely. A grave decree once faced an entire Jewish community, threatening them with total annihilation. Alarmed, the Baal Shem Tov summoned his two colleagues—the hidden *tzaddikim* Rabbi Mordechai and Rabbi Kehot. "We now constitute a *beit din*," declared the Baal Shem Tov. "Let us find a means of nullifying this terrible decree."

The Baal Shem Tov's soul ascended heavenward. He passed swiftly through myriad chambers as he tried his utmost to abolish the frightful decree, but the ruling seemed irreversible. The community was doomed. Despondent, the Baal Shem Tov began descending, when he suddenly stopped in astonishment. There, emanating from one of the Heavenly chambers, shone a brilliant light, a shimmering radiance that seemed unusually ethereal even in these spiritual spheres. The Baal Shem Tov divined that this chamber was created in merit of a simple villager, a laborer who recited *Tehillim* as he worked, finishing the entire book of *Tehillim* five times a day.

Descending to earth, the Baal Shem Tov immediately traveled to meet the simple laborer. He found the simple Jew hard at work, his lips moving to the rhythm of *Tehillim*. "Tell me," asked the Baal Shem Tov, "if you knew your spiritual merits could save an entire Jewish community, would you forfeit those merits to save them?"

The villager did not hesitate in the slightest. "If I have a portion in the World-to-Come," he declared, "I transfer it all toward this cause!" His sincere words caused a great uproar in Heaven, and the decree was promptly abolished.

In similar vein, the Baal Shem Tov explained the verse (Psalms 106:2), 'Who can recount the mighty acts of G-d, or proclaim all His praises?' Proclaiming all G-d's praises—by reciting the entire book of *Tehillim*—enables us to effectively crumble Heavenly prosecution, which are the 'severe acts' of G-d." (*Yemalel*, the Hebrew for *recount*, can also mean *crumble*).

R. Hirshel, one of the Baal Shem Tov's disciples, took this teaching to heart. A simple digger of wells, Hirshel was far from a Torah scholar, but his deeds were permeated with unusual piety. He fulfilled the *mitzvot* with meticulous care, far beyond the letter of the law. Even his eating habits exemplified unusual piety: Hirshel ate his bread with salt alone, choosing to avoid any sort of fatty spread that could make his meal more palatable. Zealously careful about the laws of *kashrut*, he drank only water and, throughout his life, never tasted meat.

Hirshel had committed the entire *Chumash* and *Tehillim* to memory and recited their sacred words constantly—whether digging wells or walking the streets to and from work. Though he barely understood the meaning of the words he uttered, Hirshel reviewed the sacred texts constantly, imbuing every moment of his waking hours with spirituality.

Said the Baal Shem Tov: "In Heaven, the opinion of Hirshel the digger is given careful consideration!"

The Baal Shem Tov's teaching had far-reaching ramifications even many decades later. The year 5603 (1843) was intensely difficult for the third Rebbe of Lubavitch, Rabbi Menachem Mendel—known as the *Tzemach Tzedek*. The Russian czar planned to sign insufferable decrees into law, decrees leveled against Russian Jewry and the teachings of Chasidus, placing the spiritual lives of countless Jews in jeopardy. Distraught with worry, the Tzemach Tzedek traveled to Liozna, to the resting place of his righteous mother, Rebbetzin Devorah Leah, and implored her to intervene in Heaven on his behalf, for success in his mission.

Suddenly the Tzemach Tzedek saw his mother. "I tried my utmost to arouse Divine mercy," she revealed. "In fact, I even merited to enter the radiant chamber of the Baal Shem Tov, where I relayed your fears and the threat facing Russian Jewry. 'Grant my son the ability to nullify this evil decree!' I beseeched him. 'Give me some means of protection to pass on to him which will enable him to thwart those who plot against Chasidus!'

"The Baal Shem Tov turned to me and said: 'Tell your son the verse, 'And the fear (*chitat*) of G-d enveloped the cities...so that none pursued the sons of Jacob' (Genesis 35:5). *Chitat* forms the acronym of the three books of *Chumash*, *Tehillim* and *Tanya*. Your son is proficient in all three, having committed them to memory, word by word, letter by letter. Whoever is fluent in these three is capable of destroying all obstacles, thereby removing all forms of Heavenly concealment.'"

Divine Providence

Another foundation of Chasidic teaching centered on Divine Providence—G-d's constant and specific supervision over every detail of His handiwork. Divine Providence, taught the Baal Shem Tov, extends to every element of Creation, at every time and in every place. When two Jews meet, he averred, their encounter reflects a Divine orchestration of events, bringing them together to strengthen the observance of Torah and its commandments. Rather than suffice with charitable or social commitments, it behooves the pair to learn from one another, each influencing his partner to further their Torah and *mitzvot*.

The Baal Shem Tov taught a cardinal principle: "A person is

enjoined to learn something from every occurrence in this world," he said. "Everything one sees or hears contains a vital lesson, highlighting a practical application in his service of G-d."

According to the Baal Shem Tov, Divine Providence affects every facet of Creation, extending to the tiniest, seemingly insignificant details. A single leaf, a thin stalk of straw—all these are supervised and ordained by the Infinite One. Divine Providence regulates how often a falling leaf should turn, or where it should finally rest. There is a specific Divine intention within every physical occurrence.

Moreover, G-d coordinates numerous causes to effect a single act in regard to Creation, and everything is with evident Divine Providence. For example, on a glorious summer's day, a sudden wind may strongly blow, detaching some leaves from a tree, removing straw from thatched rooftops, or fluttering loose straw around the yard. But then, after a few minutes it's all over, and all is calm once again. This demonstrates that G-d summoned the wind to facilitate certain Divine intentions for these specific elements.

This teaches an important lesson. If, for insignificant leaves and straw, Divine Providence controls every aspect of their movements, we can infer that concerning G-d's beloved children—the Jewish Nation—this applies in a much greater sense, in a manner that defies description!

To further illustrate this principle, the Baal Shem Tov offered the following illustration: "In a large forest, a tall mountaintop, or a wide valley, lies a field of tall, unkempt grass. The area is untouched, unexplored by humans. The grass sways and bends in the wind, toward various directions—right, left, back and forth. Each of these movements is Divinely ordained, systematically orchestrated by G-d's precise desire. Similarly, G-d regulates the exact time-span of this grass, specifying how long it will exist in months, days and hours. During this time frame, G-d ordains how often the grass will sway, and toward which direction."

Said the Baal Shem Tov, "This is what is meant by the verse 'And you shall go to the place where G-d will choose to make

His Name rest (dwell) there' (Deuteronomy 26:2). *You shall go to the place*—when a Jew travels it is not mere happenstance. Rather, *G-d has chosen* man's steps, having divinely ordained man's movements. So when the person arrives at the new location, it is in order to *make His Name rest (dwell) there*"—to spread G-dliness in the world.

Within the Simplest Jew

Toward the end of the 18th century, it still remained common to find grown adults partially or completely illiterate. Barely able to stumble through the daily prayers, these unlettered Jews could never hope to grasp even the most basic of Torah texts. Humbled by their intellectual handicap, they tried serving G-d to the best of their ability, performing the Torah's commandments with genuine feeling and deep faith. Peddlers, artisans, merchants—all tried to compensate for their ignorance with good deeds and wholehearted fervor. Yet, in the eyes of the scholarly world, these Jews were an embarrassment, an aberration to Torah-true life. The learned shunned the ignorant masses and condemned their ignorance.

The Baal Shem Tov energized these simple Jews by revealing their intense spiritual worth, thereby elevating their morale. Recognizing genuine sincerity and devotion, he removed their cloak of shame and unworthiness, and replaced it with a brilliant light of purpose. Guided by his teachings, the Torah world took a second look at simple Jews, perceiving their merits in a far better light.

"The greatest scholar must learn from the unassuming sincerity of the unlearned Jew," taught the Baal Shem Tov. "Though ignorant, they accept G-d's rule willingly, and serve Him with devotion. Their *mitzvot*, permeated with the wholehearted joy that stems from deep faith, generate great delight in the Heavens."

Through highlighting the essential qualities found within all Jews, the Baal Shem Tov revealed the innate spiritual character of every soul, regardless of background or stature. "Every Jew is precious before G-d," he declared. "G-d's love is comparable to the overwhelming affection parents have toward an only child born in their old age, and on a far greater scale! Moreover, G-d does not only love the soul. He cherishes the Jewish body as well. This love extends from the simplest individual to the most scholarly."

Drawing on the description of G-d's initial appearance to Moshe Rabbenu (Exodus 3:2), the Baal Shem Tov interpreted the Biblical verse in a manner that emphasized this ideal: "*And G-d appeared to him in a fiery thorn bush*—the barren thorn bush represents the simple, unlearned Jew," he explained. "Their unassuming sincerity and warmth, based on pure faith, is the fire of the thorn bush.

"*And the bush was not consumed*—The great yearning of the unlearned to serve G-d is never satisfied. By contrast, the scholar satisfies his quest for G-dliness through study and innovative Torah thoughts. Thus, G-d showed Moshe the great worth of the simple Jew. The ever-burning fire exists within the simple and the sincere, not within the accomplished scholar."

(Rabbi Schneur Zalman of Liadi—the founder of the Chabad-Lubavitch movement—elaborated on this idea, coupling the Baal Shem Tov's teaching with practical application. "G-d showed Moshe the true meaning of leadership," he observed. "A leader chosen to guide others toward redemption is empowered to touch and illuminate every Jew, to reveal the spiritual radiance that blazes within the simplest soul.")

"We represent G-d's *tefillin*, as it were," taught the Baal Shem Tov. "What is written in G-d's *tefillin*? 'And who is like Your Nation, Israel, a unique people on this land' (*Brachot*, 6a). Learned scholars are symbolized by the head-*tefillin*, which are placed near the mind, the seat of intellect. Conversely, the hand-*tefillin* represent the simple Jews, who serve G-d by merit of good deeds and sterling character.

"It is important to note that the hand-*tefillin* are donned before the head-*tefillin*. This denotes the superior worth of the simple Jew, whose firm faith, unfettered by intellectual achievement, forms a total subjugation to G-d's Will. Such unquestioning obedience contains more spiritual worth than all the scholarly achievements of the learned combined."

The Baal Shem Tov went even further, stressing that the merits attained by simple Jews serve to protect the scholars! "Our Sages compare the Jewish Nation to a grapevine," he explained. "'Scholars are the grapes; simple Jews are the leaves' (*Chullin*, 92a). Just as the grapevine would ultimately wither and die without the protection afforded by its leaves, similarly, without the spiritual merit of simple Jews, scholars would lose valuable spiritual protection."

The Baal Shem Tov befriended the simple Jews. Every Sukkot, he danced and sang with his unlearned brethren, preferring to share his spiritual enjoyment with those who exhibited sincere joy.

Years later, his disciple and successor, the *Maggid* of Mezritch, commented on his mentor's boundless love toward every Jew. "Had the Baal Shem Tov known the true worth of simple Jews the way he perceives it now in the World-of-Truth," he declared, "he would have loved them with even more passion!"

Rabbi Schneur Zalman of Liadi had this to add: "The Baal Shem Tov was the Avraham of Chasidus. Just as the first Patriarch dedicated his entire life to spreading an awareness of G-d even among the simplest people, the Baal Shem Tov, too, devoted his life to the simplest Jews, drawing them ever closer to the warmth of Torah and *mitzvot*.

"The *Midrash* states: 'Until Avraham, the world functioned in darkness and uncertainty. When Avraham came, the world began to shine with purpose.' The same applies to the Baal Shem Tov, the Patriarch of Chasidus: Until his time, the light of spirituality shone brilliantly for scholars and learned men, but unlearned folk remained enshrouded by the darkness of ignorance. When the Baal Shem Tov began his Divine work, the light of spirituality shone for simple Jews as well."

The Baal Shem Tov strove to bring the light of Torah closer to even the most ignorant Jews. At times, he expounded Chasidus on a simple level, his choice of words specifically geared toward those with mere rudimentary knowledge of Torah. His closest disciples—all scholars of stature—were totally dedicated to their Rebbe, yet they harbored slight resentment against the simple folk who occupied so much of their master's time and attention. Yet, despite their feelings, the students would review and delve into those teachings too.

One day the Baal Shem Tov's students gathered to review the complexity of a new teaching, marveling aloud at the sheer depth of knowledge evident in their master's words. "In truth," they decided unanimously, "the Baal Shem Tov's path is intended for the scholarly and righteous—those well-versed in all areas of Torah, who cleave to G-d through pious deeds." Their message rang clear: the Baal Shem Tov belonged to his elite circle of disciples.

Hardly had they finished speaking when the Baal Shem Tov arrived unannounced. "I adore the simple Jews; they are G-d's greatest treasure," he admonished his startled disciples. "The Prophet Malachi (3:12) declared, *[Israel] will be my desired land, says the L-rd of Hosts*: Just as the wisest of all men can never ascertain all of nature's secrets, so, too, we cannot begin to fathom the intense spiritual treasures hidden within every Jewish heart. Indeed, they *truly* are G-d's desired land."

"It is my greatest hope," concluded the Baal Shem Tov, "that I can empower these simple Jews, and enable them to bring forth a bountiful 'harvest'—as befits those who are called 'G-d's desired land.'"

"Learn from these simple Jews!" he instructed. "Let them show you the true meaning of sincerity and trust, unquestioning faith, belief in the righteous, *Ahavat Yisrael*, and other fine traits. The simple Jew—he is the true servant of G-d!"

In accordance with the Baal Shem Tov's words, his disciples began observing simple Jews more closely, realizing how, in reality, the unlearned were far better attuned to the real meaning of spirituality. "Just watch R. Pesach the water-carrier!" commanded the Baal Shem Tov. "Observe how he enters the synagogue."

His disciples were well acquainted with the water carrier, an illiterate fellow who earned his living by carrying heavy buckets of water through the streets. That day, as the humble water carrier entered to *daven Minchah*, the Baal Shem Tov's disciples stood scattered around the synagogue, eyes affixed upon the door. Entering the foyer, R. Pesach immediately made his way to the sink and proceeded to wash his hands with the utmost care, rinsing and wiping between every finger. As he crossed the threshold, R. Pesach's face changed visibly, physically affected by his palpable fear of G-d. Glancing in awe at the Holy Ark, R. Pesach recited the verse, "I have set G-d before me always" (Psalms 16:8), his face turning various shades of red and white with emotion.

Humbled, the Baal Shem Tov's students left the synagogue deep in thought. They—the scholarly and righteous disciples of the Baal Shem Tov—could learn much from this simple water-carrier. How true were the words of their saintly master regarding the virtues of simple Jews!

On another occasion, the Baal Shem Tov interpreted a single verse of prayer in a manner that illustrated the essential difference between the sincere and the accomplished. At a gathering of learned scholars, the Baal Shem Tov sat in silence as various scholars debated with one another, each bent on proving the authenticity of his particular innovation. Declared the Baal Shem Tov: "*[O G-d] look down and see our shame* (Lamentations 5:1)—Help us recognize our shameful display of arrogance and self-promotion...."

Later, when the Baal Shem Tov arrived in a village populated by unlearned Jews, he witnessed their altruistic efforts as, together, they raised large sums of money to redeem jailed captives. Driven by a true desire to assist their fellow Jews, these simple villagers displayed an extraordinary measure of genuine *Ahavat Yisrael*. Declared the Baal Shem Tov: "*[O G-d] look down and see our shame*—Observe how they risk their lives because of their love of fellow Jews!" (The Baal Shem Tov translated *cherpah*, shame, as *cheref*, risk.)

Appreciative of their sincerity, one Rosh Hashanah the Baal Shem Tov chose to blow *shofar* with the simple Jews and young children. He instructed his disciple Rabbi Yaakov Yosef to blow *shofar* for his other disciples, while he joined the unlearned in their prayers. "Father in Heaven!" the congregation implored fervently. "Please, have mercy on us!"

"Their sincere cries pierced the Heavens," observed the Baal Shem Tov later. "This cry was more effective than anything else possible."

On a different occasion, the Baal Shem Tov was alarmed to perceive a severe decree threatening several Jewish communities with annihilation. Summoning his disciples, the Baal Shem Tov instructed them to begin a schedule of fasting and penance, but all their combined efforts proved fruitless. Hoping to succeed in merit of communal intervention, the Baal Shem Tov and his students turned to the local rabbi and convinced him to establish a day of fasting and prayer.

On the scheduled date, hundreds of men, women and children gathered in the synagogue, raising their voices in prayer and anguish. Crying remorseful tears, they repented for their sins and asked for Divine mercy. Suddenly the Baal Shem Tov turned to one of his disciples, the righteous Rabbi Nachman of Horodenka, and exclaimed jubilantly: "It is over! The decree has been annulled!" The Baal Shem Tov's face radiated pure joy and his disciples rejoiced at this unexpected salvation.

Later, when he was alone with his disciples, the Baal Shem Tov revealed details on the annulment: "The decree seemed irreversible," he began. "Even when the congregation recited *Tehillim*, I could not discern the slightest weakening in the decree. On the contrary—the spiritual adversary fortified his arguments against the community, increasing the severity of their collective punishment. Suddenly, intermingling with our prayers, a woman's cry could be heard: 'Master of the Universe!'

she beseeched. 'I am but a simple mother of five children, yet, when they begin crying, I cannot bear to ignore their entreaties. Dear G-d, You have so many children crying out to you—why, even a closed heart would become receptive to such wailing! Father in Heaven, save Your children!'

"Silenced by her deep faith, the Heavenly adversary abandoned his efforts and slunk away in shame. These sincere words, uttered by a woman who could not even read the Hebrew alphabet, shattered an otherwise powerful prosecution. A few simple sentences effectively annulled the entire decree."

This was not the only time unconventional prayer saved a community. One year, on the awe-inspiring day of Yom Kippur, those gathered in the Baal Shem Tov's *shul* in Mezibush could not help but notice the Rebbe's frightening demeanor. Ashen with grief, the Baal Shem Tov spent an inordinate amount of time concentrating on his prayers, a river of tears streaming down his cheeks. His disciples watched with growing alarm as the Rebbe's spiritual devotions intensified well beyond his customary fervor.

Surmising that a grave Heavenly decree was troubling their master, the Baal Shem Tov's disciples redoubled their supplications, trying to avert whatever calamity threatened the Jewish nation. Soon the congregation at large was swept up by their frightful cries, hearts trembling in fear at the looming danger. Terrible wailing rent the air as each and all inspected their past misdeeds, making a resolute commitment to improve their fulfillment of the Torah and its *mitzvot*.

The skies darkened and stars slowly began to appear, but the Baal Shem Tov remained oblivious to the physical realms of time and space. His lips moved continually, his eyes stayed firmly shut in concentration. The Heavenly decree must have reached such terrifying proportions that the Baal Shem Tov was prepared to keep the Yom Kippur prayers going in the hope of arousing Divine mercy. Men and women sobbed aloud, trying to silence the Heavenly adversary. Their inner introspection and deep sighing intensified; the very walls seemed to be running with tears.

Near the *chazzan* stood an unlettered teenager, a poor shepherd who tended flocks of sheep in the nearby forest. Unable to read the Hebrew alphabet, the shepherd lad regularly attended the Rosh Hashanah and Yom Kippur services in the Baal Shem Tov's *shul*, staring into the *chazzan's* face. At this moment, when the congregation became visibly anxious, the shepherd also felt deeply distraught. If only he, too, could pray along and help his brethren in their time of need!

His mind racing, the shepherd recalled the various sounds of farm animals and birds he knew so well. Long hours spent shepherding his flock had enabled him to mimic all these calls perfectly, yet he prized the cry of the rooster most. The shepherd's emotions peaked, cresting into tearful action and he loudly cried, "Cock-a-doodle-doo! G-d, have mercy!"

The congregation stopped their devotions, aghast at the sacrilegious outcry disturbing the holiest prayers of the year. Those standing near the young shepherd reached out threateningly, gesticulating for him to keep silent or leave the building. "But I am also a Jew!" protested the youngster loudly. "Let me pray! Your G-d is also my G-d!"

Rabbi Yosef Yuzpa, the elderly *shamash*, stepped in quickly, calming passions on all sides. "The boy can stay," he said firmly. "Let him be."

Suddenly a commotion arose. The Baal Shem Tov's face shone with fiery radiance; his movements bespoke joy. The Baal Shem Tov and his disciples were hurrying through the final paragraphs of prayer, their faces suffused with elation. The Baal Shem Tov quickly began the repetition aloud, singing the words to the tune of a sweet melody. He recited the closing verses of the *Neilah* prayer with grateful emotion, ending the prayer with a blissful melody of appreciation.

That night, the Baal Shem Tov's disciples sat anxiously at their master's meal, hoping to hear an explanation of the day's events. The Baal Shem Tov did not disappoint them. "Today I perceived a terrible decree looming in Heaven," he began. "An entire Jewish community was threatened with destruction, G-d forbid. As I increased my devotions, hoping to have the decree annulled, a most unusual thing happened: I myself became the subject of Heavenly displeasure! Angels working for the adversary suddenly came before the Heavenly Court to accuse me of bringing other Jews to sin! 'The Baal Shem Tov sends Jews to work in small villages and busy crossroads,' they charged. 'By bringing them into close proximity to gentile peasants, he has made it easier for them to emulate the evil habits practiced by their gentile neighbors. The Baal Shem Tov is causing his fellow Jews to live a gentile life.'

"I watched in disbelief as the Heavenly Court accepted the charge and began investigating certain Jews who had moved to smaller villages per my instructions. To my chagrin, they found details that, indeed, seemed to strengthen the prosecutor's argument. They began debating my future, trying to decide how to punish me, when a mighty voice began reverberating throughout the Heavens: 'Cock-a-doodle-doo! G-d, have mercy!'

"This sincere outburst shook the Heavens, arousing G-d's Infinite mercies. Both decrees were promptly abolished. Upon witnessing this unexpected salvation, I swiftly concluded the prayers with songs of joy and praise." The Baal Shem Tov finished his narration, leaving his students to contemplate the incredible powers found within the truly sincere Jew.

A LASTING VISION

As related above, the Rebbe's boundless love for ignorant Jews would perplex even his closest disciples. One summer day, between the years 5513 (1753) and 5515 (1755), a large crowd of guests arrived in Mezibush to spend the upcoming Shabbat with the Baal Shem Tov. These were simple, unlettered folk— artisans and laborers, farmers and cattle growers, market peddlers, street vendors, and small-time merchants.

Friday night, at the festive Shabbat meal, the Baal Shem Tov showered these simple Jews with special attention. One received leftover *kiddush* wine from the Rebbe's personal goblet; others secured individual slices of his *challah*; still others merited to receive pieces of fish and meat from his plate. His disciples stared incredulously as the Rebbe even permitted one of the guests to use his cup for *kiddush*! As the meal progressed, the disciples found themselves questioning the Baal Shem Tov's benevolent attitude toward these simpletons.

On the morrow, the Baal Shem Tov ate alone with his students. This had developed into a customary schedule of sorts: all guests were invited to the first and third Shabbat meals, but the second—the meal eaten early Shabbat afternoon—remained reserved for the Rebbe's select disciples. After the prayers, the students assembled in the dining hall to wait for the Baal Shem Tov's arrival, while the simple guests hurried through their meal and retired to the synagogue to recite *Tehillim*.

The Baal Shem Tov entered the dining hall and arranged his students' places at the table according to specific order. The Baal Shem Tov began the meal by delivering a mystical discourse and, when he finished, his disciples broke out in meditative song. Together they sang as one voice, spiritually enthused by the deep insights shared by the Baal Shem Tov. "Compared to yesterday, this is so much better!" some thought quietly as they gazed at the Baal Shem Tov's radiant visage. "It is so frustrating to share our meal with ignoramuses—people who can't even hope to understand any of the Rebbe's words...."

"Besides," they thought, "why does the Baal Shem Tov show these unlearned Jews such affection anyway?"

Hardly had the thought crossed their minds, when the Baal Shem Tov's face turned deeply serious. The Rebbe became pensive as he sat in deep meditation until, suddenly, he resumed expounding Torah, this time choosing to elaborate on the inherent spiritual goodness found within the Divine service of the simple, sincere Jew. When he finished, his disciples resumed singing, realizing that the Rebbe perceived their unspoken question and had addressed his words to them.

The Baal Shem Tov continued sitting in a state of deep meditation, his face burning with fierce intensity. Opening his eyes, he glanced at each student with a penetrating look. "Place your right hand on the shoulder of your neighbor," he commanded. "When the circle is complete, continue your singing."

Mystified, his disciples hurried to fulfill his bidding. Soon a human chain surrounded the table, each side ending at the Rebbe's chair. The disciples sang different melodies as the Baal Shem Tov sat immersed in thought. "Close your eyes now," he said as they finished. "Do not open them until I tell you to."

The disciples closed their eyes and the Baal Shem Tov placed his hands upon the shoulders of those sitting near him, effectively completing the circle. At that moment, his disciples felt transported to the highest celestial spheres as the sweetest strains of song and prayer intermingled with deep emotion reached their ears. The voices swirled and rose, intense outbursts of love channeled through the sincere recitation of *Tehillim*:

"*Ay!* Dear G-d! G-d's pronouncements are pure (Psalms 12:7); Dear G-d! Test and prove me, sanctify my heart (ibid. 26:2); Compassionate Father! Be gracious; I trust in You, my soul finds shelter in Your wings (ibid. 57:2); *Ay! Gevald!* Father in Heaven! Let G-d arise; his enemies will scatter, his foes shall flee (ibid. 68:2); *Ay, Ay!* Merciful Father! Every bird has a home, a swallow a nest (ibid. 84:4); Dear Father! Return us, G-d who assists us; erase Your anger from us" (ibid. 85:5).

Though the disciples sat with closed eyes, rivers of tears coursed down their cheeks. Overcome by intense spiritual fervor flowing through their being, their hearts contracted with emotion, beads of sweat forming on their faces. "What devotion!" they thought in wonder. "If only G-d would help us attain such spiritual greatness!"

The Baal Shem Tov removed his hands from the shoulders of those sitting nearest him and the heavenly sound dissipated instantly. "You may open your eyes," he instructed. "Resume your singing."

When the singing subsided, a complete hush fell on the room. The Baal Shem Tov, still deep in meditation, opened his eyes and said: "The songs and spiritual bliss you experienced—these are the Divine repercussions caused by the sincere recitation of

Tehillim by those simple Jews in the next room. These words of *Tehillim*, drawn from the innermost recesses of their hearts and imbued with complete faith, generate the greatest Divine satisfaction."

The disciples were silent. They now understood how even the simplest Jew possessed extraordinary spiritual capabilities, in a measure that truly deserved the Baal Shem Tov's fullest attention. By merit of their unassuming sincerity, these simple Jews had attained lofty spiritual heights, rightfully earning the Rebbe's respect and admiration.

THE INTERNAL DIFFERENCE

Among the Baal Shem Tov's many followers were two individuals totally dissimilar in nature and bearing. R. Nosson was a wealthy fabric merchant from Brody, an accomplished scholar who spent hours toiling in Torah and performing *mitzvot*. Yet, despite his spiritual stature, R. Nosson spent little time refining his own character traits, preferring instead to focus on intellectual achievement. The father of a large family, R. Nosson taught his sons to follow his example and raised them to become great scholars who, like their father, ignored any suggestion of self-refinement.

R. Avraham, another follower of the Baal Shem Tov, was a simple Jew who lived in the tiny village of Belishtzenitz. Practically destitute, R. Avraham could hardly earn enough money to feed his family. Neither could he boast of any scholarly achievement, yet he served G-d to the best of his ability. Wholehearted joy permeated his *mitzvot*, and he worked constantly on his character, refining his manner toward others and elevating his inborn traits.

One week, R. Nosson and R. Avraham both arrived in Mezibush to spend a few days with the Baal Shem Tov. That Shabbat, the Baal Shem Tov delivered a discourse based on the verse, "When you spread out your hands [in supplication], I shall conceal my sight from you [says G-d]. Even if you pray profusely, I shall not hearken, for your hands are bloodied" (Isaiah 1:15).

Observed the Baal Shem Tov: "*When you spread out your hands*—even if you distribute charity with an open hand, *I shall conceal my sight from you*, because your charity was performed by rote, without true empathy for the suffering and humiliation felt by the pauper. This is not true charity. In fact, *your hands are filled with blood*—this constitutes cold-blooded 'murder.'"

After the discourse, R. Nosson and R. Avraham reviewed the Rebbe's words, each internalizing the Rebbe's words in a radically different form. Analytical by nature, R. Nosson contemplated the various intellectual implications learned from the Rebbe's teaching. He thought carefully into the ramifications of the two manners expressed in the discourse—the cold, aloof bearing of the brain, and the compassionate feelings generated by the heart.

R. Avraham, by contrast, channeled the Rebbe's words into practical application. According to his understanding of the Rebbe's words, it was imperative for him to refine his character traits, to become more receptive to the suffering of others. The Baal Shem Tov's words reverberated in his ears, giving him no respite. "Charity performed by rote, even in generous measure, constitutes murder," thought R. Avraham glumly. "What can I say about my charity?" Returning home, R. Avraham worked diligently on his character traits, heightening his concern for others. With time, he became a kinder person, ever more warm and receptive to the plight of his fellow man.

Months passed. On Pesach night, as the Baal Shem Tov sat at the *seder* table surrounded by students, he began discussing the incredible Divine pleasure caused by the sincere service of the unlearned Jew. As he spoke, the Baal Shem Tov commanded his disciples to close their eyes and place their hands on the shoulder of their neighbor, forming a human chain around the table. The Baal Shem Tov then placed his hands on the students sitting closest to him, and began singing softly.

Suddenly a vision appeared. The Baal Shem Tov's disciples saw R. Avraham sitting in a small room lit by a tiny kerosene lantern. A few earthenware vessels lay on a rickety table. Though their surroundings were modest, R. Avraham and his family celebrated the *seder* with true festivity, spending the night in joyous thanksgiving.

As the students watched in surprise, R. Avraham and his family faded away and a different vision filled the room. They saw an elaborately set table, bedecked with a lavish tablecloth. Gleaming vessels of gold and silver mirrored the radiant light of the sparkling candelabra. R. Nosson's family had gathered in the bright, spacious room, and were participating in the *seder*, yet something was terribly wrong. The participants were surly, impatient, hardly able to sit in ease. Irritable and unfriendly, they seemed to abhor each other's company. Their *seder* was totally orphaned of festive flavor.

The Baal Shem Tov removed his hands and the vision disappeared. "Witness the difference!" he declared. "See the integral difference between one who works on his character traits and one content with intellectual advancement alone!"

"R. Avraham is, undoubtedly, a simple person, yet he works hard on refining his character. This has enabled him to perceive the inherent good within every Jew and has brought him to a state of perpetual contentment and joy. Even when he has no food to feed his children on Pesach—R. Avraham is still genuinely happy! By contrast, R. Nosson is content with his intellectual advances. Yes, he does serve G-d with both heart and mind—a worthy goal in itself—but he lacks the perfection attained by the merits of positive deeds.

"This," concluded the Baal Shem Tov, "is the inner meaning of the verse, 'Better a dry crust of bread with peace than a house full of sacrifices and fighting' (Proverbs 7:1). Inner contentment is the key to true happiness."

Unconditional Love Toward Fellow Jews

"*Ahavat Yisrael* forms the entrance to G-d's courtyard," taught the Baal Shem Tov. "To love a fellow Jew is, in essence, to love G-d, for all Jews are G-d's children. If you love a father enough, you will undoubtedly love his children as well."

The Baal Shem Tov imbued the mitzvah of *Ahavat Yisrael* with fresh meaning, teaching that all Jews deserve the unconditional love of their brethren. "When one hears an uncomplimentary report about another Jew, even if he does not know the individual referred to, he should be very deeply pained. For one of these two is certainly in the wrong: If what they are saying about the individual is true, then *he* is defective; and if not true, then the talebearer is in an unhealthy situation."

The Baal Shem Tov portrayed the Jewish nation as a single, undivided entity, and declared that each person decides his own destiny when passing judgment about another. In essence, verbal criticism or praise about others mirrors our personal strengths and shortcomings. "Whatever is spoken about another person befalls the speaker," he asserted. "One who speaks kindly about others, praising their merits and good deeds, deserves the same reward and Divine favor as the individual who actually performed those good deeds! Conversely, one who slanders others—readying them for Divine punishment—is himself deserving of the selfsame retribution!

"This extends even further," continued the Baal Shem Tov. "One who chooses to justify another's misfortune, without feeling the slightest trace of empathy or the inclination to arouse G-d's mercy—this alone arouses Heavenly displeasure, initiating careful scrutiny of *his* actions and speech. Yet, one who really empathizes with the pain of others, and intercedes with G-d on their behalf, will enjoy full recompense for his compassion."

The Baal Shem Tov taught that *Ahavat Yisrael* can demand personal sacrifice, to the extent of self-negation. He said, "In order to do a favor for a fellow Jew—a material favor and certainly a spiritual one—be prepared to put your own ambitions aside. This applies even when you are helping a complete stranger."

He also said: "A soul may descend to this world and live seventy or eighty years, in order to do a Jew a material favor, and certainly a spiritual one."

He further taught: "The commandment to put our unquestioning faith in G-d applies to personal hardship. When confronted by disaster, we place our trust in the Almighty and double our efforts to find salvation. Our trust remains intact even in face of seemingly insurmountable obstacles. However, when disaster strikes a fellow Jew, it is forbidden to rely on faith alone and remain complacent, assuring the afflicted that 'G-d will definitely come to your aid.' Instead, it behooves us to implore the Almighty on their behalf, beseeching Heaven to assist and provide salvation."

The Baal Shem Tov also revealed the extraordinary spiritual pleasure caused by the genuine brotherhood and camaraderie of fellow Jews. He declared: "The warm blessings showered by good friends has such favorable Divine repercussions, that it rivals the continuous defense and arousal of Heavenly mercy effected by the angel Michael!"

He also exclaimed that "when a Jew sighs in distress over the misfortune of another, this sigh shatters the strongest arguments presented by Heavenly adversaries. Spiritual walls of steel buckle. Conversely, when a Jew rejoices in the happiness of his friend and blesses him with further success—his blessing is as favorable before G-d as the prayer offered by Rabbi Yishmael the High Priest in the Holy of Holies!"

INNER INTERPRETATIONS

To further illustrate the tremendous merits of *Ahavat Yisrael*, the Baal Shem Tov brought three novel interpretations to the following verse: "Hear the causes between (*bein*, in Hebrew) your brethren and judge righteously" (Deuteronomy 1:16).

The first interpretation centered on the word *bein*. Normally translated as "between," *bein* is also associated with the Hebrew word *binah* ("knowledge"), leading the Baal Shem Tov to explain the Biblical verse in this fashion: "Those who *hear*—who have the capacity to sense spiritual worth—sense the boundless love G-d has towards every Jew. They readily discern that all Jews are precious before G-d. This leads to *knowledge between your brethren*, that each Jew becomes knowledgeable and aware of the precious spiritual worth within every individual."

The second interpretation explained the verse according to the literal translation of *bein*—"between": "Those who *hear*—who perceive spiritual merit—are *between your brethren*, they associate with all elements of the Jewish nation and derive spiritual pleasure from every Jew individually."

According to the Baal Shem Tov's third interpretation, spiritual gain is dependent on, and fashioned by, one's perception of his fellow man. "In order to *hear*, to attain a spiritual ability that discerns inner worth, it is imperative to come *between your brethren*—to mix and associate with all Jews, for even the unlearned are our brethren."

On another occasion, the Baal Shem Tov interpreted the prohibition against slander to underscore the importance of *Ahavat Yisrael*. Drawing on the verse, "Let not your heart harbor hate against your brethren; rebuke your neighbor, lest you incur sin" (Leviticus 19:17), the Baal Shem Tov taught:

"If you notice that another person hates you, thereby transgressing the prohibition against hating a fellow Jew, use his negative feelings as a catalyst for self-introspection. Perhaps, in fact, his spiritual service is far better than yours, and he finds your spiritual aspirations wanting. His hate is, no doubt, based on *your* spiritual faults.

"To resolve this predicament—*rebuke your neighbor*. Confront your friend; proffer an explanation! Let him hear why *your* service of G-d is better; prove his suspicions to be baseless. Then, when he recognizes your righteousness, his hate will automatically dissipate.

"Why, in truth, should you be burdened with this responsibility, forced to reveal the merits of your spiritual path in order to deflect hate? *Ahavat Yisrael demands this step!* For, due to *Ahavat Yisrael*, you will be pained to see your friend transgressing a Biblical prohibition. Your feelings of boundless love will impel this initiative, and thereby remove his unsightly sin!"

Indeed, the Baal Shem Tov saw *Ahavat Yisrael* as a continuous driving force, a never-ending ambition to imbue life with kindness and friendship. "Our Sages declare (*Avot* 2:3) that Torah without work cannot endure," he taught. "'Work' denotes our efforts in furthering *Ahavat Yisrael*. A scholar or layman who studies Torah, yet does not come to a deep appreciation of *Ahavat Yisrael*—his Torah is worthless and cannot endure."

"Many Jews are born to irreligious parents," he explained further. "These unlearned people never received a proper Jewish education. It behooves us to inspire these lost souls, to show them the light of Torah. For some, this becomes their sole purpose in life—to bring others closer to Torah and *mitzvot*. This is expressed in the song of the Psalmist, 'Those who go down to sea in ships, who work in mighty waters [see G-d's wonders]' (Psalms 107:23).

"When born "at sea"—i.e., thrown into the unpredictable currents of this material world—some are shielded from the forceful waves by their protective "boat" of Torah and *mitzvot*. Starting with birth, their righteous parents worked hard to instill them with values based on Torah and *mitzvot*, effectively guarding them from materialistic pitfalls. Others, however, are born without this crucial shield—their parents are irreligious, apathetic to the merits of Jewish education. These souls are pained, doomed to live in perpetual agony. (*Aniyot*, the Hebrew word for *boats*, can also be interpreted as *agony*, from the word *aniya*.)

"Meritorious individuals carry the responsibility of *working in mighty waters*," continued the Baal Shem Tov. "They reach out to these ignorant Jews and offer them spiritual protection. Through inspiring those drowning in the raging waters of our material world, souls otherwise lost are redeemed from ignorance, guided back to their true Source."

"Helping such people has tremendous spiritual ramifications," said the Baal Shem Tov. "This is the inner interpretation of the opening *Mishnah* of *Bava Metzia*, "When two people find a [lost] cloak and each claims, 'I found it first; all of it is mine,' the cloak is evenly divided between them." The manner in which this law is interpreted in the Heavenly Academy illustrates the importance of *Ahavat Yisrael*:

"*When two people find a [lost] cloak*—Reuven notices that Levi has left the true path of Torah and informs his friend, Shimon, of this situation. Dismayed by his friend's report, Shimon exerts all effort to help Levi and eventually succeeds in bringing him to full repentance. In retrospect, both people "found" the same "lost" soul.

"Later, the souls of both Reuven and Shimon claim, *'I found it first; all of it is mine'*—each insisting that they alone are responsible for Levi's repentance and return. Each demands full Heavenly recompense for having brought Levi to observe Torah and *mitzvot.* 'I told Shimon about it first,' protests Reuven, 'all of the reward is mine!'

"'But I actually helped Levi repent!' Shimon objects. 'All Reuven did was talk! Mere words pale in comparison to my concrete actions! All the reward belongs to me!'

"After evaluating their demands, the Heavenly Court rules that *the cloak is evenly divided*—both souls share equally in the Divine reward. This ruling highlights the great merits of *Ahavat Yisrael,* a mitzvah whose reward extends to each and every person involved, no matter their measure of involvement."

HIS ENDURING LESSON

The Baal Shem Tov's approach to *Ahavat Yisrael* forever changed universal perception of this mitzvah. Due to his influence, this cornerstone of Jewish life extended to even total strangers and unlearned folk. Every Jew, regardless of stature or scholarship, deserved the unconditional love of his brethren.

As related earlier, in his younger years, the Baal Shem Tov worked as a teacher's assistant in the town of Brody. After rounding up the local children every morning, he walked them to *cheder* and back home again at night. As they marched together, the Baal Shem Tov kissed the children with deep emotion. His successor, the *Maggid* of Mezritch, once declared, "I wish I could feel such love and fervor when kissing the mantle of the *Sefer Torah,* as the Baal Shem Tov felt when he kissed young Jewish children studying *Alef-Bet!*"

Once, as he sat in the presence of his students, the Baal Shem

Tov described his deep love toward even the simplest Jew: "There once lived an unlearned Jew who barely knew how to mouth the daily prayers and recite *Tehillim*. Yet, he loved every Jew fiercely, with every fiber of his being. His thoughts, his words, his actions—all revolved around the cardinal principle of *Ahavat Yisrael*. He helped whomever he could in whatever way possible, celebrating in their joyous occasions and grieving at their misfortunes.

"Let the Heavens and the earth bear witness!" pronounced the Baal Shem Tov. "Let them declare the immense spiritual worth of this unlearned Jew. After his demise, when he appeared before the Heavenly Court, the celestial judges reviewed his meritorious life—one lacking in scholarship, but rich in unconditional *Ahavat Yisrael*. 'This soul deserves the greatest spiritual reward,' they ruled unanimously. 'His portion in *Gan Eden* will be among the towering scholars, *tzaddikim* of old who loved each and every Jew with fiery intensity."

The Baal Shem Tov preached *Ahavat Yisrael* wherever he went. Chasidic leaders later extolled his far-reaching influence, and revealed that even the Baal Shem Tov himself had attained lofty spiritual heights through this mitzvah. "By virtue of *Ahavat Yisrael*, the Baal Shem Tov merited *ruach hakodesh* and the revelation of Elijah the Prophet," observed Rabbi Schneur Zalman of Liadi. "The Arizal merited these Divine gifts through his performance of *mitzvot* with unbridled joy, but the Baal Shem Tov attained them through the unreserved love of his brethren."

Said Rabbi Yosef Yitzchak Schneersohn, sixth Rebbe of Lubavitch, "Until the Baal Shem Tov, people coupled *Ahavat Yisrael* with Torah scholarship, showing kindness and appreciation only to scholars. The Baal Shem Tov revolutionized *Ahavat Yisrael*, initiating a movement that expressed boundless love toward every Jew for one reason alone—his identity as a Jew."

Rabbi Yosef Yitzchak also said: "The Baal Shem Tov devoted his life to *Ahavat Yisrael*, to the extent of self-sacrifice. He heard the anguished sigh of a single Jew living in a forsaken corner of the world, a Jew he had never met. Sorely troubled by another's misfortune, the Baal Shem Tov would intercede on his behalf until he could effect salvation."

And, in the name of Rabbi Mordechai Bayever, a colleague of the Baal Shem Tov: "*Ahavat Yisrael* became the foremost responsibility of the Baal Shem Tov's disciples. Each was enjoined to choose a close friend. To be the Rebbe's disciple without a friend was an anomaly. The Baal Shem Tov planted the roots of *Ahavat Yisrael* within even the simplest of Jews, teaching them to view others through the lens of unconditional *Ahavat Yisrael*, to focus on the positive aspects of their fellow man."

The Baal Shem Tov's impact on our perception of *Ahavat Yisrael* remains inestimable. Rabbi Shalom DovBer, fifth Rebbe of Lubavitch, stated: "It is impossible to accurately evaluate the depth and breadth of the Baal Shem Tov's *Ahavat Yisrael*. This priceless inheritance, as faithfully transmitted by his disciples and successors, has become our worthy heritage today."

Initiated Intervention

THE CITY OF DENBURG was host to a teeming Jewish community that included many followers of the Baal Shem Tov. Among them lived Rabbi Moshe Chaim and his wife Miriam, a long-suffering couple who had weathered many tribulations in life. After enduring childlessness for many years, the couple was finally blessed with three girls, but the infants all died within a short period of time. Rabbi Moshe Chaim and his wife grieved deeply and the entire community mourned with them.

One year, during the intermediate days of Pesach, a group of local Chasidim decided to visit the Baal Shem Tov, in far-off Mezibush. Prepared to complete the entire journey by foot, the group was headed by Rabbi Gedaliah Baruch, one of the leaders of the Chasidic community in Denburg. Hearing of their ambition, Rabbi Moshe Chaim and his wife decided to join the group, hoping to secure the Rebbe's blessing for healthy children. They had heard much about the Baal Shem Tov and his miracles and were confident the Rebbe could help them.

And so, on the second day of Iyar, the childless couple joined the large group leaving Denburg for Mezibush. It was a grueling journey, one that alternated between dusty roads and unkempt inns, but the Chasidim hardly noticed these trivial discomforts. The true purpose of their journey—seeing the Baal Shem Tov in person—made material annoyances unimportant.

Upon their arrival, Rabbi Moshe Chaim and his wife were allotted a scheduled time for a private audience with the Rebbe. Entering the Baal Shem Tov's holy room, the couple burst into bitter tears as they bewailed their childless lot, beseeching the Rebbe for his blessing. The Baal Shem Tov listened carefully, but remained ominously silent and soon indicated that the audience had neared its end. The disheartened couple left the Rebbe's room, hoping they could meet the Baal Shem Tov again during their stay.

Indeed, a few days later, the couple was readmitted into the Rebbe's chamber, where tears flowed like water as they implored the Rebbe to bestow his blessing for healthy children. When their second meeting ended without result, the couple was forced to secure a third audience. Yet again, despite their heartfelt pleas, the Baal Shem Tov kept his silence. Overcome by emotion, Miriam swooned and fell to the floor. Later, after being revived, the poor woman could barely regain her composure as she wept unrestrained, bemoaning her dismal fate.

During the time they spent in Mezibush, the childless couple witnessed the Baal Shem Tov perform astonishing wonders for people stricken with all sorts of ailments. Terminally ill patients were cured; barren women conceived; impaired individuals regained their senses, and many others experienced open miracles. Crestfallen, the couple could hardly believe the magnitude of their misfortune. The Baal Shem Tov—divinely empowered to assist the suffering—had apparently despaired of reversing their childless destiny. After all, their heartfelt pleas had been met with deep silence.

Their friend, Rabbi Gedaliah Baruch, also sensed that something was amiss. Deeply familiar with the Rebbe's conduct, he perceived that the childless couple faced serious spiritual barriers, yet this staunch Chasid refused to relinquish hope. As one of the foremost disciples of the Baal Shem Tov, he knew that concerted effort by others could shatter severe Heavenly prosecution and he hurried to consult with his friends. "We will gather a quorum of men," they suggested. "Let us spend three days immersed in prayer and *Tehillim* while abstaining from food and drink, asking G-d to bless this unfortunate couple with offspring. Afterwards, we shall see how the Baal Shem Tov reacts to our efforts."

Rabbi Gedaliah Baruch and his colleagues kept their commitment secret. Day and night they prayed and fasted together, imploring G-d for Divine mercy. If only their friends could bear children! So deep was their concern, so overwhelming was their compassion, that nothing else mattered to them. Energized as a group, they continued to storm the Heavens for three consecutive days, hoping to effect salvation.

As the evening shadows lengthened on the third day, the exhausted group began the evening prayer, thoroughly spent by their devotions. Suddenly the Rebbe's attendant appeared in the doorway: the Baal Shem Tov was summoning them to join him in a festive *seudat mitzvah*. "A *seudat mitzvah*?" they echoed in surprise. "To celebrate what occasion?"

The attendant shrugged his shoulders. "The Rebbe gave no explanation," he replied.

That evening, a large crowd gathered in the *shul* of the Baal Shem Tov. Surrounded by scores of disciples and guests, the Rebbe sat at the head of the table, his face radiating spiritual delight. He delivered mystical discourses based on the verses, "Love your fellow as yourself" (Leviticus 19:18) and "How good and pleasant is it when brothers dwell together" (Psalms 133:1), elaborating at length on the virtues of unconditional *Ahavat Yisrael.*

After relating various stories highlighting the theme of *Ahavat Yisrael*, the Baal Shem Tov turned to the assembled crowd and declared: "When friends gather to arouse deep Divine mercy for a suffering comrade, they are capable of shredding Heavenly decrees—even those that would normally prevail for seventy years! Their devoted efforts transform curses into blessings, converting death into extended life!"

Rabbi Gedaliah Baruch and his friends stole furtive glances at each other across the table. Nothing could be hidden from the Baal Shem Tov. Evidently, their fasting and tears had borne fruit; now even the Baal Shem Tov was celebrating in their success. The *seudat mitzvah* was, in essence, a clear indication that better times now awaited the childless couple. Elated, Rabbi Gedaliah Baruch hurried to tell Rabbi Moshe Chaim and his wife to seize the moment and ask for the Baal Shem Tov's intervention. The couple rushed to the Baal Shem Tov and the Rebbe immediately blessed them. "You will give birth to a son," he prophesied, "a boy who will live many healthy years."

Overjoyed, the couple returned home, waiting with firm belief for the Rebbe's blessing to materialize. The very next year, on the second day of the Hebrew month Iyar, Rabbi Moshe Chaim's wife gave birth to a baby boy whom they named Shlomo. During the festive meal following the circumcision, Rabbi Gedaliah Baruch rose to address those gathered at the celebration. "Look at the extraordinary rewards of pure faith!" he observed. "In merit of their unwavering faith in the righteous, Rabbi Moshe Chaim and his wife had their lifelong wish fulfilled on the second of Iyar—the precise date they set out to meet the Baal Shem Tov one year ago!"

At about the same time, Rabbi Gedaliah Baruch's wife, Basha, gave birth to a baby girl, whom they named Yocheved. When these two children grew up, they were married, and Shlomo became one of the central pillars of the Chasidic community in Denburg. True to the Baal Shem Tov's blessing, he lived to the hoary old age of one-hundred-and-twelve years, never experiencing the slightest discomfort or malady until his final day.

Humbling the Angels

ON ONE OF HIS MANY JOURNEYS, the Baal Shem Tov arrived in a particular village and headed straight for the marketplace, the teeming hub of activity for local townsfolk. A curious crowd of men, women and children—sincere, unlearned Jews—gathered as the Rebbe rose to address his attentive audience. The Baal Shem Tov spoke about *Ahavat Yisrael*, emphasizing the merits of unconditional kinship and true camaraderie. "The extraordinary love G-d shows every single Jew," he said, "gives us an inkling into the *Ahavat Yisrael* we must show every Jew."

To illustrate the deep import of his words, the Baal Shem Tov mentioned Rabbi Yaakov—a local scholar renown for his scholarship and assiduity. A proficient Talmudist, Rabbi Yaakov had committed the entire Talmud to memory, together with the commentaries of *Rashi* and *Tosfot*. "Picture Rabbi Yaakov deep in study," began the Baal Shem Tov. "He is tackling a complex *Tosfot*, analyzing the complicated intricacies evident in every part of the lengthy commentary, when his youngest son bursts through the door and tells him a novel thought. Struck by the child's sense of innovation, Rabbi Yaakov interrupts his studies to play with his charming son, enjoying every moment he spends entertaining the boy.

"Such is the power of a child!" declared the Baal Shem Tov.

"Only Rabbi Yaakov's child is capable of distracting his eminent father, enabling them to play happily together. Similarly, G-d oversees and controls every detail of Creation, burdened, so to speak, with the loftiest secrets of the celestial worlds. Yet, when a Jew comes before G-d with a heartfelt prayer or an impassioned plea—G-d turns away from all His important "obligations," ready to assist the Jew in whatever measure possible. Such is the scope of G-d's love for His children!

"Early in the morning," continued the Baal Shem Tov, "when a Jew rises and runs off to the synagogue to pray with a *minyan*; later in the day, when he stops everything to *daven Minchah*; in the evening, when he puts exhaustion aside to hear an *Ein Yaakov* class before *Maariv*; after *Maariv*, when he returns home and repeats the Torah class for his family—G-d then turns to His celestial angels and boasts:

"At the dawn of Creation, when I consulted with you—My lofty angels—whether or not to create man, the response was: 'What is man worth to arouse Your remembrance?' Look closely now; see your mistake. The spiritual advances of man supersede the spiritual service of celestial angels!

"Angels have no wife or children who demand constant sustenance; they have no worldly troubles or impediments; no taxes or property fees. Yet, lowly man has all these distractions—a wife and children he must feed, bills and taxes he must pay, continuous obstacles he faces every day in his physical world. He is troubled and distracted, worried both day and night, burdened by the full weight of Exile. Despite all this, he acts superbly, bringing spirituality into every facet of his life as he serves G-d with all of his might and soul."

Concluded the Baal Shem Tov: "Visualizing this powerful statement of spiritual satisfaction—how G-d derives immense gratification from every mitzvah performed by Jews on this material plane—should propel us to ever-greater heights, and energize us with renewed vigor and strength in our service of G-d."

THE POWER OF SINCERITY

Sincere Blessings

A SINCERE BLESSING uttered by simple Jews arouses Divine compassion. On one occasion, the Baal Shem Tov overheard an individual bless his friend. "G-d will surely help!" he exclaimed.

The Baal Shem Tov turned to his disciples and observed, "With these few words, this man has saved hundreds of thousands of Jews from Heavenly prosecution."

Sincere Words

THE BAAL SHEM TOV ONCE TOOK his disciples to a distant village, where he planned to spend time in the company of two very different individuals. First they visited a simple tanner who spent his days curing animal hides. The tanner's lips moved constantly as he worked, having accustomed himself to recite *Tehillim* throughout the day. Despite his ignorance, the tanner knew it was forbidden to say *Tehillim* with unclean hands. Thus, during the actual curing of the hides, when his hands were dirty and soiled, the simple villager refrained from reciting these holy words of *Tehillim*.

Upon entering the home of the tanner, the Baal Shem Tov instructed his disciples to form a circle and place their hands on each other's shoulders. "Now close your eyes," he said, as he began singing a pensive melody. Closing their eyes, the disciples were astounded to see the tremendous Heavenly uproar caused by the *Tehillim* emanating from the poor hovel.

Afterwards, the Baal Shem Tov and his disciples went to visit a famed scholar who lived in the same village. A veritable recluse, the scholar shunned the outside world and spent his entire day immersed in Torah and prayer. In fact, the scholar had even merited to witness a revelation of Elijah the Prophet! To publicize this fact, whenever the scholar conversed with others

9 1

in learning, he always concluded his words by saying, "This is what I received from Elijah the Prophet."

During their visit, the Baal Shem Tov summoned his students together. "Close your eyes once more," he commanded, "then place your hands on the shoulder of your neighbor." The disciples quickly formed a circle again and closed their eyes, waiting as the Baal Shem Tov sang quietly to himself. Suddenly, they recoiled in horror: a vision of slithering snakes and scorpions appeared before their eyes! Frightened, they withdrew their hands and the circle was broken.

"Now I will explain everything to you," the Baal Shem Tov addressed his disciples. "True, someone who fasts continuously for forty days and removes himself from worldly affairs will merit to see Elijah the Prophet. Anyone who fasts for this period of time will see Elijah—even a servant or a maid! However, this does not guarantee revelation of the *soul*. This ascetic scholar is plagued by conceit and self admiration; he is obsessed by his great worthiness. Despite having merited to see Elijah the Prophet, his entire being is permeated with the snakes and scorpions of arrogance that stems from the original snake that sinned in the Garden of Eden.

"Try comparing him to the unlearned tanner!" concluded the Baal Shem Tov. "Why, every word of this simple Jew penetrates the Heavens! It is worthwhile for all of you to hear him utter a blessing."

Having achieved the purpose of their visit, the Baal Shem Tov and his disciples left the village. Later, when they heard about the passing of the simple tanner, the Baal Shem Tov gathered ten of his disciples and returned to the village. Once there, the Baal Shem Tov himself participated in the burial.

On another occasion, the Baal Shem Tov and his disciples spent Shabbat in a tiny village. On Shabbat afternoon, they watched in surprise as a simple villager rounded up a group of friends and led them to his house. Inside, the tables were laden with an abundance of food and drink in honor of the third Shabbat meal.

Through Divine intuition, the Baal Shem Tov perceived that these actions of the simple villager had aroused great satisfaction in Heaven. Perplexed, the Rebbe decided to approach the villager and ask for an explanation. "Why do you spend such an exorbitant amount of money on the third Shabbat meal?" asked the Baal Shem Tov.

"I have good reason for this," confided the simple villager. "I heard that every Jew is granted an additional soul on the Shabbat day—a soul that departs with the conclusion of Shabbat. I have also heard people wishing aloud that, when the time comes for them to depart this earth, they will expire in the company of Jews."

"This is why I spend so much money on the third Shabbat meal," explained the villager. "Since my additional soul is about to depart from this world, I make a festive meal with my friends. This way, my additional soul can depart in the company of fellow Jews."

Greatly pleased by the sincerity of this response, the Baal Shem Tov now understood why this simple villager effected such immense Divine satisfaction.

Sincere Interpretations

T HE HIDDEN *TZADDIK* RABBI KEHOT—a follower and confidante of the Baal Shem Tov—often mingled with simple and unlearned Jews. As was the practice of many hidden *tzaddikim*, Rabbi Kehot spoke warmly with these Jews, many of whom often felt dejected by their shameful ignorance. Rabbi Kehot befriended them, offering words of support and encouragement to those he met, and energizing all with his pleasant demeanor.

One day, as Rabbi Kehot walked by the marketplace, he met a group of horse dealers talking about their horses. Rabbi Kehot was therefore quite interested when he suddenly overheard two of these horse dealers discuss a verse in *Tehillim* (32:9). "Be not like a horse, like a senseless mule, that must be muzzled with bit and bridle while being adorned to prevent it from approaching," quoted one of the dealers. According to the literal meaning, the Psalmist exhorts man to accept the validity of chastisement and reproach—unlike the horse that requires a restraining muzzle to prevent damage to others.

The illiterate horse dealer had not the slightest inkling into the accepted interpretation of these words. Instead, his sincerity and earnestness illuminated this verse with totally different meaning: "Horses don't appreciate the true importance of the bit placed in their mouth," explained the dealer to his friend.

"Instead of realizing how beneficial this is for the driver—who uses the bridle to steer his horses in the right direction—the horse thinks the bit is there to improve his chewing habits! Therefore, says the Psalmist, 'Don't be a fool like the horse. Instead, recognize that all your G-d given capacities are for a solitary purpose—to utilize them for the service of G-d.'"

Impressed by the novel insight, Rabbi Kehot resolved to repeat this tidbit on his next visit to the Baal Shem Tov. Indeed, when he later repeated these words to the Baal Shem Tov, the Rebbe's face became aflame with emotion. The Baal Shem Tov burst into meditative song, reflecting deeply on the inherent truth realized by the simple horse dealer.

In another instance, the interpretation of an unlearned Jew brought salvation to the Baal Shem Tov's very own village. A fierce drought once hit the town of Mezibush. The burning sun radiated heat day after day, while the villagers scanned the sky in vain for the slightest sign of rain. In desperation, the entire Jewish community filled the synagogue, crying for G-d's mercy.

A simple Jew stood out among the congregation. Though he prayed and cried aloud like all the others, this simple Jew kept repeating a single verse: "And He will stop up (*atzar*) the heavens, so that there shall be no rain" (Deuteronomy 11:17).

Inexplicably, the Baal Shem Tov perceived that precisely these words were having the desired effect. Soon a strong wind began blowing heavy clouds across the sky and a drenching downpour soaked the village. Determined to understand the power behind these unusual words, the Baal Shem Tov approached the simple Jew. "Tell me," he said warmly, "why did you choose to keep repeating exactly this verse and no other?"

"My reasoning was simple," answered the illiterate Jew. "I translated the word to mean beseeched G-d to *squeeze* (*atzar*) *the heavens* so much until *there will be no rain* left in them. Instead, all the rain should come down on earth and water our village."

These prayers, having been uttered with utmost conviction, brought salvation for the entire Mezibush. Though the unlettered Jew erred in his interpretation of the verse, his pure intentions had pierced the Heavens, overturning the harsh decree leveled against the inhabitants of Mezibush.

To further enhance their sincerity, the Baal Shem Tov often stopped in the marketplace of various villages to address the simple Jews and encourage their spiritual efforts. Through his words, the Baal Shem Tov brought the simple villagers great satisfaction, impressing them with the realization that they, too, possessed the ability to attain lofty spiritual levels.

Once, as the Baal Shem Tov arrived in a small, remote village, he gathered all the Jewish residents—men, women and children—and relayed a verse from *Tehillim*, illuminating his words with the teachings of Chasidus. This time the verse was, "Fortunate ("*Ashrei*" in Hebrew) is the nation you choose and draw near to dwell in your courtyard, with the goodness of your house, the holiness of your sanctuary" (Psalms 65:5):

"*Ashrei* forms an acronym for *Amen Yehay Shmay Rabbah*. There are those who attain the spiritual level of G-d's courtyard; others achieve the level of G-d's house; still others elevate themselves to the level of G-d's Sanctuary. However, through the sincere recital of *Amen Yehay Shmay Rabbah*—all these levels are attained!"

The Baal Shem Tov's words infused the simple villagers with renewed enthusiasm and excitement, prompting them to answer *Amen Yehay Shmay Rabbah* with a heightened level of awareness.

Sincere Faith

IT WAS A HOT SUMMER DAY when the Baal Shem Tov arrived in a small drought-stricken agricultural village. The Jewish farmers wandered listlessly about, their crop and produce ruined by the heat. To make matters worse, pestilence broke out in the farms, threatening all their livestock as well. For days on end the villagers waited for rain, but the heavens were unyielding.

Being sincere, G-d-fearing Jews, the villagers had resolved to improve their ways and better their spiritual standing. Repentance and prayer filled the village. Yet, despite their efforts, the sun continued to beat mercilessly on the village. In desperation, they decided to hire a *maggid*—a traveling preacher—who would arouse them to true and complete *teshuvah*.

Soon the *maggid* arrived in the village. The entire Jewish population assembled in the synagogue, waiting to hear the *maggid's* message of repentance. As customary in those times, the *maggid* began heaping scorn and condemnation on the hapless Jews, rebuking them roundly for their grievous "sins" and painting a bleak picture of punishment and Divine retribution. Frightened by his grim depictions, the poor Jews burst into a fit of wailing and weeping that seemed to shake the very synagogue itself.

Sitting quietly among the crowd, the Baal Shem Tov could hardly bear the distress of his fellow brethren. Turning to the *maggid*, he exclaimed, "Why are you harassing these Jews? Jews are good people!"

The Baal Shem Tov then turned around to the devastated audience. "Dear Jews," he called out. "Come, let's dance together and I promise you that rain will arrive after *Minchah*."

The congregation stared at the stranger in suspicion and fear. Was this perhaps another freethinker with a penchant for mocking their sincere efforts to attain repentance? Or maybe he was an imbecile with a tendency of ridiculing others?

Sensing their hesitation, the Baal Shem Tov began speaking to the assembled Jews about the importance of having unwavering belief and trust in G-d. Supporting his words with quotations from the Sages, the Baal Shem Tov explained how G-d's salvation is instantaneous, effective in the blink of an eye, and how a Jew must demonstrate concrete faith in G-d. His pure words made a tremendous impact on the simple Jews, arousing their innate and absolute trust in G-d. A large circle quickly formed outside. The villagers danced joyously with the Baal Shem Tov, demonstrating complete faith in Divine salvation and hoping for a miracle.

It was not long in coming. Soon a strong wind began blowing rain clouds across the sky. A soaking downpour drenched the dancers as they lifted their parched lips skyward. The Baal Shem Tov blessed his brethren, assuring them ample sustenance for all their needs.

Sincere Tears

As THEY DID EVERY DAY, dozens of sincere worshippers gathered in the synagogue of Zaslov in the quiet pre-dawn hours of the morning. They had just completed reciting the entire *Tehillim* before the morning prayers, when two strangers appeared in the synagogue, identifying themselves as personal emissaries of the Baal Shem Tov. The righteous pair—Rabbi Nachman of Horodenka and Rabbi Dovid Furkas—revealed they were on a special mission. "The Baal Shem Tov needs sixty gold florins to fulfill the mitzvah of releasing captives," they announced. "Due to the urgency of the situation, he has sent us to Zaslov, asking everyone to contribute toward the required amount and send it directly to him via special messenger."

The congregation quickly composed a list of households devoted to the teachings of the Baal Shem Tov, and selected a *beit din* to decide the precise amount of money expected from each family. After completing their list, the *beit din* chose several people, charging them with the mission of collecting money for this urgent mitzvah. "Collect money from all these families!" instructed the *beit din*. "If someone does not have any money available, take collateral from him, which he can redeem later when he pays up."

The prayers began exceedingly late that day, but they were

permeated with special joy and gratitude. For their part, the Baal
Shem Tov's emissaries and some of the local scholars went to the
nearby *mikveh*. Upon their return, they began contemplating the
teachings of Chasidus as a prelude to *davening*, relying on the collectors to raise the money.

The messengers of the *beit din* had meanwhile wasted no time
in soliciting funds from those on their list. The Jews of Zaslov
were overjoyed at the opportunity to participate in the great
mitzvah and fulfill the Rebbe's bidding. Hence, hardly three
hours passed before the collectors raised the entire sum of sixty
gold florins. They kept a detailed list recording the particulars of
every contribution—who had given money; who had promised
pledges and gave collateral; and who had loaned money to be
drawn against the collateral.

Returning to the synagogue, the collectors found Rabbi
Nachman, Rabbi Dovid, and the members of the *beit din* deeply
engrossed in prayer. So involved were they in beseeching G-d's
mercy that they did not even notice that the collectors had
entered the synagogue! The collectors, however, were impatient.
Satisfied with the fulfillment of their mission, they felt an urgent
need to send the entire sum of money off to its designated purpose without delay. "A Jewish family is wasting away in prison!"
they protested hotly. "Every moment is precious!"

Others in the group were not as sure. "We have no right to
disturb our esteemed leaders," they countered. "It's only proper to
wait until they finish their prayers. Besides, don't you think the
Baal Shem Tov already knows we completed our mission? Don't
be fools! The Baal Shem Tov doesn't need our puny efforts to fulfill this mitzvah. Due to his boundless love of other Jews however, the Baal Shem Tov has provided us with the opportunity to
participate in this great mitzvah and reap its bountiful rewards."

The debate stopped in mid-sentence as the sound of crying
filled the synagogue. Turning to the entrance, the collectors were
surprised to see three women standing in the doorway. One held
a candlestick; another held a *kiddush* goblet; the third held a
down pillow.

The women continued wailing, looking at the collectors in distress and grief. Apparently, their respective husbands were away at work, and the collectors had not visited at these homes during their rounds. The collectors knew the husbands very well—one was a tailor who worked in a nearby town; the second peddled wares in scattered villages around the countryside; and the third shuttled between roadside inns, teaching children of Jewish innkeepers who lived far from the Jewish schools in larger towns.

"We heard that the Baal Shem Tov sent messengers to collect money for a great mitzvah," the women sobbed. "We waited and waited, but no one came to our house! Please give us a share in the mitzvah! We purposely hurried here with our expensive items, so you can hold them as security. When our husbands come home with money, we will redeem our belongings for their full value."

Members of the fundraising group stared at each other in astonishment. "But we can't do that!" they protested. "The *beit din* ordered us to collect money from specific families. We were given a detailed list of people; your names don't appear on our list at all. We can't take anything from you—no collateral, no money."

This revelation prompted a fresh bout of tears from the distressed women. "We are not even on the list?" they wailed. Sorely grieved at not having been deemed worthy to participate in the Rebbe's cause, their cries of anguish rose with emotion, piercing the hearts of Rabbi Dovid, Rabbi Nachman, and the others still engrossed in prayer.

Noticing that the collectors had returned with the necessary funds, the *beit din* quickly concluded their prayers and convened to address the concerns of the three sincere women. Well aware of the destitute conditions prevalent in these homes, the *beit din* initially expressed extreme reluctance to sanction the donations. Yet, despite their misgivings, the *beit din* finally acceded, and accepted the securities offered by the poor women. At eleven o'clock a special messenger—a simple, unlearned Jew who patched shoes—was sent to bring the entire sum of sixty gold coins to the Baal Shem Tov.

Meanwhile, a large feast had been prepared in the study hall as residents of the village gathered to celebrate the inestimable privilege of assisting the Baal Shem Tov in his holy work. The community felt honored by the Rebbe's attention to their village, having granted them the merit of participating in *pidyon shvuyim* and sending two great *tzaddikim*—Rabbi Nachman and Rabbi Dovid—to grace the village with their presence.

Rabbi Nachman, Rabbi Dovid, the *beit din,* and the collectors all sat down to partake in the meal—a simple affair of black bread, salted fish, cucumbers and vodka. A feeling of wholehearted joy and contentment pervaded the atmosphere as Chasidim sang and danced with one another. It was, indeed, a true display of pure, untainted joy in fulfilling G-d's mitzvah.

Rabbi Nachman and Rabbi Dovid addressed the crowd. They explained some teachings of the Baal Shem Tov and expounded Torah thoughts of their own. Though brief, their words contained deep Kabbalistic ideas, and the crowd listened in silence. After each talk, the crowd burst once more into spirited song and dance, savoring their good fortune of hosting such illustrious guests.

Before the conclusion of the meal, Rabbi Nachman and Rabbi Dovid chose to highlight the sincere request of the three poor women who had begged to participate in the Baal Shem Tov's mitzvah. "The Baal Shem Tov has tremendous regard for simple Jews," they said. "The Rebbe often makes the following remark: 'With their sincere recital of *Tehillim* and wholehearted love of fellow Jews, simple Jews elicit higher Divine grace than great *tzaddikim!*

"'Our Sages tell us that G-d exacts punishment when the righteous sin ever so slightly. Simple Jews however, are spared such scrutiny. G-d, who does not rule despotically over his creatures, values their sincerity. The simple, unlearned Jew serves G-d wholeheartedly, arousing great Divine satisfaction.'

"Deep truth glimmered in the tears of these women," continued Rabbi Nachman. "They possessed one overwhelming desire: that their absent husbands have a share in the Rebbe's mitzvah of *pidyon shvuyim*. The mitzvah is so precious in their eyes, and they consider the Rebbe so holy, that they burst into pained tears when their names were found missing from the list."

"These tears are so precious in the eyes of G-d! The archangel Michael and his 180,000 hosts of favorable advocates find incredible spiritual sweetness and pleasure in these tears! These pure, heartfelt tears have enough power to annul terrible Divine accusations leveled against Jews."

To illustrate his words, Rabbi Nachman related a story to the enthralled crowd, describing how the earnest prayer and tears of a simple Jewish woman had once saved entire communities from annihilation.[1] "Tears like those shed by the poor women today are true tears," concluded Rabbi Nachman. "We can only hope to shed such tears during the holiest time of the year—the holy day of Yom Kippur...."

1. See page 66.

Sincere Joy

T HE WARM GLOW OF FLICKERING CANDLES brightened darkened
homes across Mezibush as Jewish residents inspected every nook
and cranny for the slightest particle of *chametz*. It was the night
preceding the Pesach festival, about 1756-57, and Jews everywhere were searching their property for unwanted leaven. In the
home of the saintly Baal Shem Tov, a group of disciples and
guests had gathered to watch the Rebbe perform *bedikat chametz*,
waiting to witness the Rebbe's intense spiritual joy as he fulfilled
the mitzvah. Yet, as they watched the Baal Shem Tov, they knew
something was terribly wrong.

The Rebbe went through the motions abruptly, his perfunc-
tory manner completely devoid of spiritual pleasure. His manner
was grim, almost despondent. After he finished checking the
house for *chametz*, the Rebbe secluded himself in his room for
many hours, totally ignoring the crowd of guests who had arrived
for Pesach. Alarmed, the students sensed impending doom.
Evidently, the Baal Shem Tov had perceived a terrible Heavenly
prosecution leveled against the Jews.

Late that night, the Baal Shem Tov suddenly exited his room
and selected ten disciples. "You will form my *minyan*," he said
somberly. "After immersing in the *mikveh*, you will all recite the
Tikkun Chatzot prayer near my room, meditating intently on spe-

cific Kabbalistic formulae. I will pray, alone, in my room."

"If you hear my voice silenced," said the Baal Shem Tov, "cease saying *Tikkun Chatzot* immediately. Instead, recite special *Tehillim* with extreme concentration and intense focus, continuing until I awaken."

Faces drawn with anxiety and worry, the students went to immerse in the nearby *mikveh*. Positioning themselves near the Baal Shem Tov's room, they began reciting *Tikkun Chatzot* with great fervor, imploring G-d for mercy and compassion. They could hear the Rebbe's voice intermingling with their own; grief and anguish evident in his every syllable. Suddenly they could hear the Baal Shem Tov's voice no longer, and the students quickly turned to reciting *Tehillim*, punctuating their prayers with tears and sighs.

The door opened quickly and Rabbi Tzvi—the Rebbe's scribe—entered, his face white with horror. "Woe is to us!" he cried in dismay. "The Rebbe is lying on the floor, completely lifeless!"

Gripped by fear, the students resumed reciting *Tehillim* with renewed concentration and fervor. As daybreak came, other students arrived to study and pray—only to find a group of worried disciples already reciting *Tehillim* near the Rebbe's door. The ten disciples described the shocking events of the past few hours, and the new arrivals quickly rushed off to the *mikveh*. Upon returning, they too began reciting *Tehillim* with the others, concentrating intently on Kabbalistic intentions aimed at restoring their master's spirit. At long last, their prayers bore fruit, and the Baal Shem Tov opened his eyes once more.

The fainting spell had so weakened the Rebbe that his concerned students were forced to carry him by chair to the *mikveh*. As he rose from immersing in the water, the Baal Shem Tov's face turned deathly white and his eyes bulged frighteningly. His students recognized that expression all too well: the Rebbe was in a higher, more supernal world.

Upon returning to the synagogue, the Baal Shem Tov addressed his students, his words heavy with anxiety. "Today's prayers carry special significance," he said. "When you pray, concentrate on the meditations normally reserved for the Rosh Hashanah liturgy."

This unusual instruction only served to heighten the feelings of tension and unease already prevalent in the room, and the disciples watched anxiously as the Rebbe himself began leading the prayers. During the repetition of the *Amidah*, the disciples listened in awe as the Baal Shem Tov added *Anenu*, the special prayer reserved for fast days and other times of distress. Fully aware that a catastrophe of immense magnitude faced the Jewish nation, the disciples prayed with unusual fervor and devotion, fear evident in every word they uttered.

At the conclusion of the prayers, the Baal Shem Tov addressed his students again, expounding on the need for absolute faith in G-d. "The essence of faith is aroused when no other form of salvation seems possible," he explained. "Even when every door of hope appears barred, it is important to retain unwavering faith, to rely on G-d that all will turn out for the best. In fact, joy strengthens faith." Saying this, the Baal Shem Tov instructed his disciples to fast the entire day, and they all left the synagogue.

Until then, the disciples had been eagerly awaiting the afternoon hours of *erev* Pesach, a time when the Baal Shem Tov would join them in baking *matzot* for the upcoming festival. It had always been a time of spiritual delight and elation but now, after the harrowing events of the previous night and morning, the disciples were no longer sure of what to expect. To their relief, the Baal Shem Tov seemed in much better spirits after he immersed in the *mikveh* again before noon. Exhibiting the customary joy and enthusiasm he showed for every mitzvah, the Baal Shem Tov baked his *matzot* for the upcoming holiday, while his students secretly rejoiced at their master's return to his usual self.

Their relief was premature: before *Minchah*, the Baal Shem Tov again instructed his students to meditate on the Kabbalistic intentions normally reserved for Rosh Hashanah. Afterwards, when the Rebbe recounted the order of the Pesach Sacrifice, the students again noticed his mood become anxious and morose. As dusk gave way to night, the Baal Shem Tov began the festival evening prayer, joy and anguish intermingling with every word.

That night, as the Baal Shem Tov sat at the *seder*, he seemed unusually shaken and embittered. Though the Rebbe recited the Haggadah in his usual sing-song, his disciples discerned an unmistakable element of distress and supplication. Adding to their disconcertment, the Baal Shem Tov abandoned his yearly practice of expounding Chasidic teachings on various sections of the Pesach story. Instead, he read through the Haggadah fairly quickly, reciting it all in one unbroken chain.

The Baal Shem Tov's anxiety deeply upset his disciples, and they were particularly distressed at the Rebbe's unwillingness to share his newest interpretations of the Haggadah, something they longed for greatly. If now, at the height of the Pesach celebration, the Baal Shem Tov could not find reason for joy then surely all was lost.

Suddenly the sound of laughter filled the room. The disciples looked up in absolute amazement to see the Baal Shem Tov laughing merrily, his eyes closed in concentration, his face aflame with an unearthly fire. His laughter grew stronger and stronger—until it appeared unrestrained and endless.

After some time, the Baal Shem Tov opened his eyes and looked lovingly at his followers. "*Mazal tov, mazal tov!*" he announced joyously. "Blessed be His great Name, Who has chosen the Torah, His servant Moshe, and His nation Israel. Even those at the lowest level of our nation—even the simplest Jew— can attain the lofty spiritual level of 'Israel.' These simple Jews do more good for Israel than Yisralik the Baal Shem Tov!"

Overcome with emotion, not a single student could muster the courage to ask the Baal Shem Tov for an explanation. However, seeing their bewilderment, the Rebbe decided to explain matters for himself. "On the day before Pesach," he began, "I perceived a terrible threat leveled against a sizeable Jewish community some four-hundred families strong. On the first day of Pesach—which, this year, coincides with a gentile holiday—the gentiles would initiate a pogrom, and smite the entire community.

"I was in terrible anguish. All night long we stormed the Heavens with our prayers, trying to arouse Divine mercy, but nothing helped. When I realized how bleak the future appeared, I was aroused to awaken and heighten our level of uncompromising faith in G-d, and that is how I ushered in the Pesach festival. And then, as I sat by the *seder* tonight, I suddenly envisioned a remarkable sight:

"In a nearby village lives a simple couple who, unfortunately, have not been blessed with children. The husband, though modestly learned, is a towering example of sincerity and good deeds. As he sat down to his lonely *seder*, he began reciting the Haggadah aloud for his pious wife, narrating the story of our bondage in Egypt and the various troubles and tribulations experienced by the Jews. Suddenly his wife burst into tears. 'Why are you crying?' her husband asked in concern. 'Is something upsetting you?'

"'Of course!' she replied sadly. 'You just read from the Haggadah, *Our burden—this refers to [the horrors wrought on] our children, as it says: "And every baby boy shall be cast into the Nile"'* (Exodus 1:22).

"'So, what's there to cry about?' said her husband. 'G-d redeemed us from that terrible place!'

"'But even now we still suffer in Exile,' retorted his wife. 'Believe me, if G-d would have granted us a son, I would never act the same way to him as G-d does to us. Are the gentiles who harass and torment us more worthy in His eyes than the Jews, His very own children? Besides, I distinctly remember reading many times in our Torah that G-d constantly remembers His covenant with the Patriarchs in our favor—yet see how we suffer!'

"'G-d is righteous in all His ways'" (Psalms 145:17), replied her husband.

"His wife would not be placated. 'Where is His attribute of mercy?' she asked repeatedly. 'Just tell me, where is it?' They continued arguing back and forth throughout the *seder*—the husband defending G-d's inscrutable ways, while the wife lamented her bitter reality.

"Wearied by the exhaustive preparations for the holiday, the couple felt increasingly tired as the *seder* wore on, and quickly felt the effects of the four cups of wine. As they drank the fourth and final cup, the couple was suddenly overcome by ecstatic joy, experiencing the relief and elation of the Jews during the Exodus. Casting their earlier arguments aside, husband and wife began to dance, celebrating the Pesach redemption with genuine joy.

"When the wife began defending the Jewish people, her sincerity caused a great tumult in Heaven. The defending angels loudly supported her and tried to annul the decree, but the prosecuting angels rose up in anger and began speaking evil against us. Seeing this, I became greatly depressed. Who could tell—perhaps the opposing angels would have the upper hand after all?

"The turmoil continued as long as the couple kept up their arguments. And then the unbelievable occurred: husband and wife got up to dance, expressing true happiness in the Creator's kindnesses. This wholehearted joy shattered any remaining argument of the prosecuting angels; the decree was promptly torn to shreds. As I perceived this, my despair turned to joy, and I began laughing aloud."

Having concluded his narrative, the Baal Shem Tov placed his handkerchief on the table. "Quickly!" he commanded. "Grab a piece of my handkerchief and close your eyes!"

His disciples scrambled to touch the handkerchief. Closing their eyes, they suddenly envisioned the childless couple, dancing together in their faraway hut. Round and round they went, pure bliss shining in their eyes. The Baal Shem Tov's disciples could not help but marvel at these simple Jews, and at their sincere appreciation of G-d that had saved hundreds of families from annihilation.

Sincere Charity

Not always could the Baal Shem Tov channel salvation and blessing for those in distress. Once, when approached by a person in great need of Divine intervention, the Baal Shem Tov perceived insurmountable Heavenly opposition blocking his efforts to help this individual. "But please do something," sobbed the anguished individual. "Only the Rebbe can help me with his prayers!"

The Baal Shem Tov, who radiated intense love and concern for every individual Jew, felt deeply pained at the thought of turning someone away empty-handed. He tried everything in his power to arouse Divine mercy, but to no avail. The gates of Heaven seemed locked.

In desperation, the Baal Shem Tov rose from his seat, approached the bookcase that stood in his room, and selected the first volume his fingers encountered. It was the Talmudic tractate of *Bava Batra*, and the Baal Shem Tov opened the book at random. His eyes fell on the open page and he read the following, "'You have blessed the work of his [Job's] hands' (Job 1:10). Said R. Shmuel the son of R. Yitzchak: Whoever merely took a coin from Job was blessed with success (*Bava Batra* 15b)."

The strange circumstances prompting his reading of this Talmudic phrase seemed a clear orchestration of Divine

Providence. This was obviously a celestial hint, an indication of how to effect deliverance for this distressed individual. Evidently, only someone blessed with spiritual success in his charity could come to the rescue—but who?

Absorbed in thought once more, the Baal Shem Tov began thinking about the people he knew. Suddenly the name of Rabbi Shabsai Meir of Brody crossed his mind. Rabbi Shabsai Meir was a prosperous businessman who had not let fortune turn his head. Though his tremendous wealth increased with time, Rabbi Shabsai Meir continued living unpretentiously, spending his days in a quiet and unassuming manner. Simple furnishings graced his modest home; plain clothes comprised his wardrobe.

Only one thing had changed: Rabbi Shabsai Meir began giving larger amounts of money to charity, constantly praying that his contributions be blessed with success. "Grant me the ability to give charity with a wholesome heart," he prayed fervently. "May those who receive charity from me be blessed with prosperity."

His sincere acts of charity—many performed in secret—made such a favorable impression in Heaven that his prayers were duly accepted. The Heavenly Court ruled that Rabbi Shabsai Meir deserved to be blessed with success in his charity. As such, whoever received a donation from Rabbi Shabsai Meir suddenly experienced good fortune and success.

Remembering this, the Baal Shem Tov understood that only Rabbi Shabsai Meir could execute deliverance for this anguished individual. "Go to Brody," instructed the Baal Shem Tov. "When you get there, contact Rabbi Shabsai Meir. He's a very hospitable person who will undoubtedly invite you to his home for Shabbat. After Shabbat, offer thanks for his hospitality and ask him to bless you in merit of his great acts of charity."

The unfortunate fellow did as the Baal Shem Tov instructed. After spending a wonderful Shabbat in the home of Rabbi Shabsai Meir, he approached his host nervously, well aware that this was his sole opportunity to arouse Heavenly mercy. "Please bless me," he begged desperately. "Empowered by your legendary acts of charity, ask G-d to show mercy and save me."

Moved by his heartfelt plea, Rabbi Shabsai Meir blessed the man with deep feeling. And, true to the Baal Shem Tov's word, the individual finally merited salvation.

Sincere Reaction

THE BAAL SHEM TOV'S STUDENTS were most disconcerted to find his *Rosh Chodesh* meal going terribly wrong. They felt distanced from the Rebbe. Instead of the customary joy and singing that pervaded every *Rosh Chodesh* gathering, the Rebbe acted withdrawn and troubled. The students tried various means of gladdening the Rebbe's spirits, but the Baal Shem Tov seemed not to notice them.

Suddenly the door swung open and a simple, unlearned villager by the name of R. Dovid entered. As if by prearranged signal, the Baal Shem Tov broke out in a radiant smile, and began showering the simple Jew with attention. He let R. Dovid sit near him and even gave this simple Jew a piece of the *challah* over which he had said the *Hamotzi* blessing! The usual spiritual delight had been restored to the *Rosh Chodesh* festivities, but now the Baal Shem Tov's students felt downcast at their inability to gladden their master, while a simpleton had succeeded by his presence alone.

Sensing their distress, the Baal Shem Tov turned to Rabbi Dovid and sent him out on an errand. He then addressed his disciples, explaining why R. Dovid had the Rebbe's grace. "This simple villager has committed an act of supreme self-sacrifice, one seen rarely in this world," revealed the Baal Shem Tov.

113

"Throughout the year, R. Dovid—a terribly impoverished fellow—scrimped and saved as many coins as he could from his meager earnings, and put them into a special collection. After a year, the mountain of small coins amounted to a respectable amount, and R. Dovid traveled to the city to purchase the finest *etrog* he could find.

"On his way home, R. Dovid encountered difficult roads and swollen rivers. He traveled carefully, slowly, ensuring that nothing would happen to his precious *etrog* to render it invalid, G-d forbid. He came home, exhausted to the bone, only to find his hungry wife and children waiting for him with sad faces, their emaciated bodies weakened by hunger. Enthused by his find, R. Dovid rejoiced with his *etrog*, completely oblivious to the malicious stares of his wife. 'How could he forget about his family and squander so much money on an *etrog*?' thought the angry woman. 'Why, he is happy at our expense!'

"Soon the woman could bear it no longer. With a cry of bitter rage, she reached out and broke the top of the *etrog*, rendering it invalid for use. R. Dovid did not feel the slightest tremor of anger. "She is right," he said quietly. "I am probably unworthy of owning such a fine *etrog*. Indeed, how does a simple person like myself expect to use such an expensive *etrog*?"

"With the festival of Sukkot rapidly approaching, R. Dovid decided to join in with the other villagers and bless the communal *etrog*. He took a battered vessel from the table, sold it at the pawnshop, and used the few coins to buy his individual share in the community *etrog*."

Concluded the Baal Shem Tov: "Do you still wonder why the mere presence of R. Dovid filled me with delight? Know this: Since the time Abraham sought to sacrifice his son for G-d, there has never been such a test...."

Sincere Kindness

Eliezer Lipa's cart rode slowly through the streets of Tarnow, water sloshing noisily in his huge barrels. The water carrier nudged his horse slowly along the familiar route, but his mind wandered back to his two sickly sons, Elimelech and Meshulam Zusia. How many tears had he and his wife shed over their sons! The boys did very poorly in *cheder* and hardly understood anything the teacher taught. Eliezer Lipa and his wife performed additional good deeds in merit of their children, hoping that G-d would open their minds to the holiness of Torah, but their children continued to make poor progress.

Eliezer Lipa was a very simple Jew. Unlettered and ignorant, he hardly understood the meaning of the daily prayers, yet he always made certain to participate in the daily *minyan*. Others spoke idle banter during the prayer, but not Eliezer Lipa. Pious and G-d-fearing, the water carrier loved G-d dearly, and always conducted himself in a just and forthright manner. He deeply respected those well-versed in Torah, and accorded an extra measure of respect to the rabbis and scholars in the community.

He knew his father had lived extremely differently. An eminent scholar, his father was fluent in the entire Talmud along with the commentaries of *Rashi* and *Tosfot*, yet remained an exceedingly humble person who never demonstrated the extent of his scholarship. Instead, he sat near the stove of the synagogue, earning his livelihood from simple tailoring. When Eliezer Lipa was born, his mother had died during childbirth, and his father died within the following year. A caring uncle living in a nearby village took young Eliezer Lipa into his home and raised him, but he had neither time nor ability to teach Eliezer Lipa Torah. Hence, the son of a famous scholar grew up completely ignorant.

During the daily Talmudic class taught in the synagogue, Eliezer Lipa once heard the teacher explain that G-d delights in the physical effort man expends in his daily work. Though he certainly possessed the necessary skill to occupy a more comfortable position, Eliezer Lipa took these words to heart and decided to work at the most tedious labor he could find.

When he reached marriageable age, Eliezer Lipa was betrothed to an orphan girl who worked in the house of the Tarnow *gaon*, Rabbi Moshe Meir. Eliezer Lipa's wife was a worthy equal for her husband. Though raised in the home of a rabbinic leader, the woman was completely illiterate. She had merited hearing the rabbi's wife relate many stories from the Torah, and remembered various Jewish laws she had seen the rabbi practice, but she could not pray alone or even read the Hebrew alphabet. The only things she committed to memory were the blessings recited before eating food. Despite her ignorance, Eliezer Lipa's wife was a pious woman, and she often recited *Tehillim* with her husband, repeating word-for-word as he read aloud.

The couple lived a simple life, barely making ends meet from the few coins Eliezer Lipa earned through a variety of jobs—building ovens, construction, wood chopping, gardening and weeding. After some years, Eliezer Lipa and his wife were blessed with a son whom they named Elimelech—after Eliezer Lipa's father. Later, when a second boy followed, the new baby was named Meshulam Zusia—after Eliezer Lipa's father-in-law.

During this time, Eliezer Lipa became a water carrier, bringing water into Tarnow from a river located some distance away. Fortunately, four of the wealthiest residents in Tarnow took the sincere villager as their water carrier, and Eliezer Lipa was finally able to make a respectable income and sustain his family comfortably. In addition, Eliezer Lipa brought water to some of the synagogues in the village, an honored role he shared with Zalman Dov—the other water carrier of Tarnow.

One day, as Eliezer Lipa rode with his buckets through the marketplace, he suddenly encountered an unusual sight. A stranger stood there, speaking animatedly to a circle of enthralled listeners, regaling them with words from our Sages. Unbeknownst to Eliezer Lipa, this stranger was none other than the Baal Shem Tov, who traveled from town to town encouraging the simple folk in their sincere service of G-d.

Eliezer Lipa was curious to hear what had caught the attention of the normally busy merchants and customers, including some of his closest acquaintances. As he neared the crowd, Eliezer Lipa heard the stranger begin the following story (from *Vayikra Rabbah*, 3:5): "When the Temple stood in Jerusalem," began the Baal Shem Tov, "Jews from far and near came to bring their sacrificial offerings before G-d. Once, an especially affluent individual chose a rather large and well-fed ox from his pastures and brought his sacrifice to Jerusalem. To his extreme consternation, the ox suddenly stopped at the Temple gates and refused to budge.

"Bedlam ensued. A crowd of people ran up and began trying to move the ox, but the stocky animal made a mockery of their efforts. During the commotion, a poor man arrived at the Temple with his modest—but sincere—offering of vegetables. Sizing up the situation, he offered his vegetables to the ox, and walked backwards as the huge animal lumbered toward the juicy treat. Slowly but surely, the poor man's vegetables coaxed the unruly animal to the slaughtering area, after which its remains were offered on the altar.

"Who do you think has found greater favor in G-d's eyes?" asked the Baal Shem Tov, looking into the eyes of the simple Jews standing around him. "The poor man! That very night, as the magnate dreamed in his sleep, he heard a voice emanate from Heaven that proclaimed: 'He Who dwells in the Heavens derived greater pleasure from the poor man's sacrifice than from yours!'

"Can you imagine?" exclaimed the Baal Shem Tov enthusiastically. "The magnate offered the choicest animal available—a fat, sturdy ox. Overcome with joy, the magnate then offered a thanksgiving offering and sponsored a large feast for his family and friends, while the Temple priests enjoyed their allotted meat portions from the sacrifice. The magnate felt greatly pleased by his great mitzvah, and rightfully so—after all, who could match his benevolence?

"Conversely, the poor man felt morose and dejected with his offering. 'What a miserable pauper I am,' he thought. 'What worth do my meager vegetables have compared to such a well-fed ox? And yet, how happy I am to have served G-d with what I can afford.'

"Despite this," the Baal Shem Tov raised his voice with emotion, "the Heavens themselves revealed: 'He Who dwells in the Heavens derived greater pleasure from the poor man's sacrifice!'

"G-d desires the heart, the sincerity of the person! Whenever a Jew does something for G-d, and does it with wholehearted enthusiasm, this is exceedingly precious before G-d. This meager offering—even if it is only worth a single penny—arouses greater supernal delight than the egoistic pride of the most expensive offering. G-d, so to speak, boasts about the simple Jew to his celestial angels, saying: 'Look what a beautiful thing my son has done just for me!' This delight arouses G-d to bless the simple Jew with all his needs."

The Baal Shem Tov finished his story and the crowd dispersed. Eliezer Lipa returned to his horses and water barrels, but he could not dismiss the stranger's words reverberating in his ears. As he whipped the horses and sweated to carry the heavy water barrels, Eliezer Lipa envied the poor, sincere Jew whose bundle of vegetables had caused such Divine delight, and an earnest prayer welled up in the water carrier's heart. "Please, G-d," he implored, "allow me to serve you also with a special mitzvah, to fulfill a unique deed with wholehearted joy."

And then it struck him. The ultimate kindness would be to exchange his water route with Zalman Dov, the other water carrier. Eliezer Lipa was well aware of the self-sacrifice such a move entailed: the patronage of his four wealthy customers covered over half his income! He even provided water to Rabbi Naftali, the head of the community. Zalman Dov could not hope to enjoy such profit. Many synagogues lined his route, and Zalman Dov sold them water for half the normal price, severely lowering his earnings. Yet, Eliezer Lipa realized that this would be his mitzvah, his opportunity to serve G-d with genuine joy.

Eliezer Lipa's wife reacted happily to his suggestion. "Now we will merit to supply all the local synagogues with water!" she exclaimed. "Maybe, just maybe, this act of kindness will help our sons succeed in their studies!"

Eliezer Lipa understood his wife all too well. They had never accepted the fact that their children met no success in their studies. Instead, they did everything possible to arouse Divine mercy and channel spiritual blessing for their sons. When they recited *Tehillim* together, the couple shed bitter tears as they beseeched G-d to grant their children understanding. Their charity was legendary. It was not unusual for Eliezer Lipa and his wife to give away their only food to hungry guests while they themselves fasted. Every Friday, Eliezer Lipa's wife baked two fresh *challot*, which she then distributed to the poor in merit of her two sons. Additionally, she lit two candles in the local synagogue, praying that G-d illuminate the eyes of her sons with Torah and Divine service.

Naturally, Zalman Dov was overjoyed with the proposed change, and he immediately agreed to change routes with Eliezer Lipa. The exchange was done without fanfare or publicity; none of the village residents even noticed the change. Sometimes, Eliezer Lipa's wife accompanied him to the river, herself drawing buckets of water to pour into their barrels. "What good fortune we have!" she said sincerely. "Worshippers in our synagogues now have enough water to wash their hands before the prayers." Both parents earnestly hoped that this honest sacrifice would arouse

Heavenly mercy for their sons, improving their ability to learn.

After two years, Eliezer Lipa decided to send his sons to learn in a distant yeshivah. After all, Elimelech was already eighteen, and his younger brother Meshulam Zusia had passed Bar Mitzvah age. After bidding their sons a tearful farewell, the parents returned home to an empty house. "I just had an idea," Eliezer Lipa's wife turned to him. "Let's take in two students from the local yeshivah and give them free room and board. In this merit, our sons will succeed in their studies."

Eliezer Lipa enthusiastically agreed. Soon two students were welcomed into the home of Eliezer Lipa and his wife, where they enjoyed comfortable lodgings and warm meals. For their part, the couple was gratified to hear from passing visitors just how well their sons had adapted to yeshivah life and, surprisingly, their great academic achievements. "This must be in merit of our additional good deeds," Eliezer Lipa and his wife concurred. "G-d has shown mercy on our children, enabling them to succeed in their studies." The couple was overcome with joy and gratitude.

One Friday morning, as Eliezer Lipa lugged his barrels out of the river, he suddenly heard a strange splashing sound. Peering into the barrels, the water carrier was surprised to see a fish swimming frantically around. "How happy my wife will be!" thought Eliezer Lipa. "Since I lost my earnings to Zalman Dov, we have not been able to afford fish or wine for many weeks already."

Eliezer Lipa quickly made his way home, gave the fish to his delighted wife, and went to the bath house to prepare for Shabbat. As she cleaned the fish, his wife was flabbergasted to find a glittering diamond resting inside the dead fish. Her amazement gave way to chagrin, and then to sorrow.

Upon returning home, Eliezer Lipa was shocked to find his wife in a state of mourning. "But what happened?" cried the water carrier. "When I left for the bath house a short while ago, you were so happy with the fish I found!"

His wife gave no response. After much cajoling, Eliezer Lipa's wife finally revealed the source of her distress. "I distinctly recall you telling me how G-d desires the toil of man," she said between tears. "Such a person, you said, is blessed both in this world and the next. During our life together, you keep praising G-d for enabling you to find decent labor."

"Yet now," continued his wife morosely, "I am afraid you will abandon this field of work and start dealing in business and trade, which are rarely completely free of sin."

"What are you talking about?" asked Eliezer Lipa in amazement. "You know I have been offered positions in business and trade in the past; I have always refused to even hear about it. Why should I change my mind suddenly?"

Eliezer Lipa's wife opened her hand to reveal a shining diamond, and quickly explained where she found this treasure. Eliezer Lipa's eyes darkened. He recalled hearing how a Talmudic sage received a golden table leg from Heaven to alleviate his poverty, only to learn it had been deducted from the Divine reward awaiting him in the World-to-Come. "Come, let us forget about our worries," said his righteous wife. "Shabbat is almost here; we must greet it with joy. We will decide what to do with the diamond after Shabbat is over."

The next day, during the Shabbat meal, Eliezer Lipa retold the story of the Talmudic sage whose wife suffered terrible embarrassment due to their extreme poverty. While all her neighbors bustled around their kitchens on Friday and filled their ovens with *challot*, her home was empty. Seeing her distress, her husband prayed for Divine assistance, and a golden table leg descended from Heaven. However, that night as they slept, the wife dreamed she sat in the Garden of Eden, surrounded by many people sitting at golden tables with three legs. Imagine her alarm and consternation to realize her very own table was missing a leg! When she awoke, she implored her husband to pray again—this time asking G-d to retract the leg—and his prayers were effective.

"I heard a similar story when I worked for the rabbi," said his wife. "It was about a childless scholar, (the father of Rashi), a diamond merchant, who was being forced to sell his most precious diamond to decorate an idol in a distant land. As he stood on deck of the ship, the scholar threw the diamond into the ocean, rather than transgress the prohibition of idol worship. G-d then blessed him with a son who became a towering Torah scholar and the foremost commentator of the Torah."

After *Havdalah*, Eliezer Lipa became thoughtful again. "We finally heard good news about the scholastic gains of our children," he said. "Yet now, it appears G-d is testing us. We must be strong and strengthen our faith!"

"Excellent!" replied his wife. "But first we must tell the *rav* of our find. Maybe it belongs to someone; he will instruct us how to fulfill the commandment of returning lost objects."

Eliezer Lipa dutifully did as his wife instructed. He showed the diamond to the *rav*, explained the surrounding circumstances, and asked the *rav* for the proper procedure on announcing a find. "Generally speaking, you are correct," said the rabbi. "Normally we are enjoined to declare all finds publicly, so we can identify the owner and return it accordingly. Your case, however, is different. The fish evidently found the diamond in the river bed, in which case it rightfully belongs to whoever catches the fish. G-d has given you a small fortune; all you must do is separate a tithe for charity."

Returning home, Eliezer Lipa told his wife that the diamond was rightfully theirs, and the righteous couple immediately decided to give its *entire* worth to charity. After having the precious stone evaluated, Eliezer Lipa and his wife sold the diamond and distributed its value among the poor—half for needy scholars, and half for impoverished families. For his part, Eliezer Lipa continued his water route as usual. Life resumed as normal: Besides the rabbi, not a soul knew of their find.

A year passed and soon word came from Elimelech announcing his engagement. His future father-in-law had assured Elimelech he would support him for many years, enabling the young scholar to continue studying uninterrupted. The water carrier and his wife were overjoyed with the good news, and their joy increased tenfold when their younger son Meshulam Zusia returned from yeshivah. He had grown into a kind-hearted young man with an earnest look of piety about him. When he found the two students staying in his home, Meshulam Zusia arranged regular study periods with them, in addition to their yeshivah schedule. Despite the vehement protests of his father, the boy helped along with the water route, drawing water from the river into his father's buckets.

After six months, Meshulam Zusia returned to yeshivah. Eliezer Lipa continued his hard labor with a jubilant song in his heart, deeply impressed with the spiritual values of his children. Wading out into the water one morning, Eliezer Lipa was startled to feel something hard and cold between his toes. As he raised his feet out of the water, the water carrier was shocked to find a gold coin! He bent down into the water, searching carefully around with his hands, until he felt a broken earthenware vessel imbedded in the sandy riverbed. Eliezer Lipa dug around the vessel, loosening it enough to secure a solid grip, and raised out a jug brimming with gold and silver coins. Eliezer Lipa hid the vessel among his water barrels, delivered water to his customers, and returned home with his newly-found treasure.

Needless to say, this latest find threw Eliezer Lipa and his wife into a dejected state of mind. "Apparently, G-d still wishes to test us," they concluded. "We need to fortify ourselves against this test, and continue living our previous lifestyle." The couple buried the treasure in the basement, and resolved to distribute these riches to charity.

Soon news arrived that their younger son was engaged. Like his older brother, Meshulam Zusia's father-in-law had agreed to support him during his years of study, and this information gladdened Eliezer Lipa greatly.

Close to five years passed, and Eliezer Lipa's health began to fail. No longer could he draw water from the river, or drag heavy barrels up and down the streets of Tarnow. The water carrier sold his route to a fellow villager on the condition he received a small percentage of the earnings, as per the instructions of the local *rav*. Hence, while a veritable treasure lay buried in their basement, Eliezer Lipa and his wife lived a humble life of frugality, using the treasure for charitable donations exclusively.

Meanwhile, Eliezer Lipa's uncle suddenly fell ill. Though childless, the uncle was deeply proud of Eliezer Lipa's righteous children and, when he passed away, he bequeathed his entire inheritance to Eliezer Lipa—including many houses and estates. Upon hearing this good news, Eliezer Lipa gave his humble home away to the water carrier he recently hired, and entrusted him with full profit of the water route. "Be sure to give the synagogues their full share of water," he warned. "I am selling you the business based on this understanding alone."

Taking along their meager possessions and all the remaining treasure, Eliezer Lipa and his wife moved into the spacious home of their departed uncle, located on the outskirts of Tarnow. Once there, they invited other Jewish couples to live in the vacant homes scattered around the various estates. These were destitute scholars with large families, and Eliezer Lipa's generous move meant a new lease on life for such financially strained people. Every household received a large garden, perfect for growing their own vegetables. Eliezer Lipa rented out the windmill to one of the local residents, and let local farmers plant their grain on the huge expanse of land surrounding his estates.

With time, the rewards reaped by Eliezer Lipa and his wife for their extraordinary good deeds and legendary kindness became apparent to all. Their two sons became great *tzaddikim* in their own right, renowned throughout the Torah world for their piety and scholarship. Eliezer Lipa and his wife enjoyed great inner contentment from the spiritual achievements of their revered sons, far more than anything possibly gleaned from physical riches. Their sincerity and devotion to serving G-d continue to live on, perpetuated by the worthy lives of their two sons who became brilliant diamonds in the Chasidic chain—the celebrated Rabbi Elimelech of Lizhensk (author of *Noam Elimelech*) and Rabbi Meshulam Zusia of Anipoli.

The Sincere Porter: Hirshel Goat

IT WAS A TYPICAL DAY in the marketplace of Brody. Merchants haggled loudly with prospective customers; fowl clucked, animals brayed and mooed, as people dashed about in search of a bargain. The raucous cacophony of sounds did not disturb the large crowd that had gathered around a scholarly looking speaker. The unknown preacher—the Baal Shem Tov—spoke warmly to the simple Jews, inspiring them to increase their devotion to G-d. The Baal Shem Tov described how the sincere prayers and *Tehillim* uttered by the simplest Jews cause G-d supreme gratification, even rivaling the scholarly accomplishments of venerated sages.

The Baal Shem Tov suddenly glanced up in wonderment. A simple Jew walked slowly by, a sack of flour lying heavily on his shoulder. His face was pale and drawn, his clothes were torn and frayed, and rivulets of sweat ran down his cheeks. Simple straw slippers covered his feet. Yet, rising above his head was a pillar of dazzling bright light, radiating with such intensity that the Baal Shem Tov could not help but stare in astonishment. In fact, the shining light appeared similar to the rays of radiance that shone from the face of Moshe Rabbenu! "He must belong to the circle of hidden *tzaddikim*," thought the Baal Shem Tov. "And yet, I know nothing about him."

The porter continued walking through the marketplace and the Baal Shem Tov heard the merchants call out to the porter sarcastically. "Hirshel, carry your packages in peace!" said one. "Hirshel Goat, bear your burden peacefully!" called another.

"Be well, be well," responded the simple Jew, nodding his thanks.

The Baal Shem Tov quickly turned to the two other *tzaddikim* who had accompanied him to Brody—Rabbi Yechezkel and Rabbi Efraim. "Do you recognize the Jew with the pillar of fire?" he asked. "Does he belong to the circle of hidden *tzaddikim*?"

Rabbi Yechezkel and Rabbi Efraim were equally bewildered. "No, we don't know him at all," they responded. "To the best of our knowledge, he is not a member of our group."

Puzzled, the Baal Shem Tov turned to the local merchants in the marketplace, trying to glean information about the righteous porter. "Oh, him?" said the merchants mockingly. "He's a goat-keeper. He has four goats at home, because he claims to have a particular affinity for goat's milk. We call him 'Hirshel Goat.' His wife died ten years ago, so Hirshel lives alone with his goats in one of the ramshackle huts near the end of the city."

The Baal Shem Tov's astonishment increased. He resolved to follow Hirshel around on his errands, to try to discover his meritorious deeds. Yet, even after a few days of careful surveillance, the Baal Shem Tov remained genuinely puzzled: How could a simple tender of goats merit such sublime spiritual radiance?

Deeply pained at his inability to perceive the porter's true worth, the Baal Shem Tov prayed fervently, imploring G-d to reveal the secret merits of the goat keeper. When his prayers went unanswered, the Baal Shem Tov decided to fast for three days in the hope of unlocking Hirshel's secret way of life. For three days, the Baal Shem Tov fasted and prayed in the *hekdesh*, the communal boarding house that offered free lodging to travelers and homeless paupers. On the third day, as the Baal Shem Tov left the *hekdesh*, he met Hirshel the goat-keeper standing outside. "I am very hungry and weak," said the Rebbe, "and I would particularly enjoy a cup of goat's milk. I heard you sell this particular sort of milk; perhaps I can buy some?"

"Certainly!" answered Hirshel joyously. "Come with me and I will give you milk, but not for money. I am also a Jew, and I am enjoined to share my bread and belongings with fellow Jews. I won't take a penny from you!"

The pair walked silently through the streets of Brody, finally reaching a row of old, decrepit homes at the outskirts of the city. Most of the houses lacked proper roofing, many had broken windows, and all were in urgent need of basic repair. Hirshel pushed open the door of his home and the air was suddenly filled with the sound of loud bleating. The goats rushed toward Hirshel, licking his hands and feet as they frolicked excitedly around their beloved owner.

Hirshel greeted his goats warmly, stroking them gently and calming them with soothing words. Soon, the goats stood ready for their milking. Hirshel sat down to milk the goats, offered his guest a cup of warm milk, and soon the pair were engaged in conversation. To the Baal Shem Tov's surprise and delight, Hirshel revealed his daily schedule and, in doing so, removed the shroud of secrecy surrounding his sacred work.

"All her life, my righteous wife Rachel Leah cared for the poor, sickly people in our village," said Hirshel. "Whenever a destitute family had a child, my wife was there to help the mother and the newborn—washing, cleaning, feeding, and doing everything she possibly could. She started this mitzvah when she was very young, even before our marriage, and continued uninterrupted until the day of her death.

"Ten years ago, Rachel Leah passed away. A few days after her demise, she appeared to me in a dream and related everything she experienced after leaving our physical earth. 'I felt myself being escorted before the Heavenly Court,' she told me. 'They were busy reviewing every aspect of my life when suddenly a large group of souls appeared—the selfsame sickly women and children I had helped throughout the years. They told the Heavenly Court how I assisted them and, in merit of these good deeds, I was immediately escorted into *Gan Eden*.

"'I have come to reveal a secret,' my wife continued. 'In Heaven, special regard is shown to those who spend their lives helping other Jews. Since you are a simple Jew, unable to gain merit through the study of Torah, I have a suggestion how you can attain great spiritual reward: Help the sickly and suffering, and offer assistance to birthing mothers. However, keep your deeds secret. Do the deed for its merit alone, without fanfare or publicity.' Saying this, my wife disappeared and I awoke.

"Upon pondering her words, I decided to purchase four goats. Whatever money I earn from peddling, I use to buy superior grain for feeding the goats. Thus, they produce healthy, nutritious milk, of inestimable value for invalids or birthing mothers who have no means of acquiring medication. I distribute the milk secretly, leaving full containers on doorsteps of needy households. Thank G-d, my milk has healed many of the sick and needy.

"Last night, my wife appeared to me as I slept," continued Hirshel, looking intently at the Baal Shem Tov. "She said: 'If you meet a poor man tomorrow who asks you for something, bring him home with you. Offer him some milk and tell him our secret. Through him, you can attain everlasting salvation.'"

Deeply moved by the porter's sincerity, the Baal Shem Tov resolved to stay in Brody for an entire month and closely scrutinize Hirshel's daily actions, hoping to see his worthy activities firsthand.

During the next few weeks, as the Baal Shem Tov observed Hirshel's daily schedule, he could not help but marvel at the porter's righteous deeds. Totally ignoring the good-natured taunts of local merchants and mischievous children, Hirshel performed his self-sacrificing acts of generosity in a quiet, unassuming manner. Pure faith illuminated his every deed. Seeing this, the Baal Shem Tov readily understood Hirshel's great spiritual reward, and found him deserving of the dazzling pillar of light that shone above his head.

The Baal Shem Tov met with Rabbi Efraim Tzvi, the leader of the hidden *tzaddikim* of Brody, and suggested he draw Hirshel into his circle of hidden saints. After due consideration, Rabbi

Efraim Tzvi resolved to ask Heaven whether or not the simple goat keeper was worthy to join this select group. Indeed, Hirshel's initiation received affirmation from Heaven and he soon became a member of the hidden *tzaddikim*. Rabbi Binyamin Beinish the carpenter—another hidden *tzaddik*—began teaching the porter Torah. With time, simple Hirshel became an outstanding scholar and righteous *tzaddik*, having attained ever greater heights in both scholarship and piety.

After five years, Heaven instructed Rabbi Hirshel to relocate to the city of Anipoli. There, too, he continued curing the sick, and his prayers and amulets helped heal thousands of people during the course of the following thirty-three years. Later on, Rabbi Hirshel took the wandering staff in hand, and began traveling from town to town. His last stop was Ostropol.

Shortly before his passing, Rabbi Hirshel notified the people at the *shul* that his name was Tzvi, the son of Yechiel Zalman— a *shamash* in a *shul* in Brody. He also said that he had two sons, R. Uziel and R. Gedalia, but stopped short of revealing where they could be found. On a cold day in Elul, 5521 (1761), just over a year after the passing of the Baal Shem Tov, the righteous goat-keeper passed away quietly at a ripe old age. Heavy rains fell on Ostropol that day and icy winds cut through the city. Hearing about the demise of a relatively unknown recluse, very few people ventured outside to accompany Rabbi Hirshel to his final resting place. Barely a *minyan* gathered to bury Rabbi Hirshel in the drenching deluge, and even they rushed quickly indoors after completing their difficult task.

Rabbi Hirshel's soul ascended Heavenward, where a large procession of souls gathered to meet him. They were the souls of all the hidden *tzaddikim* along with all the sickly and needy souls who had benefited from Rabbi Hirshel's charitable acts on earth. Throngs of angels created by Rabbi Hirshel's righteous deeds continued to gather, clamoring to see the great *tzaddik*.

As Rabbi Hirshel's soul arrived in Heaven, pandemonium erupted. The prosecuting angels accused the Jewish residents of Ostropol of a grievous sin: practically ignoring the demise of the saintly Rabbi Hirshel. "They disgraced the *tzaddik!*" roared the accusers. "Hardly ten people turned up to accord Rabbi Hirshel his final honor. In fact, the circle of hidden *tzaddikim* and their leader also deserve due punishment for allowing such an abomination to occur."

The souls of the *tzaddikim*, headed by the Talmudic Sage Rabbi Chaninah ben Dosa, began exerting their utmost effort to avert the Heavenly decree facing the Jews of Ostropol, but their desperate attempts bore no fruit. Suddenly, an announcement was heard: "Make way, make way for the soul of the righteous woman Rachel Leah, the wife of Rabbi Hirshel. 'A virtuous wife crowns her husband!'"

Rachel Leah's soul suddenly appeared, accompanied by thousands of shining souls and equally dazzling angels. "Can the Jews of Ostropol really be blamed for their apathy?" she beseeched the Heavenly Court. "Could they have known that this one-hundred year-old wanderer was, in fact, a righteous saint? He lived in the *hekdesh*, wore tattered and frayed clothing, and looked like an ignorant boor! On the contrary, the Jews of Ostropol deserve to be commended for their wonderful charity—they fed, lodged, and gave money to a total stranger for no other reason than to fulfill G-d's commandment of extending charity to those in need."

"Furthermore," continued Rachel Leah, "punishing the Jews of Ostropol means, in essence, punishing my saintly husband. After all, he is the sole cause of your prosecution!" Hearing her truthful words, the accusing angels slunk away in shame and the evil decree was abolished.

One-hundred-and-fifteen years passed. In 5636 (1875), Rabbi Shalom DovBer, fifth Rebbe of Lubavitch, merited to envision the Baal Shem Tov in his Heavenly chamber of light and hear various stories from his saintly soul. Among them was the story of "Hirshel Goat," the simple goat-keeper who merited to become one of the foremost *tzaddikim* of his day, and whose righteous deeds illuminated the Heavens themselves.

SPREADING THE WELLSPRINGS

Denburg

IN THE CITY OF DENBURG, there lived a poor shoemaker by the name of Rabbi Gedalia Boruch. As was the norm in those times, the scholarly and wise had their specific synagogue; artisans and merchants had theirs; and the poor, unlettered Jews worshipped in the *Chevra Kaddisha* synagogue.

Rabbi Gedalia Boruch chose to frequent the latter synagogue. He mingled freely with the unlearned worshippers, befriending whomever he could, and even volunteered to give a *Chumash* class. Apparently, the shoemaker knew more than he cared to reveal, for he taught *Chumash* and *Rashi* with the greatest ease, simplifying the text so that even the most ignorant laborer could understand. The congregants were grateful for this chance to improve their meager knowledge of Torah. Denburg's scholars spurned them, ridiculing their appalling illiteracy, and the shoemaker was the first person who cared enough to teach them.

Basha, the shoemaker's wife, had also earned the admiration of the city's poor. She possessed wide familiarity with natural medicines and folk healing and her uncanny ability at correctly diagnosing ailments made her very popular. Basha excelled in deeds of kindness, and knew intuitively how to care for the sick and elderly extra gently. Invalids and paupers were constantly knocking on her door, many waiting just to find a sympathetic

132

ear. Moreover, whatever income Basha earned from her "clinic" was immediately distributed among poor brides, needy orphans, and new mothers. Needless to say, the good hearts of Rabbi Gedalia Boruch and his wife were admired all around the city.

Curiously, ever since the shoemaker made Denburg his home, strange groups of wandering beggars began appearing in the city. Though most wandering paupers were illiterate simpletons, hoping to eke out a meager living from handouts, these beggars were of a different class altogether. They exuded an aura of refinement and piety, often surprising people with their astounding knowledge of Torah.

Not that this was a unique phenomenon: at the time, many scholars of great repute voluntarily chose a life of exile, wandering from city to city as a form of penance. Guest hostels sprung up in various cities to accommodate these wandering scholars, while some cities let them reside in the *hekdesh* room—the communal free lodging for travelers and homeless paupers—adjoining the local synagogue. Yet these so-called beggars were different. They shunned the hostels and *hekdesh* rooms, choosing to lodge in the synagogues themselves.

As customary, all synagogues had regular Torah classes throughout the week, and the beggars could often be heard explaining the text being studied, continuing with messages of inspiration and hope. Using stirring descriptions, the beggars aroused the classes' participants to improve their piety and fear of G-d. No one imagined that these "beggars" were really clandestine followers of the Baal Shem Tov, who, devoted to their mission of spreading Chasidism ever outward, had taken the walking staff in hand to inspire other Jewish communities.

One week a peculiar thing happened. Two traveling *maggidim* reached Denburg at the same time, and both specified they would address the larger community on Shabbat afternoon. At the appointed time, large crowds of people gathered in two different synagogues in Denburg, each waiting to hear a motivating message from the distinguished visitors.

In the first synagogue stood Rabbi Tevel the *Maggid*, a preacher famous for his fire-and-brimstone exhortations, who ably used his time to bring his audience to tears. In the past, his impassioned words had brought many to repent fully for their sins, largely due to his frightening warnings and imprecations. Today was no exception: Rabbi Tevel horrified the crowd with graphic depictions of Divine wrath, exhorting them to abandon their evil ways and repent for any misdeeds. Tears flowed freely as his audience imagined the terrible Divine punishments awaiting them.

Many blocks away, in the second synagogue, stood a disciple of the Baal Shem Tov, a member of the wandering group of Chasidim. He described the great merits found within even the simplest Jew, whose very essence is permeated by the sterling characteristics of "mercy, bashfulness and kindness" (*Yevamot 79a*). The Chasid elaborated on the great rewards prepared for every Jew in *Gan Eden* and in the future resurrection. "Every Jew is holy, worthy of reward," he pronounced, "as the Prophet explicitly says: 'Your Nation are all righteous'" (Isaiah 60:21). These words of encouragement made a tremendous impact on his listeners, infusing them with renewed life and hope.

After the speakers concluded, both audiences streamed out onto the streets and began comparing notes. Rabbi Tevel's listeners came away with a bitter taste in their mouths, their life's accomplishments tainted by doom and gloom. Conversely, the Chasid's listeners were fairly bursting at the chance to do more *mitzvot*, having just been energized with new life. All agreed that Rabbi Tevel the *Maggid* had done the community a disservice by his preoccupation with detecting sins and faults and depicting their torturous stay in Purgatory, while the Chasid—who stressed the merits of all Jews—had done them a true kindness with his refreshing message.

This experience served as an eye-opener for the Jews of Denburg. They accorded the traveling beggars new respect, not realizing that a poor shoemaker living in their midst was actually responsible for bringing these saintly guests.

Four years passed before Rabbi Gedalia Boruch finally

revealed his true identity. On the festival of Shavuot, hundreds of people crammed into the *Chevra Kaddisha Shul* for the morning prayers and listened attentively as the Torah portion describing *Matan Torah* was read. Suddenly Rabbi Gedalia Boruch could be seen threading his way through the crowd. He ascended the *bimah*, banged on it for attention, and turned to address the startled worshippers.

In a voice charged with emotion, Rabbi Gedalia Boruch described the scene at Mount Sinai, where our forefathers received G-d's Law with "awe and dread, fear and sweat" (*Brachot* 22a). He spoke of the intense spiritual revelation they witnessed—one not to be repeated ever again—and applied the content of the festival to contemporary life. "On this date every year, we reaffirm our commitment to the Torah," he declared. "Today we stand at the foot of Mount Sinai, ready to accept the sacred Torah once more. What joy and happiness we feel on this special day! We thank G-d for the inestimable kindness He has shown us, to find us worthy from among all the nations to become His chosen people, and bless us with the Torah and its commandments.

"In our present day, we must be even more thankful to G-d," the shoemaker went on to say. "A towering *tzaddik* has been revealed in our generation, a *tzaddik* who speaks positively about his fellow Jews and forges a spiritual path based on unconditional *Ahavat Yisrael*, positive character traits, and serving G-d with joy." Rabbi Gedalia Boruch continued speaking for some time, relaying snippets of various Chasidic teachings and enthralling the crowd with incredible stories of the Baal Shem Tov and his wondrous miracles.

Rabbi Gedalia Boruch descended from the *bimah* and went to a different *shul*, leaving the congregation in an uproar. Apparently, the simple shoemaker was not so simple after all! Unperturbed by the commotion, Rabbi Gedalia Boruch went to the other two major synagogues in the city—*Poalei Tzion* and *Shomrim Laboker*—and repeated his speech for the worshippers.

The shoemaker's inspiring words and stories spread quickly

throughout Denburg. That evening, in synagogues all around the city, groups of people excitedly reviewed the shoemaker's speech. On the following day—the second day of Shavout—a large crowd gathered in one of the synagogues, and Rabbi Gedalia Boruch addressed them again. He explained the mitzvah of *Ahavat Yisrael* in light of the Baal Shem Tov's teachings, inter-twining his words with stories of unlearned, sincere Jews who served G-d with uncomplicated faith. Uplifted by the fact that they, too, counted as worthy Jews, the simple city-dwellers were extremely appreciative of the shoemaker's encouragement. No one had ever told them how much they truly mattered.

In ensuing days, the content of Rabbi Gedalia Boruch's latest speech found grateful listeners all around Denburg. So many clamored to hear Rabbi Gedalia Boruch again that the *shamash* of the city's main synagogue invited him to address the congre-gation on Shabbat afternoon. "I accept," replied the shoemaker humbly. "I will talk about the first *Mishnah* in *Avot*."

That Shabbat afternoon, a huge crowd gathered in the main synagogue. Having heard much about the shoemaker's earlier lec-tures, the leading scholars of the town also assembled in the *shul*, waiting to hear what an "ignorant" shoemaker could offer. Rabbi Gedalia Boruch elaborated on the first *Mishnah* of *Avot*, stressing the importance of uninterrupted tradition and unwavering belief in *tzaddikim*. The crowd listened in rapt attention and all—even the scholars—left profoundly affected by his words.

"The shoemaker seems to be a learned person," agreed the scholars afterwards. "Perhaps he can give a regular Torah class." Representatives of the main synagogue invited Rabbi Gedalia Boruch to lecture on *Pirkei Avot* during the long summer *Shabbatot*, and the shoemaker readily agreed. As time progressed, those attending the class became steadily aware of the shoemak-er's impressive erudition, and people accorded him new respect. His constant mention of the Baal Shem Tov and his Chasidic teachings bore fruit: soon large groups of people became devoted followers of Chasidus.

Rabbi Gedalia Boruch now turned his attention to the fledgling scholars of the city, reaching out to the many students that filled the study halls of Denburg. He taught them Chasidic philosophy as expounded by the Baal Shem Tov, and the most gifted students were drawn to the Rebbe's approach. In a little over two years, the shoemaker was able to bring a sizeable group of new Chasidim with him to Mezibush.

The group spent two months—Elul and Tishrei—in the Baal Shem Tov's company, learning and living with his teachings and customs. They returned to Denburg as new men—full of life and vitality; deeply committed to the Chasidic path of spiritual service; and permeated by the ideals of unconditional *Ahavat Yisrael* and fine character traits.

Upon their return, these new Chasidim spread word of the Baal Shem Tov's teachings to all their acquaintances. Slowly but steadily, the city of Denburg became a Chasidic stronghold. Synagogues scheduled allotted times when people could come hear wondrous stories of the Rebbe, as told by one of his followers. For many, particularly the downtrodden and broken-hearted, this became the focal point of their week. The Rebbe's deep concern for all Jews, amply evidenced in the weekly stories they heard, was a beacon of hope that illuminated their daily lives.

Many years passed, years of progress and Chasidic growth. The Baal Shem Tov passed on from this world and the Chasidim of Denburg became devoted followers of the successors in the Chasidic dynasty—the *Maggid* of Mezritch, Rabbi Mendel of Horodok, and Rabbi Schneur Zalman of Liadi.

One day, Rabbi Gedalia Boruch appeared before his friends and relayed a startling message. "I merited to see the Baal Shem Tov in a dream last night," he said with obvious delight. "The Rebbe said to me: 'Gedalia Boruch, it is time you joined us in our world....'"

Another person would have been deeply grieved to hear such a terrible premonition, but not Rabbi Gedalia Boruch. Already well advanced in years, he accepted his fate with joy and felt privileged to receive this warning.

His weakened state had prevented him from attending synagogue, so a quorum of men came to his house every day for the services. After every prayer—*Shacharit, Minchah* and *Maariv*—the group studied *Mishnah* and a chapter of *Tanya*, which they followed with a short, informal discussion. They reminisced about past travels to the Baal Shem Tov, Rabbi DovBer, Rabbi Mendel of Horodok and Rabbi Schneur Zalman of Liadi, and recalled different Chasidic figures they had met on their travels.

"There's a special request we want to make," the group said to Rabbi Gedalia Boruch one day. "When the time comes for you to enter the World-of-Truth, and you are reunited with our Chasidic leaders in their spiritual chambers, please remember us and arouse Divine favor on our behalf. If possible, we would like to meet privately with you, to relay our personal needs...."

Rabbi Gedalia Boruch agreed wholeheartedly. His friends met privately with him, each detailing their specific requests, and Rabbi Gedalia Boruch assured them he would try his utmost to accommodate their desires.

Two weeks later, on the fast of the tenth of Tevet, Rabbi Gedalia Boruch felt his demise was near. It was evening, just after the fast, and his friends were gathered around a table set with food and drink, singing and talking. "My time has come," Rabbi Gedalia Boruch suddenly announced. "Please, help me sing the songs we heard at the Baal Shem Tov's table. I want to relive the memories I have of the Rebbe expounding Torah, of the times we were together. "

Overcome by emotion, his friends began singing the melodies they often heard at the Baal Shem Tov's table. It seemed as though the Rebbe sat there in the room with them, as though the Chasidic brotherhood had gathered together once again to hear the Baal Shem Tov speak. The hours slipped by unnoticed, and soon the night sky gave way to the earliest hints of dawn. As it got lighter outside, the group finished their meal to begin preparing for *Shacharit* and Rabbi Gedalia Boruch confided this would be his last *Shacharit* on earth. "Let us strengthen ourselves to pray with complete concentration," he implored.

After a spiritually uplifting service, the group sat down to pursue their daily studies, which they later followed with *Minchah* and *Maariv*. "Remember us for good before our masters," they repeated to the saintly shoemaker. "Mention our names before the great *tzaddikim*—the Baal Shem Tov, Rabbi Dovber, and Rabbi Mendel."

Rabbi Gedalia Boruch thought deeply. "Write your requests on paper," he replied. "When I am buried, be sure to put your requests in my grave."

After *Maariv*, the shoemaker began relating his life's story, telling his friends how he had first heard of the Baal Shem Tov and the circumstances surrounding his initial encounter with the Rebbe. Shortly after he finished his story, Rabbi Gedalia Boruch returned his soul to its Maker.

Chasidim of Denburg were hard hit by the loss of their local patriarch. To further perpetuate his memory, special *Mishnayot* and *Tanya* classes were set up in every synagogue around the city, enabling people to study Torah in merit of their beloved mentor. Due to the shoemaker's efforts, Chasidus continued to inspire hundreds of families living in Denburg and the surrounding environs.

Kalisk

No ONE KNEW THE IDENTITY of the stranger who appeared one day on the streets of Kalisk. The stranger made himself at home in the local study hall, spending his days immersed in Torah. Students learning in the study hall knew only that the stranger's name was Rabbi Chaim and that he exhibited unusual marks of greatness. He possessed a remarkable grasp of Torah; was able to discuss the most complex tractates with ease; and never seemed to waste a moment. Quiet and reserved, Rabbi Chaim totally ignored the daily hustle and bustle of the study hall, devoting all his energies to his studies instead.

Naturally, it did not take long for the students to test the new arrival. Whatever questions they posed him, Rabbi Chaim answered them at great length, until he had completely satisfied their toughest questions. Otherwise, he lived in a world of silence. The students quickly began noticing that the scholarly stranger lived a righteous life of prayer and penance. He fasted often. Even when he did eat, his "meals" consisted of bread and cold water. On Shabbat, Rabbi Chaim ate *challah* and drank *cholent*-water, and, in honor of the holy day, he allowed the water to be warm instead of cold.

Neither did Rabbi Chaim leave at night. As the last students filed out of the study hall, the scholar would lay down on a bench to sleep, using a coarse wooden stump as a "pillow." His ascetic sleeping habits drew the attention of the students and earned him the nickname: Rabbi Chaim "Wood." With time, one of the younger students approached Rabbi Chaim to ask for an explanation regarding his frugal bedspread. "Isn't this a strange custom?" said the boy. "Do you really enjoy such an uncomfortable sleep?"

"The Talmud (*Brachot* 57b) states that 'sleep is a sixtieth of death,'" retorted Rabbi Chaim. "You tell me—is it necessary to sleep long and comfortably? You could waste your whole life on comfortable sleep, luxuriating in the shadow of death!"

From the little they could glean of Rabbi Chaim, everyone knew one thing for certain: the scholar held nothing against the new group who were studying and spreading Chasidism. Whenever he heard people deriding Chasidim and their new-fangled ideas, Rabbi Chaim would raise his voice in protest. "Have you nothing better to do than speak evil of fellow Jews?" he complained. "Were I not so weak and old, I would visit their Rebbe myself!"

There were older students, too, in the study hall. These were married men fortunate enough to be supported financially by their working fathers-in-law, enabling them to sit and study undisturbed for years. Numbering twenty in all, the older students enjoyed whenever they could get Rabbi Chaim to tell them one of his original Torah thoughts, or when the scholar deigned to deliver a *pilpul* for their benefit. As his influence in the study hall increased, Rabbi Chaim began explaining the benefits of exiling oneself for the purpose of spiritual refinement. He often said, "It is imperative to fulfill the words of our Sages: 'Exile yourselves to a place of Torah' (*Avot* 4:14). You boys would be much better off if you would travel elsewhere to learn Torah."

Many students became receptive to this idea, and they asked Rabbi Chaim for advice in choosing just the right location for exile. Rabbi Chaim gave them specific instructions, tailoring his responses to their individual needs. For the brightest students—headed by Rabbi Avraham, a scholar of great repute—Rabbi

Chaim chose a remote village situated in the district of Wohlyn, an area already influenced by Chasidism.

A few years passed when, one day, the students began returning to Kalisk. The Jewish community looked on in surprise to see these normally taciturn scholars smiling and happy. Gone were the aloof expressions and reserved demeanor. Instead, the scholars chatted happily with others, exuding a collective feeling of warmth and friendliness as they rejoined their families and resumed their studies in the local study hall.

A greater surprise lay in store for the Jews of Kalisk: When the scholars began their morning prayers, they exhibited all the signs of Chasidism—they prayed aloud, interspersed their devotions with song, and some even clapped or tapped the table as they sang beautiful melodies. Even their learning had changed: the scholars often paused their studies to sing with deep-felt emotion, charging the air with spiritual fervor, completely unlike the manner of scholars.

Upon their return, Rabbi Chaim—the once reticent scholar—also underwent a transformation. He spoke freely with the students, each deeply enjoying the other's company. Worse still, when the scholars spoke with Rabbi Chaim, they often broke off...to laugh! Whoever saw scholars laugh?

Hardly had the community recovered from their initial shock, when something occurred that completely overwhelmed Kalisk. Late at night, the scholars had joined Rabbi Chaim in a *farbrengen*, right in the study hall! They brought potatoes, warmed them in the fireplace, and placed a bottle of strong spirits on the table. The group sat down to sing and tell stories, followed by joyous dancing that lasted hours. Rabbi Chaim then addressed the students, breaking out in song again, and soon a large circle filled the study hall, the dancers weaving and crisscrossing the room as Rabbi Chaim danced in the center.

This latest incident caused utter bedlam in the city. People discussed these unusual events excitedly, hardly believing what had transpired. Worse still, no one knew how to make sense of this unusual behavior. Did scholars eat potatoes and drink vodka in a holy place of study? Was it not shameful for grown men to dance with uninhibited enthusiasm? And what of Rabbi Chaim: how did the shy scholar suddenly become a skillful orator and leader?

After a few weeks, sensational news shook the city to its core. The true identity of Rabbi Chaim was finally revealed: he was none other than one of the foremost disciples of the Baal Shem Tov, charged with the mission of bringing Chasidism to Kalisk. Among the society of secret *tzaddikim*, Rabbi Chaim "Wood" was really known as Rabbi Chaim the *Porush*. To crown his efforts with success, Rabbi Chaim had temporarily donned the cloak of bashfulness, pretending to be withdrawn and uninterested in others. After gaining the respect of the students, he succeeded in sending them off to Chasidic communities, where they internalized Chasidic teachings and customs.

For days afterward, this revelation dominated all conversation in Kalisk. Residents could hardly believe the success of the Baal Shem Tov in bringing Chasidism to their community. For their part, Rabbi Chaim and his followers remained oblivious to the commotion around them and continued in their pursuit of Torah study and prayer. Soon they began a new *minyan* in a room adjoining the study hall, where they *davened* in the slower pace of Chasidim, songs and gesticulations accompanying their prayer. The entire Jewish community turned out to gaze through the windows and doors of the *minyan* room, fascinated by the unfamiliar customs and mannerisms of the Chasidim.

As time went on, Rabbi Chaim's group began reaching out to others in Kalisk. They spoke to the scholar and the layman; to the merchant and the peddler. Chasidism seeped steadily into the homes of Kalisk as people heard more and more about the Baal Shem Tov and his spiritual path.

Rabbi Chaim—the once reserved scholar—revealed his long-hidden skills as he began giving steady addresses from the *bimah* of various synagogues. The Jewish community was amazed to discover that Rabbi Chaim was an orator of rare talent whose captivating speeches mesmerized audiences. It became impossible to hear Rabbi Chaim speak and remain impassive. In fact, his speeches had such a profound affect on his listeners that, within three months, almost the entire Kalisk had become staunch Chasidim of the Baal Shem Tov.

Time would tell that Rabbi Avraham—the brilliant student sent by Rabbi Chaim to learn in the district of Wohlyn—would later become famous as Rabbi Avraham Kalisker, one of the foremost disciples of Rabbi DovBer, the *Maggid* of Mezritch, disciple and successor of the Baal Shem Tov.

Slutsk

Rabbi Boruch of Vyezin belonged to the inner circle of hidden *tzaddikim*. A prosperous lumber merchant, Rabbi Boruch became an anomaly of sorts: he was the only member of the circle to be both a hidden *tzaddik* and a rich businessman! First a disciple of Rabbi Yoel Baal Shem of Zamoshtch, then a disciple of Rabbi Adam Baal Shem of Ropshitz, the wealthy Rabbi Boruch remained deeply committed to Chasidus and strongly wished to contribute to its success.

Rabbi Boruch lived on an estate not far from Slutsk, a bastion of strong anti-Chasidic sentiment. He built a large synagogue and *hachnasat orchim* lodge, places where his friends—the hidden *tzaddikim*—could feel at ease when visiting the area. Yet, Rabbi Boruch had grander plans in mind. He established a beautiful yeshivah on his estate, accepting only the brightest students the area could offer. Students entering the yeshivah doors could be no younger than fifteen, no older than sixteen.

Conditions at the yeshivah were demanding. Each and every student committed himself to study for six uninterrupted years, with the knowledge that they could not leave yeshivah grounds for a single day! Moreover, all students were expected to study with exceptional assiduity, while resolving not to let the slightest disturbance bother them. For his part, Rabbi Boruch financed the entire project—he purchased enough food and clothing for the entire yeshivah student body, and made sure his charges had all they needed.

Little wonder then that Rabbi Boruch's yeshivah grew in stature, until it became the most sought after place for serious students. Dozens clamored for acceptance and, indeed, the yeshivah grew immensely, until hundreds crammed the large study hall. Most were young men supported by their working fathers-in-law, enabling them to study unhindered.

In truth, however, Rabbi Boruch had a secret agenda: his yeshivah would serve as the impetus for Chasidus, lessening the deep-seated animosity toward Chasidim and Kabbalists in general. This cornerstone of the yeshivah's education could only be done secretly, by planting certain ideas within the minds and hearts of his students to make them more receptive to the fundamentals of Chasidus. Though students did not study Chasidus or Kabbalah openly, somehow their studies focused on the same fundamentals taught by the hidden *tzaddikim*. In effect, Rabbi Boruch's yeshivah made these students completely open and receptive to the teachings of Chasidus.

The yeshivah molded its students into learned scholars, deeply pious Jews who followed a spiritual path taught by their founder, Rabbi Boruch himself. The hidden *tzaddik* dared not entrust anyone else with this vital role. He—and only he—would supervise the spiritual growth of the yeshivah, to ensure it followed the teachings of Rabbi Adam Baal Shem. Rabbi Boruch educated the students in progressive stages, instilling them with essential Chasidic values.

His obsession with the yeshivah did not diminish Rabbi Boruch's business successes. As his prosperity grew, Rabbi Boruch purchased large tracts of land, which he later rented out to his fellow Jews at extremely low prices, making it easier for many to earn a decent living. Dozens raised bountiful crops on his fields; others netted the many fish that coursed through his rivers; still others worked the flour mills and inns. These magnanimous deeds made Rabbi Boruch a household name among Jews living in the area, earning him a constant stream of blessings and good wishes.

In fact, during the annual meeting of the "Council of Four Lands" held that year in Slutsk, Rabbi Boruch received honorable mention at the assemblage. Dignitaries of various districts thanked Rabbi Boruch for his dedicated service in improving the often depressing lot of their brethren, publicly expressing their admiration for his successes on both material and spiritual fronts. "Rabbi Boruch worries also for the physical needs of his fellow Jews," they lauded the businessman. "His untiring efforts are a boon for our brethren living in this district."

Few knew of Rabbi Boruch's hidden ambition to bring others closer to Chasidism. His yeshivah grew and grew, planting the kernels for future Chasidic growth among hundreds of students. By studying subjects conducive to the teachings of Rabbi Adam Baal Shem, these students later lent a willing ear to the Rebbe's path.

Time progressed and, in his later years, Rabbi Boruch heard that Rabbi Adam Baal Shem had transferred the mantle of leadership to Rabbi Yisrael Baal Shem Tov. "I have done this at the express request of Achiya Hashiloni," Rabbi Adam revealed. "In Heaven, they want Rabbi Yisrael to lead our generation."

Despite his seventy-five years, Rabbi Boruch immediately summoned his sons and set off together for Tlust to meet with the new Chasidic leader. Imagine their tremendous surprise when, upon entering the Baal Shem Tov's room, the Rebbe called them all by name and specified every detail of their lives! A further surprise awaited Rabbi Boruch: "Your destiny lies in *Eretz Yisrael*," instructed the Baal Shem Tov. "When you return home, make the appropriate preparations for your trip. I guarantee you will merit long life in the Holy Land."

Returning home, Rabbi Boruch began putting his affairs in order. Years of growth and success had turned his lumber business into a thriving enterprise, yet Rabbi Boruch had no qualms about leaving everything behind in order to fulfill the Rebbe's instructions. He formally signed off the business to his children, entrusting them also with his spiritual inheritance—management of his yeshivah. "I hope you will run the yeshivah with the same spirit I did," he told his children. "Our students must continue to follow the Baal Shem Tov's path. Furthermore, in order to ensure your continuing commitment to Chasidus, you must visit the Baal Shem Tov at least once every three years."

After concluding his final preparations, Rabbi Boruch journeyed once more to the Baal Shem Tov. During his month-long stay with the Baal Shem Tov, the Rebbe entrusted him with many vital missions. Then Rabbi Baruch left for *Eretz Yisrael*. Even in his new home, the elderly Chasid remained in close contact with the Baal Shem Tov, as he continued to spread Chasidism in the Holy Land.

His sons, meanwhile, visited the Baal Shem Tov in Tlust, just as their father instructed. "I want you to develop the estates of Prince Radziville," said the Rebbe. "Develop the rivers, mills, brick factories and inns, and arrange matters so Jews will be able to settle in these areas and turn a profit." Concluded the Baal Shem Tov: "If Jews can earn a decent livelihood, they will serve G-d better!"

The Baal Shem Tov also directed them to move the yeshivah from the suburbs to Slutsk proper. Rabbi Boruch's sons clearly understood the Rebbe's rationale: Slutsk had changed greatly in recent years and the fierce opposition to Chasidism had abated. There was, truly, no reason for the yeshivah to function outside city limits anymore. Rabbi Boruch's sons wasted no time in fulfilling the Rebbe's bidding. An impressive building quickly went up in Slutsk, large enough to house the entire yeshivah comfortably. Festive celebrations draped the city in Sivan of 5500 (1740) as the building reached its final stages and stood ready to open its doors. Rabbi Boruch's sons begged the Baal Shem Tov to attend the inaugural event. "This is a rare opportunity!" they explained. "The people of Slutsk will finally be able to meet the leader of Chasidism!"

The Baal Shem Tov accepted their invitation. Arriving in time for the inauguration, the Baal Shem Tov presided over the ceremony and stayed in Slutsk for close to an entire month. Indeed, Slutsk had undergone a transformation since the times of Rabbi Adam Baal Shem. No hecklers greeted the Rebbe; no protesters disturbed the celebrations. Even the few who differed with the Baal Shem Tov kept silent, not daring to publicly voice any dissent.

Slutsk suddenly became a hotbed of Chasidism. The Rebbe's followers streamed into the city from near and far, all clamoring to get a close glimpse of the Baal Shem Tov. Chasidim continued to pour into Slutsk throughout the entire month, infusing the city with a festive atmosphere as people met up with many old friends. The Rebbe delivered Chasidic teachings to his followers, and his close disciples merited entering for *yechidut*, private encounters where they received personal guidance and blessing from the Rebbe.

In honor of the inauguration, some residents of Slutsk brought a large stone to complete construction of the yeshivah. "A stone brought by Jews for a synagogue or study hall is precious!" declared the Baal Shem Tov. He related the story of Rabbi Chanina ben Dosa, the Talmudic sage who desired to bring a polished stone to the Temple in Jerusalem, and whose efforts were assisted by five angels in the guise of laborers (*Kohelet Rabbah* 1:1). The Baal Shem Tov then expounded Torah on the stone, marking it for future prominence. For decades to come, residents of Slutsk pointed out the stone with great reverence, fondly recalling the Rebbe's precious visit that graced their city forever.

NEW REVELATIONS, NEW TEACHINGS

The *Maggid*

RABBI DOVBER, WHO WOULD LATER become known as the famed *Maggid* of Mezritch, had heard much about the Baal Shem Tov. Incredible stories of the Rebbe's legendary powers circulated freely among the masses and many embarked on the journey to Mezibush, hoping to meet the Baal Shem Tov personally and merit his blessing. Upon returning, they told of the astounding miracles they had witnessed, vividly describing the Baal Shem Tov's supernatural ability to help others with his prayers.

At first, the *maggid* spurned any notion of visiting the Baal Shem Tov. Such a journey would entail an irreversible waste of time and he could not afford to forfeit even a second of learning Torah. Yet, despite his initial reservations, the *maggid* finally chose to travel to Mezibush and judge the Baal Shem Tov's greatness for himself.

Rabbi DovBer had good reason not to rely on the hearsay of others. Considered one of the most prodigious scholars in his generation, the *maggid* was thoroughly proficient in the Talmud and subsequent *halachic* codifiers. He also possessed considerable knowledge of Kabbalah, the esoteric dimension of the Torah. Profoundly erudite, the *maggid* spent his days immersed in the study of Torah, and refrained from the slightest waste of time.

Hence, after two days on the road, the *maggid* began regretting his decision. His misgivings proved accurate after all; he found it impossible to maintain his regular study schedule while traveling. Having already started out however, he resolved to complete the trip to Mezibush.

Upon his arrival in Mezibush, the *maggid* went directly to the Baal Shem Tov's home and secured an audience with him. Seeing the *maggid*, the Baal Shem Tov began relating a story. "On one of my recent trips, I had no food for my gentile wagon-driver. I finally found a poor gentile carrying a sack of bread, so I was able to purchase some bread for the driver."

The *maggid* looked at the Baal Shem Tov in surprise. Here he had squandered hours of precious learning to travel and meet the Baal Shem Tov—only to be rewarded with empty prattle? Disappointed and disheartened, the *maggid* left the Rebbe's room and returned to his studies.

On the following night, the *maggid* decided to meet the Baal Shem Tov again, hoping to hear Torah insights from the legendary leader. "You know," said the Baal Shem Tov as the *maggid* entered, "once when I was traveling I couldn't find any hay for my horses. I was lucky to find some hay after a while, and I was able to feed them."

The *maggid* could hardly believe his ears. Losing patience with the Baal Shem Tov and his seemingly meaningless stories, he resolved to return home immediately. He rushed back to his lodgings and announced to his wagon driver: "We are leaving!" "I want to go home right now! We'll wait here a bit for the moon to rise, but then we must set out straight for home."

By midnight, the moon had illuminated the surrounding countryside sufficiently and the wagon driver consented to depart. The *maggid* approached the wagon and was about to step inside when he suddenly noticed the Baal Shem Tov's attendant standing before him. "The Baal Shem Tov summons you," said the attendant.

Surprised, the *maggid* decided to follow the attendant, and he entered the Baal Shem Tov's room. "Do you know how to study?" inquired the Baal Shem Tov.

"Yes, I do," responded the *maggid*.

"So I hear. Are you knowledgeable in Kabbalah?"

"Yes."

The Baal Shem Tov summoned his attendant and instructed him to bring a Kabbalistic work titled *Eitz Chaim*. Opening the book to a certain page, he pointed to a specific paragraph and showed it to the *maggid*. "Here!" he said. "How do you explain this particular piece?"

The *maggid* read the paragraph and interpreted it to the best of his ability. A look of displeasure crossed the Baal Shem Tov's face. "You know nothing!" he asserted.

Baffled, the *maggid* reread the paragraph. After a few minutes of contemplation, he turned to the Baal Shem Tov. "I definitely explained it correctly," challenged the *maggid*. "If, however, you are aware of a different interpretation, please let me hear it as well. Then I will decide which of us is correct."

"Stand up!" ordered the Baal Shem Tov, his face aflame like a burning brand. As he began reading the paragraph aloud, dazzling light filled the house and a wall of fire encircled the Baal Shem Tov. Visions of various angels appeared in the room as the Baal Shem Tov read their names aloud from the Kabbalistic paragraph. The *maggid* almost collapsed in sheer fright at the sight of this spiritual revelation.

The Baal Shem Tov finished reading and the awesome sight disappeared instantly. "Indeed, you read it correctly," the Baal Shem Tov turned to the *maggid*. "However, your study lacks *soul*."

Overawed, the *maggid* instructed his wagon driver to return home alone. He stayed with the Baal Shem Tov and studied his teachings, rising in stature until he joined the Rebbe's circle of select disciples.

This was hardly the only time the *maggid* witnessed supernatural phenomena occurring in his master's room. On another occasion, the Baal Shem Tov actually commanded his student to address a wayward soul.

In those days, students of the Baal Shem Tov were privileged to stand watch outside the Rebbe's room at night, reciting

Mishnayot aloud until the new day dawned. The students alternated among themselves, to assure that everyone shared this special merit. Once, as the *maggid* stood watch outside the Rebbe's room, he suddenly heard the Baal Shem Tov call his name. "Go to the next room and get my new walking stick," said the Rebbe urgently. "But hurry, I need it quickly!"

The *maggid* dashed into the nearby room and returned shortly with the stick in hand. He gave the stick to the Baal Shem Tov, but the Rebbe immediately returned it to him. "Give the walking stick back to the person standing in front of you," commanded the Baal Shem Tov. "Tell him: 'The Rebbe is unwilling to take the present you have offered, because he is unable to help you.'"

The *maggid* glanced around quickly and looked at the Baal Shem Tov in consternation. No one else was in the room besides them, yet experience had taught him not to question the Rebbe's bidding. He thrust the stick out into the empty air and repeated the Baal Shem Tov's words. A feeling of overwhelming dread came over him as he felt someone take the stick out of his hands. The *maggid's* knees knocked together violently as he watched the stick vanish entirely.

Seeing the *maggid's* alarm, the Baal Shem Tov hastened to compose his student. "Don't be scared, my son," he said reassuringly. "This fellow transgressed every prohibition in the Torah. Just before his demise, he presented me with a fancy staff and now, after departing this world, he expects a form of rectification for his soul in appreciation for his gift. However, though I tried strenuously for many months now, I simply cannot find any way to mend his misdeeds. The sinner keeps returning, begging and pleading for me to intercede on his behalf. Now you understand why I told you to return the stick: I simply cannot help him."

At times, the *maggid* served as an intercessor of sorts between his fellow students and the Baal Shem Tov. Beset by tragedy and misfortune, a student of the Baal Shem Tov arrived in Mezibush one day to meet with the Rebbe. Distraught over his friend's plight, the *maggid* entered the Baal Shem Tov's room and said,

"A student with a bitter heart just arrived; he has been sorely afflicted...."

Replied the Baal Shem Tov: "When, Heaven forbid, G-d needs to punish a Jew—even with the slightest, most insignificant punishment—this causes G-d great anguish. His pain is deeper than the agony of the most sensitive father who needs to punish his son, to ensure he follows the path of righteousness.

"Every Divine punishment contains a portal of light, a radiant opening that contains the potential for reversal. Through repentance and arousing Divine mercy, an individual becomes empowered to elevate and transform the punishment, improving his circumstances to a far loftier level."

With time, the *maggid* grew in stature until he became the Baal Shem Tov's prized disciple. The unusually close bond between the Baal Shem Tov and the *maggid* found expression one year on the eve of Rosh Hashanah, when the Baal Shem Tov handed his student a *pidyon nefesh*. "I have never given a *pidyon* to anyone," revealed the Baal Shem Tov. "But to you, Rabbi Ber, I allow myself an exception. I am confident that you will not cause me damage, but, rather, only rectify matters."

The *maggid* opened the Baal Shem Tov's *pidyon* and read the following:

By the Grace of G-d

The eve of Rosh Hashanah, 5517, Mezibush

Yisrael, son of Sarah, [prays for] health and longevity,

May he merit binding with every soul, in their current state, and elevate them to the Source,

May all enemies and those who despise him abandon their [evil] path, and be transformed into friends.

—This will be "when G-d is pleased with a man's ways" (Proverbs 16:7).

To be inscribed and sealed for a good year among our people Israel

[The charity accompanying this] *pidyon* is one ruble per week.

The Great Mission

In the year 5519 (1759) the Baal Shem Tov dispatched one of his young disciples, R. Moshe Meshel from the village of Bezenke, with a letter to be delivered to another of his disciples, an eminent scholar called R. Chaim Rapaport, of blessed memory. In this letter the Baal Shem Tov instructed him to leave town on a certain day for the forest which was eight *parsas* to the east. There he was to study intensively the first four chapters of the laws of blessings as codified by *Rambam*, and any innovative interpretation that came to mind he was immediately to jot down in brief in order that it should not be forgotten. He was to begin that day by *davening* at daybreak, eating breakfast and setting out, making sure that nothing blocked his way. When he arrived at the forest and saw the Baal Shem Tov standing there, that was the place at which he was to sit and study as prescribed. Finally, after the *Minchah* prayers, he was to make his way safely for home.

The Baal Shem Tov also sent a letter through his young disciple R. Moshe Meshel to a potter in Lvov called R. Chaim Yisrael. He made it clear that no one was to know of this mission, and once the letter was delivered the messenger was to have no further contact whatever with its recipient.

Moreover, the Baal Shem Tov instructed him that throughout the night preceding the visit to the forest he should be on the alert that R. Chaim should recite his morning prayers no later than at daybreak; though R. Chaim was accustomed to rise at midnight for *Tikkun Chatzot*, his fatigue from the scholarly exertions of the previous day might cause him to go to sleep again. He was also to see to it that R. Chaim ate breakfast before they set out, and he was to take along a cup in case R. Chaim would later be thirsty. While accompanying him on their journey, the messenger was instructed to recite from memory the opening passage of Genesis, the Song of the Sea that begins *Az yashir* (Exodus 15:1-19) and the Song that begins *Haazinu* (Deuteronomy 36:1-43). Throughout the entire time that the elder scholar spent in the forest, the messenger was to recite *Tehillim*; if he completed the entire book he was to repeat it, and if he completed it again he was to read it a third time. Furthermore, from the morning before the journey he was to speak to no man.

The day that the Baal Shem Tov determined for R. Chaim's journey to the forest was a certain Wednesday in the month of Tammuz.

* * *

This is how R. Moshe Meshel from the village of Bezenke later told the story:

At midday on Thursday I arrived at Lvov, and found the room of the Rabbinical Court over which R. Chaim usually presided. It was filled with people, and the sage was engaged in an important consultation with the elders of the community.

When I asked one of the judges, R. Moshe Yosef Yisrael, to allow me to meet him he asked me in surprise: "Don't you know about the terrible decree that the Deputy Archbishop Mikolski has just published? In the course of the coming week, until next Thursday, they will tear out the *Aleinu* prayer from all the prayer books, and from this Sunday we will not be allowed to read this prayer in any synagogue! Right now they are discussing what can be done."

Realizing that I would not be able to see R. Chaim, I went off to fulfill my second mission—to deliver the letter from the Baal Shem Tov to R. Chaim Yisrael the Potter. By the time I returned to the courtroom R. Chaim had gone home, so I handed him his letter there.

Seeing the envelope he stood up, and when he heard that I had been dispatched to him by the Baal Shem Tov his holy face lit up and he read the letter with reverent awe. Finally, he sighed and said: "The entire Jewish community of Lvov and its surrounding townships needs heaven's mercies, on account of the dreadful decree—G-d forbid—that *Aleinu* should no longer be recited in our synagogues."

The sage did not breathe a word about the letter that he had received. The members of his household and the students of his yeshivah, however, noting that R. Chaim was in high spirits, concluded that the visitor was no doubt an emissary who had brought word, orally or in writing, from the Baal Shem Tov. They recalled that whenever an oral message reached him from the Baal Shem Tov, and even more so, whenever a written message reached him, he treated that day as a festival: the penitential prayers of *Tachnun* were omitted, and he held a festive meal, a *seudat mitzvah*. Sometimes he shared with them the content of his message and sometimes he withheld it, but in the course of his Torah teachings at the table he always expounded the spiritual path of the Baal Shem Tov.

On this occasion, too, R. Chaim arranged for a festive meal to be prepared. In no time word of this reached his associates and disciples. All the elders and worthies of the community also arrived, as well as many members of the public, for all the townsmen were deeply distressed by the decree. In the middle of the festive meal the decision of the earlier consultation was announced: they would ignore the decree. At the risk of their lives, the whole community would recite *Aleinu* three times every day exactly as in the past. The coming Sunday was declared a public fast, and the *shofar* would then be sounded.

On Friday morning R. Chaim Yisrael the Potter called on Deputy Archbishop Mikolski and warned him that if he did not annul the decree he would be severely punished. Mikolski drove him out angrily. On Sunday morning, however, as he stepped down from his pulpit, he stumbled and broke his right leg and arm. He fainted from pain and was carried home. There, still suffering, he remembered that he had had a Jewish visitor on Friday. Not only that, but he recalled that he had seen that same Jew once before, in Kamenitz-Podolsk: this was the very Jew who had then warned the late Archbishop Demboski that if he did not annul his decree to burn the holy books of the Jews, he would die....

On the spot, Deputy Archbishop Mikolski ordered one of his senior priests to notify the local rabbi and his congregation that the decree was annulled forthwith: the Jews could continue to pray as they were accustomed to doing.

The glad tidings spread through the city in a moment, and for the Jews of Lvov this was a time of light and joy. They quickly sent messengers throughout the neighboring provinces, and the learned R. Chaim gave out orders: The townsmen were to complete the daylong fast; at nightfall, in time for the *Maariv* prayers, they should light many candles in all the synagogues as they usually did for a festival; the prayers should be sung to the festive melodies reserved for a festival; and *Aleinu* was to be sung to the solemn melody handed down from the saintly Maharal of Prague, as on the Days of Awe, though on this occasion the worshippers were not to prostrate themselves on the floor.

* * *

It transpires that R. Chaim Yisrael the Potter was one of the hidden tzaddikim of the time. No one knew of his comings and goings and no one took particular notice of him. After all, didn't Lvov have hundreds of good simple craftsmen who—to all external appearances—looked just like him?

He had been the emissary of the Baal Shem Tov to warn Archbishop Demboski in Kamenitz-Podolsk that if he did not rescind the decree for the burning of the Talmud and other holy books, and if did not cancel the tax that had been imposed on the Jews for the renovation of the local cathedral, he would die

160

a sudden death. Deputy Archbishop Mikolski had been there to hear Demboski's retort: "Go and tell your master that I scorn him and his threats." Demboski had then instructed the head priest to urge his colleagues to make haste and collect all the holy books of the Jews and to build a platform in the city square for the public burning. Furthermore, they were to send out couriers to summon the provincial population to witness and celebrate the vengeance that was to be wrought on the Torah of the Jews, who were hated by the religion of their countrymen. In addition, if by Tuesday, the appointed day, the Jews did not deliver the cathedral tax, Demboski authorized all the gentiles to break into the Jews' houses and stores and to rob and pillage to their hearts' desire.

His orders were immediately obeyed. Dozens of willing workers robbed the synagogues and Houses of Study and the Jewish homes of their libraries; others built an imposing platform in the city square; and yet others galloped off to spread their gleeful news in the surrounding provinces. The Jews of Kamenitz, terrified, held public fasts and prayed to heaven for deliverance.

For the next two days thousands of gentile men and women, young and old, streamed into town, excited by the prospect of a public burning and unrestrained pillage. On Tuesday morning the bells rang out from the steeple. Demboski gave orders for the preparation of the woodpile, and with all due pomp led the ceremonial procession that headed there from the cathedral. Halfway there he suddenly dropped dead. His colleagues, struck by consternation, arrived at the conclusion that the G-d of Israel had intervened to protect His Torah from their burning.

* * *

During the two days preceding the Wednesday of his journey to the forest, R. Chaim had been far busier than usual. He was so weary that if I [R. Moshe Meshel] had not been vigilant, as the Baal Shem Tov had told me to be, he would have woken up late for his midnight devotions of *Tikkun Chatzot*. Wednesday morning's sky was clouded and there were heavy torrents of rain. As soon as he stepped into the wagon that was to take him to the forest as he had been directed to do, the heavens burst with such fearful thunder and lightning that the horses, petrified, ignored the wagon-driver's whip. R. Chaim urged the driver to make progress, but nothing changed until the skies came to rest. The mere eight *parsas* took us long hours, because in addition to the mud and mire, things went wrong at every turn: the reins came loose, the saddle-straps tore, a wheel fell off, the shaft between the horses broke, and so on and on, each crisis with its own delay. Exhausted and distressed, the wagon-driver was unable to steer his horses any longer. I took his place on the driver's stand, but within twenty paces the whole wagon lurched off the road into a ditch. There we were stranded for a long time, until we finally managed to extract the wagon. It was already two o'clock in the afternoon when we arrived at the spot in the forest that the Baal Shem Tov had indicated in his letter.

No sooner did R. Chaim step down from the wagon than a fierce outburst of thunder and lightning made the horses bolt. Man and beast were frightened out of breath. In the sudden darkness the wagon-driver wept bitterly: "Rebbe! I'm terrified! I'm afraid!" R. Chaim replied: "G-d has acted thus so that He should be feared" (Cf. *Brachot* 59a). With that he went and found the place in which he was to sit, and as soon as he delved into the depths of his studies the sky cleared and the sun shone forth.

The place indicated was an open space of a few hundred cubits, about fifty cubits from the road. Here and there, among the ordered rows of old trees and at the edges of the open space, decayed foundations and remnants of diggings indicated that buildings had stood there long ago. We also saw the derelict walls of what had once been a very deep well, though now it was dry.

For about four hours the sage sat engrossed in his books. He grew so thirsty that the wagon-driver and I set out in search of water, and in a nearby thicket we found a spring.

After *Minchah* we returned to Lvov. The sage wanted me to stay with him over Shabbat, but I did as the Baal Shem Tov had instructed me and left town after *Maariv* on that Wednesday. A wagon was there waiting to be hired, I took my seat without speaking a word to the driver nor to anyone else, and on Thursday morning the wagon took me the three *parsas* to Mezibush. There, as soon as I set foot in the courtyard of the Baal Shem Tov, he beckoned to me from his window. He told me to read the entire Book of *Tehillim* three times, once before morning prayers and twice after. Until this was completed I was not to utter a word, not even to respond to a greeting. I was then to read the Song of the Sea (*Az yashir*) once, and the Song that begins *Haazinu* twice. He also instructed me not to smoke my waterpipe until after *Maariv* that evening.

Here ends the part of the story that the Alter Rebbe heard from the mouth of the *shliach mitzvah* himself, R. Moshe Meshel from the village of Bezenke.

* * *

The Alter Rebbe heard the continuation of this story from his mentor, the Maggid of Mezritch, who was an eye witness, and relayed it to his grandson, the Tzemach Tzedek, as follows:

On a visit to the Baal Shem Tov early in Elul, the learned R. Chaim Rapaport told him that ever since he had carried out his mission in the forest—to study the four chapters of *Rambam's* Laws of Blessings and to pray *Minchah* there—his eyes had been opened in his understanding of the Torah and his heart had been opened in his service of the Creator. He praised G-d for this great gift and thanked the Baal Shem Tov for having chosen him for this mission, for he had no doubt been privileged to be enriched by the radiance of some lofty soul.

At the next Shabbat table the Baal Shem Tov related the following:

About 160 years ago, in the year 5359 (1599) or 5360 (1600), one of the eminent scholars of Prague by the name of R. Shmuel Tzadok settled in Lvov. There he hired erudite tutors to guide his sons, Moshe and Yehudah Aryeh, in the paths of the Torah. Though he was a disciple of the Maharal, and an outstanding scholar, he energetically opposed the study of *Mussar*, and felt no desire to study even the writings of the Maharal (then still in manuscript), which the other disciples drank thirstily. Instead of studying ethical texts, he was drawn to the study of other disciplines, notably astronomy, for he was a friend of the celebrated astronomer and geometrician, R. David Gans.

His mentor, the Maharal, was deeply distressed by his approach to scholarship in general, in particular to his leaning to alien disciplines, and above all to his opposition to the study of ethical writings. Besides, in every question of ritual law R. Shmuel Tzadok would always take the lead in finding a lenient approach.

Among the many Kabbalists in Prague at that time there were those who followed the teachings of the learned R. Eliyahu Baal Shem of Worms. They practiced solitude, fasting and self-mortification. Groups of three or five people would go out together to a forest or field to study works of *Mussar* or *Aggadah*, and they would rebuke each other. Each man would lay bare the ailments that plagued his soul: one of them would bemoan his inclination to pride; another—to falsehood, or envy, or slander, and other such undesirable attributes. Most of them were well versed in other areas of the Torah in addition to the Kabbalah. They were punctilious in their observance of the commandments, and devoted long hours to their prayers.

The learned R. Shmuel Tzadok was hostile to the Kabbalists. At every opportunity he would insult them and scoff at their customs, to the point that he came to be called "R. Shmuel Tzadok, the opponent of Kabbalah and *Mussar*." This hostility to *Mussar*, and of course to the Kabbalah in which he had no faith, he implanted in his sons. Since his business ventures prospered— and "a rich man responds with insolence" (Proverbs 18:23)—he spoke out arrogantly against all the scholars whose views differed from his.

One day a question arose as to whether a certain woman in his neighborhood was ritually pure or not. Knowing that R. Shmuel Tzadok was reputed to be a prominent scholar, her husband sought his opinion, and he ruled that she was ritually pure. It so happened that a few days later this woman told a close friend confidentially of the query and the ruling. The friend was astonished: when she herself once had the very same case the local rabbinical judge had ruled that she was ritually impure. The poor woman, aghast, told her husband what she had just learned. They went together to the *beit din*, cried their hearts out, and asked the presiding scholar to show them how they could repent for the transgression that had come their way.

At this point the long-suffering patience of the Maharal came to an end. He summoned R. Shmuel Tzadok and rebuked him. When R. Shmuel Tzadok persisted in trying to vindicate his mistaken stand by ingenious scholarly acrobatics, the Maharal told him that he was a revived spark of the Talmudic scholar who was able to muster 150 specious arguments to pronounce a defiling reptile *pure* (Cf. *Eruvin* 13b).

R. Shmuel Tzadok and his sons and their families thereupon left Prague for Lvov. He was now advanced in years; his elder son R. Moshe was occupied all day in the tent of the Torah and in the world of ideas, and the administration of the family's business concerns was left to the hands of the younger son, R. Yehudah Aryeh.

* * *

Like his father, R. Moshe too favored foreign disciplines and studied them energetically. At the same time he was renowned for his expertise in the Babylonian and Jerusalem Talmud, in the legal works of *Rambam* and in the four *Turim*. In every field of *halachah* he sought to rule leniently, but especially in the field of *brachot*, the blessings to be recited on specified occasions. As to the study of Kabbalah and *Mussar*, he opposed it ten times more fiercely than his father had ever done.

In due course, a few years after his father's passing, he turned his back on the straight path. He bought himself an estate four *parsas* out of town, built himself a house, and moved there.

He grew accustomed to drinking wine in the company of the gentile scholars who visited him, until eventually he removed his beard and desecrated Shabbat and the festivals. His G-d-fearing wife fell ill from sheer anguish, and died, leaving no children. He later married a gentile wife, but then, far from forsaking his Torah studies, he became deeply engrossed in them. And whenever an innovative interpretation came to mind, he would write it down, even on Shabbat or festivals.

This state of affairs continued for thirty years: he never visited a *shul*, but continued to study Torah. The local Jews all knew of his lifestyle, and none of them ever crossed his threshold. If a poor wayfarer happened to come his way he would receive him warmly, give him a generous donation, and warn him not to touch any food because everything in the house was *treifah*. In addition, if the wayfarer was a Torah scholar, he would delight in the scholarly exchange of novel interpretations. And so his life went on: he ate every kind of *treifah* and *nevelah*, drank forbidden wine, desecrated Shabbat and the festivals—and studied Torah diligently.

* * *

His brother R. Yehudah Aryeh was less of a scholar than his father or brother, but he was a G-d-fearing Jew. He studied ethical texts, kept company with pious and upright people in Prague and even more so in Lvov, and in this spirit brought up his family. As old age drew near, he handed over the reins of business to his sons and sons-in-law, built a shul in his courtyard, brought ten outstanding scholars to study there fulltime, supported them and their families, and enjoyed their company. However, his distress over his brother's lifestyle caused him such acute heartache that his doctors ordered him to move elsewhere and hopefully forget its cause.

Concerned by his deteriorating health, his sons and daughters insisted that he obey. So it was that R. Yehudah Aryeh chose to return to his birthplace, Prague. He took with him several of his grandsons, the children of his sons and daughter, so that they could study in the great yeshivah there.

Arriving in Prague around the year 5377 (1617), R. Yehudah Aryeh found childhood friends. The community received him warmly and eventually appointed him as one of their wardens. Seeking among the eminent scholars of the town to determine who among them should be entrusted with the education of his grandsons, he decided to bring two of his grandsons, Avraham Moshe and Chaim Zelig, to study at the feet of the illustrious R. Yom Tov Lipmann Heller, author of *Tosfot Yom Tov*.

R. Yom Tov Lippman Heller was a disciple of the learned R. Eliyahu Baal Shem of Worms, where he had studied with exceptional assiduity for three years. After his arrival in Prague he continued with his accustomed studies of Kabbalah, and likewise emulated his master's practice of making simple and unlettered Jews, too, feel welcome in his company. This practice he passed on to the two newly-arrived grandsons of R. Yehudah Aryeh.

After four or five years, their grandfather—with the permission of their parents—married them off to daughters of the most respected families of Prague, where they continued to pursue their studies.

* * *

The reputation of R. Eliyahu Baal Shem of Worms had already spread far and wide while the Maharal was yet alive. Opposition to his teachings was sparked off by the aged scholar, R. Pinchas Zelig of Speyer. R. Pinchas Zelig's son, the learned R. Shammai Zundel, traveled about from country to country, proclaiming—in the name of his father, the generation's leading sage, and in the name of other sages—a ban of excommunication on the teachings of R. Eliyahu Baal Shem of Worms. The Maharal, accompanied by his erudite son, R. Betzalel, thereupon made a journey to Worms to see with his own eyes just who this scholar was. On his return home he published his highly-regarded view vindicating R. Eliyahu Baal Shem, whose disciples multiplied in Prague and its environs from that time on.

When R. Yehudah Aryeh returned to Prague the civil head of the community was R. Shmuel, son of R. Betzalel, only son of the Maharal. He had served in this capacity for eighteen years, having been chosen to fill the place of the renowned philanthropist, R. Mordechai Meisels, who had passed away in the year 5361 (1601). For eight years R. Shmuel had served as communal head in the lifetime of his celebrated grandfather, the Maharal, who passed away at the age of 97 on the eighteenth of Elul, 5369 (1609).

R. Shmuel was exceptionally wealthy. Every year he would fill the communal coffers with the same amount that the whole community had contributed. Half of his income was devoted to redeeming the three dues that the city's paupers—like all other citizens—were obliged to pay: the government tax, the municipal tax, and the community's tax. His good name traveled before him, for in addition to his generosity, both manifest and anonymous, to local individuals and institutions, he used to send out large sums for the support of *yeshivot* in Poland and Germany. One of the institutions which he thus supported with an open hand was the yeshivah of R. Eliyahu Baal Shem of Worms. Moreover, when R. Eliyahu Baal Shem moved to Grodno, Chelm and Lublin—the most prominent seats of learning at that time—R. Shmuel continued to support him on a generous scale, because he had heard from his grandfather, the Maharal, that from the *yeshivot* of R. Eliyahu Baal Shem light would shine forth over the Jewish people.

When R. Yehudah Aryeh settled in Prague he too helped to support the yeshivah of R. Eliyahu Baal Shem. Indeed, when word arrived in the year 5384 (1624) that R. Eliyahu Baal Shem was about to transfer one of his *yeshivot* to Prague, R. Shmuel, head of the community, and R. Yehudah Aryeh, his deputy, dispatched an emissary with a bag of money to cover the yeshivah's traveling expenses. Even before they arrived, moreover, these two philanthropists bought a courtyard with dwellings for all the students and teachers, as their private contribution.

Though the author of *Tosfot YomTov* was already about fifty years old and a celebrated scholar in his own right, he too became one of the twenty-seven handpicked scholars who studied under R. Eliyahu Baal Shem in this newly-established yeshivah. (Their mentor was fond of referring to them metaphorically as the twenty-seven letters—the entire *Alef-Bet*—with which the Torah was given, the letters with which G-d created His world.) Though most of these scholars studied there in order to progress in the revealed plane of the Torah, they were also guided in the path of the teachings of R. Eliyahu Baal Shem. From time to time they were taught Kabbalah; many of them labored with success in the refinement of their characters; and from day to day the yeshivah attracted more gifted scholars.

One of those whose exceptional progress included the study of the Kabbalah and an understanding of the teachings of R. Eliyahu Baal Shem was the young R. Avraham Moshe, grandson of R. Yehudah Aryeh. When his mentor, the author of *Tosfot Yom Tov*, perceived his awe of heaven, his lovingly meticulous observance of the *mitzvot*, and his unquenchable thirst for the study of Kabbalah, he began to privately teach him its deepest secrets. In particular, the young man was so struck by *Sefer Hapardes* of R. Moshe Cordovero that he came to know it almost by heart. Over the years his reputation grew among the scholars and Kabbalists, and R. Eliyahu Baal Shem eventually accepted him into the inner circle of his most prominent disciples.

* * *

As the years gradually clouded R. Yehudah Aryeh's recollection of his brother Moshe's sorry state, his health improved. One very old man in Prague, however, had been a friend of their father, R. Shmuel Tzadok. When he heard of what had come of his friend's son outside Lvov he approached R. Yehudah Aryeh and wailed: "I *warned* your late learned father against his lenient approach to the law! I *warned* him against his outspoken attacks on the G-d-fearing Kabbalists! But he only made fun of me and said: 'So you, too, Elimelech, are among those who see things that cannot be seen!' Your father denied the validity of the Kabbalah, and his retribution is a wicked son who wallows in abomination! Behold the judgment of the L-rd! In the very matter in which your father wantonly sinned, he was punished—with shame and disgrace more bitter than death. Your father was a great Torah scholar who took the *mitzvot* lightly, scoffing at those who observed them meticulously and scorning those who studied the Kabbalah—and G-d punished him with a son who is a great Torah scholar and transgresses all of His commandments."

As the old man's hearing and sight were failing, no one was able to explain to him what pain he inflicted upon the innocent son of his old friend by blasting forth at every encounter. And since R. Yehudah Aryeh respected him as his father's old friend, he chose to overlook the old man's insensitivity. He visited him often and heard him out patiently.

* * *

On one of these visits, R. Yehudah Aryeh took along his grandson Avraham Moshe with him. The aged R. Elimelech's customary tirade reminded him of his long-forgotten great-uncle Moshe, and he was deeply grieved by his grandfather's sorrow. He was also distressed to learn that his great-grandfather R. Shmuel Tzadok had been exceedingly lenient when handing down *halachic* rulings, and that he had often scoffed at the local Kabbalists and pietists. Until that day he had only known that his great-grandfather was a Torah scholar renowned for his innovative interpretations and expositions. Indeed, he himself had made good use of them when studying some of the more formidable Talmudic texts, notably in the Order of *Nashim*.

For this reason, that day's encounter cast his memory back to a painful private battle.

One day, long earlier, his colleagues had been unable to plumb the depths of a particularly thorny passage in the Tractate *Yevamot*. He alone, having quietly consulted his great-grandfather's commentaries on this text, was able to explain it all smoothly. His colleagues were amazed and duly impressed. For the next two days, however, by day and by night, he did not enjoy one moment's peace of mind: should he tell them the secret of his borrowed brilliance or should he not? At one point he almost decided to speak up—but then an ingenious thought crossed his mind. The Talmudic Sages, no less, taught that "envy among scholars increases wisdom" (*Bava Batra* 21a). If so, would he not be doing his colleagues a pious favor by remaining silent? Let them envy him for his seeming brilliance! After all, would the printed brilliance of some deceased scholar from a past generation lend them such praiseworthy envy...?

The claims of innocent honesty, however, threw him into turmoil. Seeing a volume of Talmud before him, which happened to be the Tractate *Sotah*, he decided to open it at random: perhaps the first statement to catch his eye would release him from his quandary. With a prayer in his heart that G-d should lead him along the path of truth he opened up the volume. Staring right at him was the following teaching (22b): "The Heavenly Court will exact justice from those who cloak themselves in pious garments that are not their own." He had his answer.

That night he did not sleep a wink: he could only picture the disgrace that awaited him. His colleagues would scorn him like a thief caught in the act. The day was no better. Despite his resolve to speak up, his tongue stuck to his palate. And when he finally succeeded in breaking his agonized silence, it was a friend, R. Chaim Shmuel, who was the first to rebuke him; the others simply looked at him with the disdain that befits a person who flaunts stolen riches. For two weeks, as he now recalled, that incident had left him utterly crushed.

* * *

The visit to the aged R. Elimelech, and the sight of his own grandfather's visible suffering, stamped a heavy imprint on the soul of the young R. Avraham Moshe. The old man's words resonated in his ears: "Your father was a great Torah scholar, but he took the *mitzvot* lightly and scoffed at those who studied the Kabbalah—and G-d punished him with a son who is a great Torah scholar and transgresses His commandments." Having studied penitential works, R. Avraham Moshe knew exactly what dire punishment awaited those who took the *mitzvot* lightly, particularly if they were Torah scholars. What was his great-grandfather now undergoing in the World of Truth? Since over thirty years had elapsed since his passing, the sufferings of *Gehinom* were now no doubt behind him, but he was possibly not yet free of the pangs of imposed restlessness. (Cf. *Rosh Hashanah* 17a and the commentaries there.)

The more he read and reread these penitential works the more was he distressed, especially since he knew that "there is no cure for the suffering of a person who shames a Torah scholar" (*Shabbat* 119b). It was clear to him that the angels of destruction were tormenting the soul of his great-grandfather with scorn and abuse because he had poked fun at people who had observed the *mitzvot* meticulously. Indeed, the Sages teach (Tractate *Kallah*, beg.) that "he who disgraces his fellow will himself ultimately be disgraced," and one of the ethical works explains this statement as follows: He who disgraces his fellow in this world will himself ultimately be put to disgrace in the World to Come, at the hands of the punitive angels.

For months on end, vexed and melancholy, R. Avraham Moshe yearned to do something to uplift and rectify his great-grandfather's tormented soul. But what could he do? He decided to consult his mentor, R. Eliyahu Baal Shem.

R. Eliyahu replied that as far as rectifying the soul of the great-grandfather was concerned, he himself would send three of his disciples to the burial place in Lvov, there to meditate upon the Kabbalistic concepts that he would specify. R. Avraham Moshe, for his part, was to make it his business to arouse his great-uncle Moshe to repent wholeheartedly and to return to the complete observance of the *mitzvot*.

To enable his young disciple to attain this goal, R. Eliyahu Baal Shem prescribed for him a detailed regimen of Divine service, and specified mystical exercises involving Kabbalistic concepts and meditations. He instructed him not to eat or drink anything, even plain water, in his great-uncle's house, though he could use the water there to wash his hands and face. Every weekday he was to conduct the midnight meditations of *Tikkun Chatzot* and recite his prayers in the house, but he was to spend Shabbat in a Jewish town about a kilometer away. Moreover, R. Eliyahu gave him a *mezuzah*. After morning prayers on his second day there he was to affix it to the front door, though without reciting a blessing over it. Finally, even after G-d made his path prosper and he aroused his great-uncle to repentance, he was never to reveal to him that he was his relative.

* * *

Moshe rose to greet his unfamiliar guest and offered him a seat. The young man was amazed: though his great-uncle must have been about eighty-six he looked like a sixty-year-old. With his broad shoulders he stood as sturdy as an oak, he was clean-shaven, and his locks and moustache and clothes all followed the fashion of the local gentiles. He was in high spirits and, according to gentile custom, at his feet lay a huge dog.

The young visitor saw from the open volume on the table that his great-uncle was studying a certain subject in the Tractate *Sanhedrin*, so he began to discuss it with him. Moshe was overjoyed at the opportunity for this exchange, and the young man for his part was impressed by his great-uncle's arguments and textual proficiency. But his mood was darkened by what he saw before him—gross features coarsened by pigfat, reddened eyes inflamed by wine, gentile fashions and long locks with no head covering.

He blurted out: "Is it possible to study G-d's Torah with an uncovered head?!"

Moshe asked in reply: "And why should it not be possible?"

R. Avraham Moshe: "Because it's insolent in the extreme."

Moshe: "What insolence?"

R. Avraham Moshe: "Insolence toward heaven!"

Moshe: "But the whole point of covering one's head is to show that one stands in awe of his Master; a person who has no Master cannot show that he stands in awe of Him. Out of respect for you, however, I'll put on my hat."

He rose to bring it, leaving R. Avraham Moshe thunderstruck, open-mouthed and speechless.

By the time his host returned, he was able to say: "Words like these oblige a man to rend his garments."

Moshe disagreed: "I'm afraid you're wrong. The law requires that one rend his garments only if he hears the Divine Name articulated, but not if he hears someone say that he does not believe in G-d."

And with that Moshe spelled out his outright denial of the Creator's existence, of the Torah's Divine origin, and of all

173

Thirteen Principles of the Faith as enunciated by *Rambam*. At the same time he insisted that he dearly loved the Torah; he liked and respected its students, and found no favor to a scholar too difficult; but he had no faith in the Creator and His commandments.

After a long discussion it was time for *Minchah*. Moshe offered his guest a bag of coins but was assured that he was in need of nothing, except that he would like to enjoy the hospitality of the house for a little while. His host went happily ahead to prepare a large furnished room, complete with a bowl and a pitcher of water, but warned him that he would not be able to offer him any food because the dishes in the house were all treifah. Once again R. Avraham Moshe assured him that he needed nothing apart from a place to stay. His host, having shown him to his room, returned to his books and resumed his studies in his accustomed manner.

* * *

Looking out of the window after *Minchah*, R. Avraham Moshe saw two carriages entering the courtyard, each of them drawn by four fine horses. Drivers and servants in fancy livery were perched at front and back, according to the custom of the local squires. As soon as the carriages reached the entrance to the building, servants in gold-buttoned coats sprang from their appointed positions, opened the doors wide, and helped the newly-arrived ladies and gentlemen step down. The guests, toying with the purple leashes tied to their little dogs' silver collars, then made their way inside with mincing steps.

A moment later, R. Avraham Moshe heard his great-uncle jovially ordering his servants to offer the guests wine and other delicacies. As evening fell, candles were lit in the main salon. The hours from then till late in the morning resounded with raucous singing and wild dancing. When the last of the guests finally collapsed in a drunken stupor, their host's servants and their own carried them all out into their carriages, closed the elegant doors, and trundled them off to their homes. In the silence that remained their host could be heard vomiting. His trusty servants carried him to his bed, and there he lay until the next afternoon.

Hearing what was going on in the house, R. Avraham Moshe wept bitterly over how his great-uncle's soul had plummeted into such a filthy quagmire. It was high time for *Tikkun Chatzot*: his bruised heart lamented the destruction of the Sanctuary, the exile of the Divine Presence, and the disgrace of G-d's people. After due self-preparation, he then prayed and studied until two o'clock in the afternoon.

As for Moshe, he finally rose, ate breakfast, and sat down to study as if nothing had happened during the night, because he was accustomed to such visits from the neighboring gentile squires.

* * *

Among the Kabbalistic meditations on the letters of the Divine Names that R. Eliyahu Baal Shem prescribed for his disciple R. Avraham Moshe, there was one that focused on the verse, "They will express the *remembrance* of Your abounding goodness, and sing of Your goodness" (Psalms 145:7). This particular meditation effects a mystical union in the supernal spheres that arouses the memory of the individual for whose benefit this exercise is undertaken: he recalls everything that he ever saw from the moment that he first opened his eyes, and everything that he ever heard from the moment that he first understood a spoken word.

It was in this meditation that R. Eliyahu Baal Shem instructed his disciple R. Avraham Moshe to immerse himself during the morning prayers—after *Tachnun*, before *Lamenatze'ach*—on the day after his arrival in Lvov.

R. Avraham Moshe fulfilled his master's spiritual directives in every detail. Finally, having completed the study sessions that followed every morning's prayers, he affixed the *mezuzah* to the front doorpost as he had been instructed by R. Eliyahu Baal Shem.

The sight of the *mezuzah* made Moshe's heart melt into tears.

"In the thirty years since I moved out here I have not laid eyes on a *mezuzah* nor *tefillin* nor a *Sefer Torah*," he exclaimed.

175

"When I was three years old, as I now recall, my devout mother, with tears in her eyes, used to pick me up twice every day, as soon as I awoke and before I went to sleep, so that I could kiss the *mezuzah* on the doorpost. My father used to make fun of her: 'How foolish of you to kiss an animal's skin!' When I was big enough to attend the local *cheder*, I used to climb up on a chair so that I could kiss the *mezuzah* myself. One day, when my father saw my mother bringing me to kiss the straps of his *tefillin*, he said: 'Does he now also have to kiss the hide of an ox or a calf?!' With this he laughed aloud, and my mother wept alone."

Sensing what profound reverberations had been stirred up by the sight of the *mezuzah*, R. Avraham Moshe saw before him the first signs of the old man's redemption. Hopefully, G-d was going to bless his path with success: his great-uncle's soul was going to be liberated from the clutches of the Evil One.

For hours on end Moshe shared his freshly aroused recollections of his childhood and youth. He spoke of himself, of his learned teachers, and of the leading sages of that generation. The more he spoke the more he was moved, until by the time he came to repeat one of the ethical teachings of R. Efraim Lunshitz, author of *Olelot Efraim*, he was aroused to the core. Suddenly he confided that these recollections had ignited in him a desire to be a Jew as he had once been. He felt that his head and arm were burning. He begged his guest to lend him his *tallit* and *tefillin*, and prayed the words of *Shacharit* with the contrite and humble tears of a true penitent.

R. Avraham Moshe concentrated his entire mind and soul on the mystical themes with which R. Eliyahu Baal Shem had armed him. Later in the day he visited the nearby Jewish town of Belz and bought a *tallit* and *tefillin*, which he brought to Moshe. About a week later, when Shabbat had passed, Moshe dismissed his servants, paid them well and gave them gifts. He left his estate with its house and contents for the gentile members of his household, packed up his library, and moved to Belz. There he bought a house near the shul and hired an attendant to see to his needs.

By way of penance, from the day he moved to Belz he tasted neither meat nor wine, but lived only on bread and salt and tepid water. Nor, throughout the nine subsequent months until his last day, did he exchange a single word with any mortal. Every week he handed the local rav a large sum of money to be distributed for charitable purposes. Finally, a few days before his passing, he entrusted to him in addition all his worldly goods to be distributed for charity.

* * *

[The Baal Shem Tov, addressing his Chasidim at the Shabbat table, now brings this saga to a close:]

The Heavenly Court handed down its verdict. For 117 years, Moshe the son of Shmuel Tzadok was to undergo the torments of *Gehinom* and the upheavals of *Sheol*. On the day in the month of Tammuz on which this period came to an end, the words of Torah which he had studied in a defiled frame of mind for thirty years had to be purified and elevated. (See Laws of Torah Study by R. Schneur Zalman of Liadi 4:3; *Tanya*, ch. 39.) For this task I chose the learned *rav* of Lvov, a Kohen, to cleanse the unclean by his profound study of the first four chapters of the laws of blessings as codified by *Rambam*, and by the *Minchah* prayer.

However, when the Evil One and his associates discovered that the suffering of Moshe ben Shmuel Tzadok was coming to an end, and that his Torah study was about to be purified and elevated by the sage of Lvov, they made fierce and desperate endeavors to sabotage his journey. But with G-d's help—here the Baal Shem Tov turned to R. Chaim Rapaport—you succeeded in your holy task. And for your part, you were then found worthy of having your eyes opened in your understanding of the Torah and having your heart opened in your service of the Creator.

With this same journey, moreover, another significant mission was accomplished. The Holy *Zohar* (*Tikkunei Zohar* 5) teaches that the waters of this nether world weep: "We want to stand before the Holy King!" From the day that G-d first divided the upper waters from the nether waters, this is the plaint of all the springs in the world. They yearn to be used for a holy purpose—for the washing of hands before prayer, for an obligatory immersion in a *mikveh*, for an immersion that heightens one's degree of purity before prayer or Torah study, for the washing of hands with a blessing that includes G-d's Name, or for a drink of water that is preceded and followed by words of thanksgiving to its Maker.

This plaint of the springs can continue for hundreds and even thousands of years—until one day a Jew washes his hands or drinks of their waters and pronounces the appropriate blessings. In the forest that lies near the estate of Moshe ben Shmuel Tzadok there is a spring. For all these 5519 years it has wept: why should it be singled out from all other springs, ever since G-d first created it, with never a solitary Jew to pronounce a blessing over its waters or to use them for a pure and holy purpose? But on that day, R. Chaim, when you drank of its waters and washed your hands there in preparation for *Minchah*, that spring was redeemed.

From this—and here the Baal Shem Tov turned to all the disciples who surrounded his Shabbat table—you may observe the detailed workings of Divine Providence. Every object that was ever created has a specific time at which it is to be uplifted and a specific individual through whom it is to be uplifted. And every single soul that comes down to this world has its own ordained purpose—what is to be its task, and what part of the world it is to rectify.

Illumination and Instruction

O NCE, JUST BEFORE THE BAAL SHEM TOV was expected to arrive, his students tried to prepare the room accordingly for their master. Well aware that the Rebbe was exceedingly fond of light, they were most distraught to find only a solitary candle in the room. They sought and searched for additional means of light, but to no avail.

The Baal Shem Tov entered the room and surveyed the gloom in displeasure. "Jews need light!" he exclaimed. "My entire goal in life is to bring light to fellow Jews...."

His students lowered their eyes in shame. "We couldn't find anything more than a single candle," they apologized.

"Go outside and snap off some icicles hanging from the roof," instructed the Baal Shem Tov. "Bring them inside and light them!"

His students rushed outside, and returned with several large icicles. They then held a match to the icicles and watched in awed amazement as the frozen water caught flame and burned brightly!

* * *

The Baal Shem Tov also impressed his followers with the importance of the spoken word. Two Jews living in Mezibush could often be found fighting with one another. Once when they met in the synagogue, the pair became embroiled in a fierce argument. "I will tear you apart like a fish!" one roared.

Summoning his students together, the Baal Shem Tov ordered them to stand near him, shut their eyes, and place their arms on each other's shoulders. The Baal Shem Tov then placed his arms on the shoulders of the two students flanking him, and the entire group recoiled in horror. Crying out in alarm, they watched as the threatening individual tore his friend into shreds!

The Baal Shem Tov removed his hands and the vision dissipated. The students clearly understood the Rebbe's message: every physical word carries tremendous spiritual weight and reverberates with spiritual significance. Hence, in the spiritual spheres, this angry threat had been translated into real action!

* * *

On another occasion, as the Baal Shem Tov sat with his students on Shabbat, he showed them a startling vision—an ox seated at a Shabbat table. Clothed in Shabbat garments, the ox was busy gorging itself on the sumptuous Shabbat feast. As the vision disappeared, the disciples looked at the Baal Shem Tov in surprise. What was an ox doing at the Shabbat table?

"You just saw a real person," explained the Baal Shem Tov. "This individual is dressed in his Shabbat best and is seated before a delectable meat dish. Yet, having totally forgotten about Shabbat, he is wholly obsessed with relishing every bite of the meat. His appetite consumes him, transforming him into the very beast he is eating. Hence, he has become an ox...."

The Baal Shem Tov then concluded with his oft-spoken observation: "A person is found where his desire is found."

Real Remembrance

THE BAAL SHEM TOV ILLUMINATED the lives of countless people, bringing life and hope to those beset by misfortune. Such was the case with R. Moshe Shlomo, a simple Jew who could hardly be considered a Torah scholar. Nevertheless, R. Moshe Shlomo was exceedingly pious and G-d-fearing, and distributed charity with an open hand. His wife Rivka was similarly pious, steadily inviting the poor and needy into their home.

Devoted heart and soul to the Baal Shem Tov, R. Moshe Shlomo often gave the Rebbe large amounts of money to disburse among his circle of hidden *tzaddikim*, most of whom were greatly impoverished. In turn, the Baal Shem Tov blessed R. Moshe Shlomo with success in his endeavors and, indeed, the Chasid soon became a wealthy man.

Unlike others, R. Moshe Shlomo became more kind and generous as his wealth increased. His charitable donations grew; his kindness extended to every person. Yet, one problem marred the happiness of R. Moshe Shlomo and his righteous wife: after fifteen years of marriage, they still remained childless. Whenever he implored the Rebbe for a blessing, the Baal Shem Tov always showered him with blessings for prosperity and good fortune, but remained strangely silent about his request for offspring.

The Baal Shem Tov's disciples respected R. Moshe Shlomo

greatly. They admired his piety, his fine characteristics and charitable work, and they, too, tried to arouse Divine mercy on his behalf. Though they beseeched the Baal Shem Tov to bless R. Moshe Shlomo with children, the Rebbe did not answer their request. Apparently, the desperate couple were fated to remain childless.

Time went on, and soon another ten years had passed. R. Moshe Shlomo and his wife realized that they would never merit to bear children, and their feelings of despair and anguish increased over time. Though their charitable deeds continued unhindered, an element of hopelessness crept into every aspect of their daily lives.

One day, the Baal Shem Tov summoned R. Moshe Shlomo and his wife. "Why are you both so despondent?" he asked. "G-d has blessed you with tremendous wealth and kind hearts, and you have dispensed charity liberally to those in need. You should be happy with your accomplishments!"

Tears came to the eyes of the distraught couple. "But what is all our wealth worth if we have no children?" they responded.

"And what is wrong with not having children?" inquired the Baal Shem Tov.

"If we have no children," said the couple, "we will not endure after death. No one will carry our name; no one will know we even existed!"

In response, the Baal Shem Tov said, "Tomorrow I am traveling to a certain town. I want you both to accompany me."

R. Moshe Shlomo and his wife readily agreed. On the following day they came to the Baal Shem Tov's home and found some of his disciples already there, also planning to join the Rebbe on his journey. A line of carriages stood waiting for them: the Baal Shem Tov used the first carriage, while R. Moshe Shlomo, his wife, and the disciples climbed into the other carriages.

The journey lasted five days. Whenever they stopped in the small towns and villages along the way, R. Moshe Shlomo distributed charity liberally, donating large sums of money to local charitable institutions. On the sixth day, as they reached a town near the city of Brody, the Baal Shem Tov instructed his driver to stop at the local inn. "We have reached our destination," said the Rebbe to the others. "We will stop here."

The group alighted from their carriages and took up rooms in the inn, spending the next few hours resting from their journey. After some time, the Rebbe summoned his entourage to his room. "Come!" he said. "Let's walk through the town together."

The group left the inn and started wandering down the narrow dirt roads of the town when they encountered a group of children frolicking in the sand. "Tell me," said the Baal Shem Tov to one of the boys, "what is your name?"

"Boruch Moshe," answered the lad.

The Baal Shem Tov turned to another boy. "And yours?" he asked.

"Boruch Moshe."

The group watched in amazement as the Rebbe methodically asked all the children their names. Two other boys also carried the name "Boruch Moshe." Another was called Boruch Mordechai; yet another was Boruch Eliyahu. A little girl could hardly wait to announce her name: "Bracha Leah," she exclaimed.

R. Moshe Shlomo and the other disciples looked at the Baal Shem Tov in astonishment. All the children seemed to have identical names! Despite their bewilderment, none had the courage to dare ask the Rebbe for an explanation. Only the Baal Shem Tov seemed satisfied; his face radiated joy and contentment, a light smile played on his lips.

The Baal Shem Tov and his entourage continued walking until they met a young girl. "What is your name?" asked the Baal Shem Tov.

"Bracha Leah," responded the girl.

Entering a side street, the Baal Shem Tov noticed a group of young girls playing together and, again, he asked for their names. His disciples listened in growing amazement as each and every girl gave an identical answer, "Bracha Leah." Continuing his walk, the Baal Shem Tov stopped a young boy and girl and asked for their names.

"Boruch Moshe," said the boy.

"Bracha Miriam," answered the girl.

The Baal Shem Tov and his disciples continued walking along various streets when the sound of young voices raised in learning reached their ears. The voices became louder as they walked, and soon they reached a local *cheder* where some twenty children studied together. Stopping at the door of the *cheder*, the Baal Shem Tov motioned for R. Moshe Shlomo and his wife to enter with him. The other disciples remained outside.

The Baal Shem Tov asked permission to question the children, and then proceeded to ask every child for his name. Based on earlier responses, R. Moshe Shlomo and his wife were hardly surprised anymore by the results: six boys carried the name "Boruch Moshe," while others carried variations. Some were just "Boruch" or "Moshe," while others shared different combinations (Boruch Avraham; Boruch Shmuel; Moshe Yosef; Moshe Yitzchak, etc.).

Meanwhile, the Baal Shem Tov's disciples were engaged in an animated conversation outdoors. "There is definitely a reason for this strange phenomenon," they asserted. "A great *tzaddik* by the name of Boruch Moshe must have lived here with his wife, Bracha Leah. The righteous have enduring impact: practically all the parents here have named their children after these great *tzaddikim*!"

The Baal Shem Tov exited the *cheder*, followed by R. Moshe Shlomo and his wife. Together with his disciples, the Rebbe continued walking through the town, stopping in every *cheder* along the way. Wherever they went, the same scenario repeated itself: the Baal Shem Tov inquired for the children's names, and almost all were called "Boruch Moshe" or something similar. Afterwards, the Baal Shem Tov visited the local yeshivah for older students, some of whom came from surrounding villages. Here, too, most students carried the name "Boruch Moshe."

The sun had begun setting as they left the yeshivah, so the weary group entered a nearby synagogue to recite the afternoon prayer. When they finished, the Baal Shem Tov approached one of the local Jews standing nearby. "Perhaps you can help us," he said. "We have noticed that most children here carry the same names Boruch Moshe or Bracha Leah. Please, what is the reason for these unusual circumstances?"

"The reason is due to the outstanding generosity of two very special people," was the reply. "Though they lived almost a century ago, their memories still remain very much alive today.

"This is their story":

* * *

Rabbi Eizik Shalom, a butcher by trade, lived in this village almost one-hundred years ago. An erudite scholar and pious Jew, he gave charity generously, and distributed meat free of charge to the local rabbi and other Torah scholars every Friday. His son, Boruch Moshe, did not exactly inherit his father's talents. From his very earliest days in *cheder*, it became apparent that Boruch Moshe did not understand nearly as much as other children his age.

The years passed, but young Boruch Moshe's scholastic achievements remained far below that of his peers. Sensing his son's inability to study, his father finally took him out of yeshivah at age fifteen, and began teaching him the art of becoming a professional butcher. Unlike his studies, Boruch Moshe took to his father's lessons like a fish to water. He married a young lady named Bracha Leah and quickly became an excellent butcher. Unfortunately, Boruch Moshe and his wife remained childless, and this greatly disturbed their happiness.

A few years after the wedding, Boruch Moshe's parents passed away, and Boruch Moshe continued his father's practice of distributing charity to all those in need. Though our young butcher became very wealthy, he did not forget about the destitute and the downtrodden, and he quickly became known for his generous ways.

To honor his parents' memory, Boruch Moshe hired the eminent scholar Rabbi Shlomo Yitzchak to teach him *Mishnayot*. Yet, despite the efforts of his illustrious tutor,

185

the butcher made absolutely no headway in his studies. Rabbi Shlomo Yitzchak tried his utmost to explain everything in the simplest of terms, but Boruch Moshe could not even grasp a solitary *Mishnah*! Naturally, this further deepened his dejection.

Meanwhile, Boruch Moshe had a habit of participating in a daily Torah class that met between *Minchah* and *Maariv* in the synagogue. Though our butcher barely understood the classes, he did sometimes glean an especially simple Torah thought, and this encouraged him to continue attending these classes. One day, as he sat listening to the *shiur*, Boruch Moshe heard the teacher mention a Talmudic aphorism, "Whoever teaches his friend's son Torah is as if he actually bore that child."

These words made a tremendous impact on Boruch Moshe. "Imagine!" he thought. "Not only am I childless, doomed to be forgotten by others, but I am even unable to raise another son spiritually, for I am an unlearned, illiterate boor." Crushed by misery, the butcher recited the evening prayer with bitter tears, and then stumbled out of the synagogue to make his way home.

As Boruch Moshe walked home, he noticed his teacher—Rabbi Shlomo Yitzchak—walking alongside him. Before long, Boruch Moshe had bared his heart to the scholar, divulging his inner torment and twofold anguish—his childlessness and his ignorance. "But all is not lost," explained the scholar in return. "Our Sages also infer that one who helps others financially, providing the support for their children to study Torah, is also considered as though he bore those children. Hire someone to teach poor children Torah; you don't have to actually teach them yourself!"

Boruch Moshe returned home a different man. Gone were his feelings of depression and misery; an exciting alternative beckoned strongly. Boruch Moshe repeated the tutor's words to his wife and voiced his intention to hire a teacher for the poor children in their village. "What a wonderful idea!" exclaimed his wife excitedly. "Let us begin immediately!" Indeed, that very week, Boruch Moshe hired the first teacher.

Years passed. Boruch Moshe grew exceedingly wealthy and, in turn, he continued hiring more and more teachers to raise poor children in the path of Torah. He continued living with his wife in their small home, preferring to distribute his wealth to charity and the teachers he maintained. All told, by the time he turned sixty, Boruch Moshe paid the salaries of thirty teachers! Due to their efforts, the village underwent a complete transformation: every single child received a wholesome Torah education, and Boruch Moshe's network of schools raised an entire generation of learned Jews.

In their later years, Boruch Moshe and his wife often discussed their charitable venture. "I understand that the children taught by our teachers are considered our very own," she once said. "But what are the practical implications? People recall our names favorably now, but who will remember us after we are gone? If only we had a son or daughter!"

"Bracha Leah, where is your faith?" said her husband, a trace of anger evident in his voice. "The holy Talmud guarantees that whoever teaches his friend's son Torah is as if he actually bore that child! We must believe wholeheartedly that we have earned the same status and merits as those of the the rightful parents of these children."

* * *

"Boruch Moshe and his wife passed away fifteen years ago," the man told the Baal Shem Tov. "The entire region mourned their passing. Practically every Jewish child in the immediate area studied in a *cheder* sponsored by the righteous couple. My brothers and I learned in one of Boruch Moshe's *chadarim*; even our rabbi studied in a school founded by Boruch Moshe! Hence, after their passing, we felt it our duty and privilege to name our children after this righteous couple who did so much for our Jewish education.

"For a long time, practically every boy born in our village was named Boruch Moshe or something similar. Every girl received the name Bracha Leah or an alternative combination. Even the elderly instruct their children to name their offspring after the righteous butcher and his wife.

"Every year," concluded the storyteller, "on the anniversary of their passing, the rabbi himself leads the entire Jewish community in prayer and says *Kaddish* on their behalf. Afterwards, a large procession can be seen making its way to the local cemetery, where the former *cheder* students recite *Tehillim* and prayers—just as children do at the graves of their parents."

The Baal Shem Tov thanked the storyteller warmly for his time. After *Maariv*, the Baal Shem Tov and his disciples returned to their inn, and the Rebbe spoke directly to the hearts of the childless couple. "You have heard everything today," said the Baal Shem Tov. "This is the meaning of the verse, 'I will give them [those who keep My covenant] a memorial in My house and within My walls, an everlasting memorial, better than sons and daughters' (Isaiah 56:5). My *house*—this refers to Torah, which is G-d's House; My *walls*—this refers to the Jewish nation, who stand firm, like a wall, to protect the sanctity of G-d's sacred Name."

When R. Moshe Shlomo and his wife returned home, they immediately hired a teacher to instruct the poor children of their town. With time, the couple sponsored more and more teachers, bringing the wisdom of Torah to every child they could reach. R. Moshe Shlomo and his wife enjoyed long life and great wealth and, upon their passing, many former students named their children after the righteous couple. As the Baal Shem Tov had shown, the selfless generosity of R. Moshe Shlomo and his wife earned them real, enduring remembrance, long after their physical bodies departed this earth.

Rewarding the Righteous

Rabbi Shimon was not the simple water carrier he appeared to be. He, along with select others, belonged to the circle of hidden *tzaddikim* who followed the spiritual path of the Baal Shem Tov. Others merely saw the plain, seemingly unlearned Jew who carried water through their streets but, in reality, Rabbi Shimon had attained a lofty spiritual stature.

One day, the Baal Shem Tov summoned the water carrier to his room. "We both desperately need large sums of money," he said as Rabbi Shimon entered. "I need funds for my crucial work of *pidyon shvuyim*, to ransom enslaved Jews from their cruel captors. I also need money to provide financial support for hidden *tzaddikim*. You need money in order to marry off your daughter to a scholarly young groom, and you need even more money to support them both later.

"I have an idea," continued the Baal Shem Tov. "Go to a certain place, where you will find a chest filled with treasure. Bring it back here; we will divide it equally."

The Baal Shem Tov gave his follower detailed instructions where to find the treasure and Rabbi Shimon hurried off to locate his new-found wealth. Upon reaching the designated area, Rabbi Shimon found a chest containing gold and precious stones. He took the entire chest and carted it away, heading straight back to the Baal Shem Tov.

The Baal Shem Tov divided the contents of the chest equally. He took half for *pidyon shvuyim* and assisting hidden *tzaddikim*,
and placed the remaining half in the hands of Rabbi Shimon.

"I will even tell you where to find your daughter's destined
mate," revealed the Baal Shem Tov further. "Go to Zludnick—in
the regional district of Vilna—and meet with Rabbi Eliyahu
Bunim, one of the foremost scholars in the area. His son is your
future son-in-law."

* * *

In another instance, the Baal Shem Tov foretold of illustrious
offspring in the merit of righteous deeds. Rabbi Yaakov Shamash,
a hidden *tzaddik* and devoted follower of the Baal Shem Tov,
maintained an unusual practice that underscored his concern for
others in need. Whenever he heard of a birth in a poor household, Rabbi Yaakov would visit the impoverished family and
lend his assistance. He stoked the furnace to heat the home; he
fed the young children; he swept and cleaned the house.

Once, the Baal Shem Tov remarked about the spiritual benefits reaped by Rabbi Yaakov's worthy activities. "Rabbi Yaakov
merits seeing G-dliness in a revealed form," declared the Baal
Shem Tov. Now, the Hebrew word for "seen" is *nireh*. By rear-
ranging the Hebrew letters to form a different word, the Baal
Shem Tov concluded by promising: "From *nireh* will come forth
Aharon."

Indeed, not much time elapsed before Rabbi Yaakov's wife
gave birth to a baby boy. The youngster was named Aharon and
grew up to become one of the most celebrated *tzaddikim* of his
time—Rabbi Aharon of Karlin.

* * *

Another Chasid, the hidden *tzaddik* Rabbi Meir Zalman, merited to receive the Baal Shem Tov's blessing for longevity. Indeed,
Rabbi Meir Zalman lived a long, full life. On his ninetieth birthday, he resolved to visit the Baal Shem Tov and secure the
Rebbe's holy blessing. "*Mazel Tov* Rabbi Meir Zalman!" the Baal
Shem Tov greeted him as he entered. "The *Mishnah* (*Avot* 5:22)
tells us, *ben tishim lasuach* (at ninety, the body is stooped)."

With a play on the words, the Baal Shem Tov alternatively translated the *Mishnah*: The son (*ben*) of the ninety-year-old (*tishim*) will speak (*lasuach*, from *sichah*, talk).

The Baal Shem Tov then began revealing the future to his faithful disciple. "You know how to speak Torah, yet you choose to remain silent—but your son Michel will speak for both of you. Michel will become a follower of my disciple's student, a student who shall reveal a new path in the service of G-d. This student will illuminate the importance of prayer and explain how it forms the preparatory basis for understanding Divinity."

"This particular student will introduce another innovation," continued the Baal Shem Tov. "He will reveal how every Jew— even the most simple and unlearned person—can perfect his spiritual service with authentic love and fear of G-d."

Indeed, Rabbi Meir's son was Rabbi Michel of Opotsk, a great scholar who became a foremost follower of a disciple of a disciple of the Baal Shem Tov—Rabbi Schneur Zalman of Liadi, author of the *Tanya*.

* * *

The Baal Shem Tov rewarded his followers spiritually as well. Rabbi Yaakov Yosef of Polonnoye was one of the foremost students of the Baal Shem Tov. He would visit Mezibush often, take great pains to serve the Baal Shem Tov in any way possible, and then return home.

Although Rabbi Yaakov Yosef was a venerated and accomplished scholar, he once sensed a decline in the quality of his studies. Normally, his brilliant mind would constantly conjure up novel Torah insights, but a significant amount of time had already passed without his slightest contribution to Torah scholarship. Alarmed at this troubling development, Rabbi Yaakov Yosef decided to visit the Rebbe and request his blessing.

Arriving in Mezibush, Rabbi Yaakov Yosef found the Baal Shem Tov about to begin his prayers. Rabbi Yaakov Yosef brought a glowing coal and lit the Rebbe's pipe. Said the Baal Shem Tov: "In merit of the flame you have brought me, may G-d's flame clearly illuminate all your future innovative Torah thoughts." Having merited such a specific blessing, Rabbi Yaakov Yosef returned home, clearly assured of future growth and achievement.

The Sound of the Shofar

THE BAAL SHEM TOV related the following parable:

There once lived a mighty king who had an only son. Wise and perceptive, the son lived up to all his father's hopes, and a warm relationship developed between them. One day, the king decided to send his son away to distant countries where, he hoped, his son could attain ever-greater levels of knowledge. The king entrusted the prince with a small fortune of money and sent him off to discover his future.

Unfortunately, within merely a few years, the prince spent his entire fortune and was left penniless. He had reached a distant land where no one had even heard of his father—the king—and they treated him with utter disdain. Wandering the streets of a foreign land, the prince decided it was enough: the time had come to return home.

Yet, the intervening years had taken such a toll on the prince that he had completely forgotten his native tongue. Hence, when, one day, a ragged vagabond appeared on the streets of the royal capital, using sign language to communicate his elevated status, the residents began to laugh and jeer, treating the prince like the town imbecile. "What a riot!" they laughed. "Can you imagine the prince walking around in tattered clothing?"

The prince tried to ignore their taunts as he made his way

toward the palace. Approaching the guards standing at the gates, the prince began communicating by an impressive array of hand signals and grunts, trying to convince them he was their prince. The guards however, had seen such antics before; they totally ignored the distraught stranger.

Despondent with grief, the prince began wailing loudly, raising his voice in a bitter cry. His cries resonated throughout the palace courtyard until they reached the king, who immediately recognized the voice of his long-lost son. Resplendent in his royal robes, the king himself exited the palace, neared the courtyard gates, and personally escorted his son back home inside.

"The spiritual soul—G-d's beloved son—is sent far away, to this material world," explained the Baal Shem Tov. "Daily tribulations and financial worries combined erase the soul's recollections of a better, spiritual world. The soul can even lose its fortunes, its native language.

"On the day of Rosh Hashanah, the soul perceives her loss and strives mightily to reenter the Divine palace, yet her spiritual failures block the entranceway. Herein lies the secret of the *shofar*. The soul's ultimate return is effected by the call of the *shofar*, whose cry reaches far beyond the Heavenly Gates and arouses G-d to bring his children inside, to achieve full repentance."

Continued the Baal Shem Tov:

"As G-d sits on the Throne of Judgment on Rosh Hashanah, the Patriarchs try to arouse Divine mercy for their children. Abraham, the epitome of kindness, implores G-d to arise and be seated on the Throne of Mercy; Isaac mentions the merits of his *Akeda* sacrifice; Jacob joins in with supplication for G-d's great mercies. Moses stands immersed in prayer while the defending angels soar with our merits and *mitzvot*, trying to silence the accusing angles that highlight our many faults.

"In Heaven, every thought, deed and action of mortal man is carefully recorded and weighed. On Rosh Hashanah, the Day of Judgment, these records are reviewed and the Patriarchs and Moses try to arouse favor on our behalf.

"Down here on earth, when a Jew is overcome with remorse

and cries out, "Our Father our King, save me! Have mercy on me!" this cry of the soul strengthens the supernal attribute of Mercy, enabling it to overcome the attribute of strict Judgment. This, in turn, ensures a sweet and prosperous New Year."

Spiritual Shoes

T HE BAAL SHEM TOV once described the events in Heaven on Simchat Torah morning:

"Synagogue services generally get off to a late start on Simchat Torah morning," he observed. "The festive *hakafot* and holiday meal stretch far into the night, and it takes more time for many to get out of bed the next day. Up in Heaven however— where they experience neither *hakafot* nor a meal—the angels begin their supernal service right on schedule. Yet, they face a predicament: Though they cannot wait to start singing praises to G-d, 'the angels above offer praise only *after* the Jews utter their praises from below' (*Chullin* 91b).

"On Simchat Torah, the angels are forced to wait quite a bit until we begin our prayers. Hence, they utilize this time to 'clean' *Gan Eden*. Imagine their consternation to find torn shoes littering the floor! 'We are accustomed to find *tzitzit*, *tefillin*, or other *mitzvot*,' exclaim the angels in surprise. 'What are worn out soles doing in here?'

"Perplexed, the angels consult with the Archangel Michael. 'Yes, the torn shoes are my merchandise,' he calms them. 'These shoes were torn during the uninhibited dancing of Simchat Torah *hakafot*. You see, those shoes are from the *hakafot* in Kaminka, these are from Mezritch....'

"Enthused with his 'find,' the Archangel Michael begins speaking about Matatron, the angel closest to G-d's radiance. 'Matatron spends his days weaving the prayers offered by Jews down below into crowns for G-d (*Torah Or* 42b from *Zohar* 37b). I could fashion a much better crown from these torn shoes!'"

Relived Again

THE BAAL SHEM TOV greeted the festivals with renewed vigor each year, reliving the spiritual connotations of the year's changing cycles. In this vein, he shed deeper interpretation into the *halachic* ruling, "One who reads the *Megillah* backwards, has not fulfilled his obligation" (*Megillah* 2:1).

Explained the Baal Shem Tov: "*One who reads backwards* refers to those who treat our yearly festivals like old-fashioned relics; observances of events that have long passed and are now irrelevant. Such a person *has not fulfilled his obligation*, for this wrongful attitude prevents him from experiencing the deep riches contained within the festivals."

Spiritual Murder

T HE BAAL SHEM TOV gave a daily Talmudic class for his closest disciples. Drawing on his unmatched erudition, the Rebbe quoted extensively from the great codifiers—*Rambam, Rif, Rosh* and other commentators. The Rebbe's analytical approach was breathtaking. As he taught, the Baal Shem Tov translated every word into Yiddish, whether explaining complex *halachic* texts or *Aggadic* material.

When they studied the tractate of *Erchin*, the group learned the saying of our Sages, "Slander kills three" (*Erchin* 15b).

Explained the Baal Shem Tov:

"Slander and tale-bearing kills three people—the speaker, the listener, and the one being spoken about. This is spiritual murder, which is worse and more far-reaching than physical murder."

On Song and Joy

THE BAAL SHEM TOV possessed a remarkable voice. Beautifully sweet, it contained incredible depth and changed effortlessly between musical notes. He sang often. The Baal Shem Tov taught that song and melody are conducive to worship of G-d, and can be utilized for spiritual advancement.

He often said, "Music touches the soul. Song causes deep inner emotion and brings man to unadulterated joy. Chasidim know that singing is part of serving the Creator."

Timeless Time

ONCE, THE BAAL SHEM TOV sent a letter to his brother-in-law, Rabbi Gershon Kitover, reproaching him for having excommunicated a Torah scholar living in *Eretz Yisrael*. The Baal Shem Tov felt his brother-in-law had acted without ample justification and, in his letter, he revealed further that a harsh Heavenly decree was leveled against Rabbi Gershon for his rash behavior.

Rabbi Gershon later wrote back to the Baal Shem Tov, admitting to the incident. "I did excommunicate the scholar," he wrote, "but that happened much after you wrote your letter!"

"True," the Baal Shem Tov later replied, "but you do not realize how things are viewed from the Heavens. Even in the lower supernal world of *Yetzirah*, ten or fifteen years can be viewed in a split second. Though it occurred later in our material time, its ramifications were already felt in Heaven."

The Scholarly Debate

I<small>N A SMALL TOWN NEAR</small> M<small>EZIBUSH</small> lived three brothers whom we shall call Reuven, Shimon and Levi. All three were outstanding Torah scholars, yet only Reuven and Shimon had become attached to the Baal Shem Tov and his teachings, and considered themselves followers of the Chasidic movement. One day, as they sat studying in the synagogue, Levi happened to ask Reuven a question concerning the Talmudic section they were studying. Reuven answered his query, and the group continued with their studies.

Soon a commotion could be heard outdoors; the Baal Shem Tov had arrived unexpectedly. The two brothers rushed off to greet the Rebbe. Many Chasidim had already gathered around the Baal Shem Tov, who began expounding Torah for his followers. After the discourse, the Baal Shem Tov set aside time to meet with his Chasidim privately. Each asked the Rebbe's blessing for his particular problems—some needed guidance in their service of G-d; others presented complex questions disturbing their studies; still others needed Divine intervention for their private affairs.

As Reuven entered the Baal Shem Tov's room, he asked the Rebbe to grant him a detailed path in his service of G-d. The Baal Shem Tov glanced at him sharply. "You carry the sin of proffering false interpretation in our Torah," he said sternly. "You explained a piece of Talmud and a commentary of *Tosfot* incorrectly."

Devastated, Reuven beseeched the Baal Shem Tov to reveal his precise sin. "I cannot remember which issue I explained incorrectly," he pleaded. "Please, I beg the Rebbe to reveal my error and enlighten my eyes with the true explanation."

The Baal Shem Tov immediately began repeating the entire subject discussed by the brothers that very morning. Reuven listened in awe as the Rebbe repeated the Talmudic section and the relevant commentators verbatim, restating Levi's question and Reuven's answer. When he finished, the Baal Shem Tov explained the flawed reasoning of Reuven's answer and, in compliance with Reuven's request, the Rebbe revealed the true resolution of the problem. Due to the complexity of the issue, the Baal Shem Tov repeated his words several times until Reuven nodded in satisfaction, confident he could repeat the Rebbe's explanation.

Soon the Baal Shem Tov left the town, and Reuven returned to his studies in the synagogue where he spent hours absorbed in thought, mentally reviewing the Rebbe's words. After absorbing every detail of the Rebbe's explanation, Reuven approached his two brothers and said, "I looked at the issue again and it seems far more complex than I originally thought. My original answer is meaningless; it raises more questions than it answers. Yet, by the grace of G-d, I believe I have found a novel way to explain this particular Talmudic piece."

"I have a proposition for you," continued Reuven. "Review the subject again a few times, and then I will tell you my thoughts on the matter." Eagerly accepting the proposal, his brothers began studying the issue again, spending every spare moment of the next few days dissecting and analyzing every element of Levi's original question and the Talmudic section at hand. "Everything makes perfect sense to us!" they finally announced. "Your answer seems to explain matters after all!"

Reuven merely smiled, and then launched into a detailed

analysis of Levi's question, revealing ever deeper layers hidden within the problem. "You see," he said finally, "what I answered is absolutely nonsensical. It does nothing to address all these elements in Levi's question."

Shimon and Levi looked at their brother in total amazement. "We never knew you possessed such scholarship!" they finally blurted. "Such breadth of knowledge! Such perception! This is unbelievable!"

Dismissing their compliments, Reuven turned back to the issue at hand. "But how do we resolve Levi's question?" he prodded. "It has become a stronger, more forceful problem!

"Didn't you say you know the answer?" protested his brothers.

"Not just yet," came the rejoinder. "Torah is acquired through toil and sweat. Try figuring it out by yourselves first!"

Shimon and Levi began grappling with the issue once again. Levi had a group of scholarly friends—antagonists of Chasidism like himself—and he resolved to discuss the matter with them. Yet, despite all their efforts, the scholars simply could make no headway in their attempts to resolve the issue, and Reuven adamantly refused to reveal the true solution.

One day, Shimon finally lost patience with his brother. "Your behavior is most unbecoming," he said bitterly. "It runs contrary to everything the Baal Shem Tov has taught us!"

Reuven accepted the rebuke silently, and then revealed everything to Shimon—his private encounter with the Baal Shem Tov, the Rebbe's admonishment, and the Rebbe's explanation of Levi's question.

His reply only served to stoke Shimon's anger. "I can't believe you hid this from everyone!" he said fiercely. "You should have told them the whole story just to prove the unequalled erudition of the Baal Shem Tov! And besides, you still haven't told *me* the answer!"

"I want them to try themselves first," countered Reuven. "Let them come and admit defeat; then I will furnish the Rebbe's answer. After they comprehend it, I will tell them it came from the Rebbe. Then—and only then—will Levi and his friends begin to grasp the Rebbe's incredible knowledge of Torah."

"You are right," said Shimon slowly, an idea forming in his head. "You know, why don't we present the question to our uncle?"

Reuven turned pale, hardly believing his brother's words. Their uncle, an erudite scholar who lived a few miles away, sat alone in a secluded room, where he learned Torah day and night for years on end. Due to his unrelenting pursuit of knowledge and assiduity, their uncle had become a known figure in the scholarly world, and his name was revered in many circles. Yet, their uncle remained a fierce antagonist of the Baal Shem Tov, having lent his support to those who opposed the Rebbe and his growing movement. "How can you even suggest such a thing?" hissed Reuven through clenched teeth. "Since our uncle said degrading things about the Rebbe, I have not even stepped foot inside his home!"

Yet, soon Reuven agreed that Shimon's idea had great merit. If their uncle would admit his inability to solve Levi's question, it would bring great fame and respect to the Baal Shem Tov, forcing their uncle to concede the Rebbe's greatness. Thus, when Levi returned to ask for the resolution of his question, Reuven suggested they confer with their eminent uncle and ask his learned opinion. "Marvelous!" said Levi. "What a brilliant idea!"

Off Levi went to consult with his friends, and soon the group decided to leave on the following day, after the very first *minyan* that prayed at sunrise. As Chasidim, Reuven and Shimon could not agree to this itinerary. The Baal Shem Tov had taught them the significance of lengthy prayer and the inestimable importance of proper preparation for communion with G-d. As such, Levi and friends set out while the two brothers remained behind, only completing their prayers in the early afternoon.

Upon finishing their prayers, Reuven and Shimon journeyed to their uncle's synagogue. They arrived to find Levi and his friends deep in discussion with their scholarly uncle, arguing over fine points in his analytical viewpoint. Their uncle had just offered an explanation, but immediately retracted it. "In

essence," said their uncle piously, "the scholarly logic I expounded contains the sheer genius of Maimonides and the acute reasoning of *Maharam Shif*. However, this answer simply will not do."

Suddenly he spied his errant nephews. "What are you two
doing here?" he asked in displeasure. "Weren't you angry at me
for slighting your leader? What do you need here anyway?"

"We came in case you have a solution to Levi's question,"
responded the pair. "We find that the greatest Talmudic Sages—
Rabbi Akiva and Ben Azzai—traveled great distances to further
their knowledge of Torah."

"You want to learn Torah?" asked their uncle snidely. "Why
don't you go to that newfangled leader of yours—perhaps he
knows a good answer to Levi's complicated query." The scholar
burst into gleeful laughter, pleased at his witticism.

"Apparently, our learned uncle does not know the answer
after all," said Reuven and Shimon plainly. "We might well do as
he says and ask the Baal Shem Tov."

Barely able to contain their fury, Levi's friends began shouting loudly at the pair. "Where is your honor for the Torah? Our
uncle is a righteous scholar who, for forty years, has studied assiduously in holiness and purity...."

"Actually, you're mistaken," interrupted their uncle. "It's
already more than forty-three years and seven months."

"...and he is scrupulously careful to eat *yoshon*...."

"He says *Tikkun Chatzot* every night at midnight and tortures
himself as a means of repentance...."

"Including rolling around in the freezing snow," added their
uncle with a righteous air.

"And now," spat Levi, "you frivolous '*Kedushah* jumpers'[1] have
the nerve to mock this outstanding sage, the scholar of our generation! For this alone you deserve to be excommunicated!"

Reuven and Shimon listened quietly. When Levi finished his
tirade, Reuven repeated Levi's question once more, highlighting

---

1. Aflame with excitement, Chasidim often jumped up and down while reciting *Kedushah*; this led to the derogatory term "*Kedushah* jumpers" used by those
opposed to Chasidism.

every aspect of the difficulty as explained by the Baal Shem Tov. Their uncle stared in disbelief. "Incredible!" he breathed. "This is true scholarship." After contemplating the matter deeply, the scholar shrugged his shoulders in amazement. "You presented the question in totally new light!" he announced. "You, Levi, also presented the question prodigiously, and is a good question; I can offer no satisfactory answer. However, the manner in which Reuven presented the question defies description."

"I will give you a parable for this," continued their uncle animatedly. "Imagine cooking a piece of fatty meat, keeping it on the flame until perfection. The fat imparts a delicious flavor and everyone enjoys a good meal. Now imagine the selfsame piece of meat seasoned with fat, flour, onion and pepper—why, it tastes entirely different, a meal fit for a king! The meat is the same piece of meat, but the end result is incomparable."

"The same is true here," concluded the scholar. "You both asked the same question, but Reuven's presentation is of entirely different quality! Well Reuven, maybe you have an answer for us as well?"

"Indeed I do," responded his nephew. "I know a good answer!"

"Since when have you become such a prodigious scholar?" his uncle peered at him in surprise. "I can hardly believe my ears! A mere half-year ago, your level of scholarship was nothing to brag about!"

"First listen to my answer," retorted his nephew. "Afterwards, I will tell you who I heard it from."

Saying this, Reuven began repeating the Baal Shem Tov's lengthy answer. Sparing no effort in elucidating every detail of the answer, Reuven reread the entire Talmudic section in question with all the relevant commentators, elaborating on every issue at length. After a few hours, they all decided to take a short break, enabling Reuven and his elderly uncle to rest from their intense mental strain.

After the break, Reuven picked up his train of thought once more, satisfactorily concluding his explanation of the Talmudic piece in question. Utter silence settled on the room as Reuven finished his presentation. "Unbelievable!" said his uncle, shaking his head in amazement. "I have never heard such erudition in my entire life. Despite my advanced years, I would walk for three miles to see this incredible scholar who revealed this explanation to you!"

"Words, just words," said Reuven. "I guarantee that when I tell you the scholar's name, you will find all kinds of reasons to renege on your word. You will present scholarly arguments to prove you cannot be held accountable for a promise made under the effects of emotional excitement."

"Not true!" cried his uncle, offended at the mere thought. "Just tell me who the *gaon* is and where he lives—I will definitely travel to him. To hear such outstanding scholarship is worth every hardship."

Levi and his friends expressed similar excitement. They begged Reuven to reveal the identity of the mysterious scholar, imploring with such intensity as if it were a matter of life and death. "We will also go learn under his tutelage," they promised. "Please tell us his name!"

After slight hesitation, Reuven decided to answer truthfully, seeing their sincerity. "Very well," said Reuven. "The *gaon* who told me this answer and showed me how to truly learn is—our leader, the Baal Shem Tov!"

He could not have hoped for a more dramatic impact. His elderly uncle looked at him in openmouthed astonishment; Levi and his friends seemed overwhelmed by shock. Reuven told them all that had transpired—his initial explanation of the Talmudic piece; the Baal Shem Tov's rebuttal; and of the Rebbe's subsequent explanation.

"I shall not sleep tonight," said his uncle. "Instead, I will wait for midnight, pray at the earliest possible time, and then I will immediately travel to the Baal Shem Tov and ask for his forgiveness. I deserve a serious reprimand, and when he forgives me I will become his student!"

Levi's friends joined in enthusiastically, but Levi himself

would not be swayed. "Come what may," he declared, "I remain opposed to the Baal Shem Tov and his teachings!" Despite this, Reuven and Shimon remained enthusiastically excited with the new adherents their leader had just gained. The uncle gave instructions to prepare a feast, and everyone sat down to eat, repeating various elements of the scholarly topic and rejoicing in the Rebbe's innovative resolution.

Within a short period of time, their scholarly uncle and Levi's friends had met with the Baal Shem Tov, attentively absorbing his teachings. Having become devoted followers of the Rebbe, the group then returned home, where they began influencing others to join the Chasidic movement. Thanks to their efforts, practically every Jew in their town and all the surrounding hamlets became Chasidim, illuminating their lives with the wisdom of the Baal Shem Tov.

Validated By Heaven

T HE "COUNCIL OF FOUR LANDS" often met to discuss pertinent issues affecting the Jewish communities in Russia, Poland and Lithuania. Composed of leading scholars of the generation, the Council strove to establish the Torah perspective on current issues. During one of these meetings, mention was made of the Baal Shem Tov and the tremendous following he had attracted. Various members of the Council voiced their protest regarding specific elements of the Chasidic movement and, after some deliberation, the Council decided that Chasidism was incompatible with Torah-true Judaism.

Concerned at the rapid spread of the Baal Shem Tov's influence, the Council decided on hasty action, hoping to curb the Rebbe's sway over the masses. "We will send three messengers to the Baal Shem Tov," they declared. "They will command the Baal Shem Tov—in the name of the Council's *beit din*—to stop spreading his teachings at once, and to desist from his unworthy activities. If he refuses, we will excommunicate him and ban his movement."

The three set out to meet with the Baal Shem Tov and were warmly welcomed upon arrival. The Baal Shem Tov conversed with them at length, startling the group with his incredible erudition. He discussed complex Talmudic issues with the utmost ease, and showed uncanny familiarity with the deepest secrets of Kabbalah. After the scholarly dialogue, the Baal Shem Tov began clarifying the basic fundamentals of Chasidism and explained some of his teachings.

Stunned, the group lapsed into silence, suddenly realizing that the Baal Shem Tov was far greater than anything they imagined. His scholarship was unsurpassed; his explanations were flawless; his erudition encompassed every aspect of Torah. They also sensed his staunch resolve, an iron determination to continue spreading his teachings. For two days and nights, the scholars engaged the Baal Shem Tov in debate. Though his arguments were superior, the Baal Shem Tov consented to meet with the "Council of Four Lands," to debate the merits of his position, and, afterward, accept any forthcoming judgment.

In the course of their conversation, the Baal Shem Tov strongly reprimanded the scholars for passing judgment in his absence, and not allowing him the opportunity to defend himself. "Such action is clearly contrary to Torah," countered the Baal Shem Tov. "Based on the verse 'Hear the causes between your brethren and judge righteously' (Deuteronomy 1:16), the Talmud infers that it is forbidden to hear the claims of one party in the absence of the other party (*Sanhedrin* 7b). Hence, your denouncement runs contrary to Torah."

Among other things, the Baal Shem Tov said the following: "The scholarly sages of our generation are familiar with the *intellectual* dimension of Torah, having appreciated Torah through their finite understanding. I, however, have come to reveal an inner dimension Torah—one associated with feelings of the *heart*."

"In the study halls of this physical earth they still debate the veracity of my movement," continued the Baal Shem Tov. "However, the study hall of Heaven is in complete harmony with my teachings. I pray that, with the help of G-d, the study halls down here on earth will also realize this truth!"

Upon hearing these emphatic words, the scholars realized their mission was doomed. The Baal Shem Tov would not be swayed; nor could they hope to influence him. "But wherein lies your power?" they asked in astonishment. "You have sixty students at most, whereas the scholars opposing you teach thousands of students in their vast network of schools!"

The Baal Shem Tov looked at his antagonists penetratingly before responding. "I will answer you by way of a parable," he said. "Imagine a farmer who sows every available space of his fields and vineyards, evenly directing his efforts to every part of the land. After spreading the seed all over his property, the farmer goes home to sleep, relying on the bountiful harvest certain to follow.

"Then there is the farmer who hoards his seeds. Though he concentrates only on a small portion of land, he invests tremendous effort in these modest plots. He works hard at hoeing, watering the land, and removing all the weeds. He rises early every morning to inspect the progress of his harvest and ensures that it is properly covered with earth. Everything is executed with painstaking precision, carefully timed just right.

"At harvest time, the difference between these two farmers becomes evident. The first farmer reaps a sizeable crop, but his produce is mostly inferior. The fruits are infested with bugs and beetles; the grain provides only dirty, coarse flour. Later, when the farmer tries replanting with seeds from his harvest, the next crop is similarly infested with insects.

"By contrast, the second farmer only garners a small harvest. Yet, his produce is of superior quality. His grain produces the finest, cleanest flour; his fruits remain without the slightest trace of blemish...."

The Baal Shem Tov had no need to interpret the parable for his scholarly guests. He returned to his room and left the group to contemplate his words. Realizing the truth of his message, two members of the group decided to stay behind and join the swelling ranks of the Chasidic movement.

Joy and Sorrow

O<small>N</small> *EREV ROSH CHODESH*, an auspicious time for prayer and repentance, many congregations would observe the prescribed order of *Yom Kippur Katan*. The city of Slutsk was no exception. Every month, on the day preceding *Erev Rosh Chodesh*, all work would come to a halt at midday. Stores and businesses would close their doors, vendors would pack up their displays, and the market would come to a standstill. Men, women and children would make their way toward the synagogue for *Minchah*, during which they would add the confessional *al chet* prayer. The *shamash* would then remind the congregation to return at midnight, in order to recite the *Tikkun Chatzot* and hear rousing words of repentance from the local *maggid*.

On one occasion, the Baal Shem Tov arrived in the city of Slutsk before *Rosh Chodesh* and joined the crowd of worshippers streaming into the synagogue. When the room was filled to capacity, the congregation began reciting *Tikkun Chatzot* together, their prayers punctuated by remorseful tears. As they finished, a hush fell on the room. The *maggid* strode up to the *bimah* and began addressing the assembled crowd with words of fire-and-brimstone, exhorting the worshippers to correct their evil ways and repent fully. His impassioned speech made an incredible impact on the audience and many broke out in loud wailing.

After the *maggid* finished his fiery words, the *shul* slowly emptied as people returned to their respective homes. Soon only a single individual was left in the synagogue—Rabbi Avraham Chaim Katzenelenbogen, the revered rabbi of the community. Sitting in his place of honor, the *rav* opened a large tome and began studying aloud, his face filled with with sorrow and grief.

The Baal Shem Tov approached and sat down near the *rav*. Purposely ignoring the rabbi's morose disposition, the Baal Shem Tov began singing a lively tune, his voice resonating with gladness and hope. The *rav* promptly interrupted his studies and stared at the guest in shock and dismay, aghast at the intentional disturbance. Yet, he resolved to let the stranger finish his song and then greet him kindly. When the Baal Shem Tov finished singing, the *rav* extended his hand in greeting and quickly returned to his book, confident that the stranger would bother him no longer. After all, he had already sacrificed some of his precious time greeting the stranger; certainly he could not be expected to waste more.

Hardly had the rabbi resumed his learning when the Baal Shem Tov began singing the same tune again, and then again, and then another time. Soon the rabbi could no longer ignore the jolly antics of the stranger sitting right beside him. "What's the matter with you?" he asked. "Why are you so happy?"

"How can I not be glad?" replied the Baal Shem Tov. "G-d has completely absolved the sins of the entire Jewish population in Slutsk—men, women and children!"

"Yes, yes," he exclaimed excitedly. "You are right!"

"If so," continued the Baal Shem Tov, "Let us dance!" The rabbi joined hands with the Baal Shem Tov and the two danced together in great joy.

(Years later, when the esteemed Rabbi Katzenelenbogen was approached to lend his support for a call of excommunication against the Baal Shem Tov and the Chasidic movement, he recalled his joyful encounter with the Rebbe and staunchly refused to sign the document.)

The next day, the Baal Shem Tov returned to the synagogue and found two scholars immersed in their studies. The young pair displayed an extraordinary measure of diligence and had not even interrupted their studies for the recital of *Tikkun Chatzot* the night earlier, nor had they heard the *maggid's* speech.

Entering the synagogue, the Baal Shem Tov sat down near one of the scholars and burst into bitter weeping. "Excuse me," said the young scholar, "but why are you crying?"

"I am crying for you," responded the Baal Shem Tov.

"Me?" asked the scholar in astonishment. "What do you mean?"

"I have great pity on you," explained the Baal Shem Tov. "That's why I am crying."

"But whatever for?" asked the bewildered scholar.

"Our Sages say that G-d cannot dwell among arrogant people," observed the Baal Shem Tov. "Your arrogance and conceit are so overwhelming that you have effectively banished G-dliness from this room. Now do you understand why I am crying?"

"Ay!" cried the scholar in alarm. "You are right!"

The Baal Shem Tov's heartfelt words found their mark. This young man later became a devoted follower of the Baal Shem Tov.

A Kosher Sukkah

ONE YEAR, ON SUKKOT, when the leading scholars of Mezibush paid the Rebbe a visit in his *sukkah*, they were most surprised to find that it was, seemingly, not *halachically* kosher for Sukkot. After closely inspecting its structural design, the scholars unanimously declared the *sukkah* invalid. The Baal Shem Tov began arguing with them, bringing various Torah sources to demonstrate how his *sukkah* did, in fact, fulfill the criteria prescribed by the Torah.

The two sides debated back and forth—the Baal Shem Tov maintaining the validity of his *sukkah* while the scholars maintained their opposition. Apparently, due to his extraordinary spiritual capacities, the Baal Shem Tov desired to elevate even problematic varieties of foliage to the realm of holiness, to be included in the performance of a mitzvah. Thus, he made the physical effort of building and sitting in such a *sukkah*, hoping to shatter the evil forces seeking to control these elements. The scholars, however, could not agree to such a move.

Finally the Baal Shem Tov opened his hand, revealing a small piece of parchment. The scholars took the parchment and, to their surprise, found it to be a note from Heaven. "The *sukkah* of Rabbi Yisrael is kosher," they read. The note was signed by the Archangel Matatron, "Minister of the Interior."

The scholars relented.

WONDERS AND MIRACLES

Curing the Mute

Slutsk, a city teeming with Jewish life, was home to many scholarly and pious Jews. Thus, when the Baal Shem Tov decided to visit the city in 5500 (1740), news of his impending arrival spread quickly throughout the community, and the residents turned out *en masse* to welcome the Rebbe.

Rabbi Uri Nosson Nota stood out among the crowd. An accomplished scholar, well advanced in years, Rabbi Uri waited desperately for his chance to meet personally with the Baal Shem Tov and describe his sorry plight. People looked at Rabbi Uri with compassion and empathy, well aware of the unfortunate circumstances he faced. Six years earlier, Rabbi Uri's son—Rabbi Shlomo—had married the daughter of Rabbi Eliyahu Moshe, a respected member of the community who lived in a village near Slutsk. Yet, barely six months had passed before the young wife had suddenly been struck with muteness. She just sat between the wall and the oven of her parents' home, refusing to utter a single word.

Six long years passed in this fashion. Rabbi Shlomo, the luckless husband, had no *halachic* recourse allowing him to terminate the marriage for, according to Jewish law, only a sane woman can accept a divorce. And so, having heard of the Baal Shem Tov's imminent arrival, Rabbi Uri hoped the Rebbe could provide relief for the unfortunate couple.

Rabbi Uri was not the only one thinking about the young couple. The woman's father, Rabbi Eliyahu Moshe, had come to Slutsk for precisely the same reason and he, too, asked the Rebbe for his blessing. After hearing their sorry story, the Baal Shem Tov summoned the fathers of both husband and wife, together with the suffering husband, and asked all parties if anyone harbored a grudge against another.

"Heaven forbid!" cried Rabbi Uri in alarm, aghast at the very thought. "Rabbi Eliyahu Moshe is a pious Jew who studies Torah regularly. His hospitality is legendary; the poor flock to his home. He offers ample support to needy Torah scholars, financing all their needs with an open hand. Furthermore, he provides my son—his son-in-law—with whatever he requires, and does so generously."

Rabbi Eliyahu Moshe also spoke up at once, extolling the fine virtues of his unfortunate son-in-law, Rabbi Shlomo. "My son-in-law has single-handedly effected a transformation in our village," he said proudly. "Since he came, he has befriended the simple, unlearned Jews in the village and teaches them Torah every day. They learn *Chumash* with *Rashi*, *Ein Yaakov*, *Midrash*, and *Pirkei Avot*.

"Until my son-in-law arrived, residents of our village were often at odds with each other, squabbling and bickering jealously about their finances. However, my son-in-law has effectively eradicated this unpleasant atmosphere. He explained to the townsfolk that G-d alone decides every aspect of our lives and He, as Creator of the world, watches over each individual, guiding them with His Divine Providence. As such, one cannot gain more than the exact amount allocated by G-d and, therefore, all forms of jealousy are totally unfounded. Due to his influence, people in our village have stopped fighting with each other, and our village has become a place of warmth and camaraderie."

Rabbi Eliyahu Moshe's voice suddenly broke with feeling. "And now," he said in anguish, "residents of our village pray for my daughter every day, asking G-d to restore her to full health. They hope and pray that my son-in-law will be able to resume a normal family life, and continue to lead them in his capable manner."

Having listened carefully to everything both men said, the Baal Shem Tov turned to all the parties assembled in his room. "With G-d's help, I will be able to heal the young woman," he pronounced. "However, I must make the following stipulation: Immediately after restoring her spirit, both husband and wife must agree to divorce. The divorce must be accepted willingly, with full consent of both parties."

A stunned silence filled the room. Both fathers began speaking at once, describing the beautiful relationship between the husband and wife and the great pain and anguish the divorce would inflict on all involved. "I am willing to give a considerable contribution to charity," pleaded Rabbi Eliyahu Moshe. "Please, cure my daughter, and do not force them to divorce each other! Let them live together in love and peace as before!"

The Baal Shem Tov would not be swayed. "This is my stipulation," he countered. "If you do not agree, I cannot help you."

The parties left the Rebbe's room, resolved to deliberate the matter thoroughly before deciding. After a few days, they returned to the Baal Shem Tov, pain evident in their eyes. "We have agreed," they said quietly. "However, we cannot promise that the woman will also agree to the divorce."

The Baal Shem Tov agreed, and, turning to Rabbi Eliyahu Moshe, he said, "Travel home and tell your daughter that the Baal Shem Tov—famed for his miraculous wonders—is in Slutsk and wants to meet her regarding an urgent matter."

Rabbi Eliyahu Moshe and Rabbi Uri looked at each other in openmouthed astonishment, trying to muster enough courage to question the Rebbe's command. "But Rebbe!" stammered Rabbi Eliyahu Moshe nervously, "my daughter has not uttered a single syllable in six years. She sits between the oven and the wall, and we can barely manage to feed her and care for her. She is totally withdrawn. How can I expect her to understand me?"

The Baal Shem Tov did not reply.

Brokenhearted, Rabbi Eliyahu Moshe and the others left the

room. "Had only the Rebbe seen my daughter," said Rabbi Eliyahu Moshe bitterly, "he would have understood the situation better. He would never have said what he said." Rabbi Uri agreed.

Rabbi Shlomo, the husband, however, did not lend his support. Having studied the teachings of the Baal Shem Tov, Rabbi Shlomo felt great closeness to the Rebbe and had already decided to become a devoted follower of the Baal Shem Tov. "We must fulfill the Rebbe's request," he said to his father-in-law. "Whatever the Rebbe says is what we must do."

"I agree," said Rabbi Uri suddenly. "If we have already agreed to the divorce, surely we should take the next step and inform the sick woman of the Baal Shem Tov's summons."

Rabbi Eliyahu Moshe returned home and found his daughter sitting dumbly in her regular place, between the oven and the wall. Turning to his wife, Rabbi Eliyahu Moshe related everything that had transpired with the Baal Shem Tov and relayed the Rebbe's assurance that he would cure their daughter. As he spoke, Rabbi Eliyahu Moshe retold some amazing stories he heard about the Baal Shem Tov's miraculous powers.

"Please, who performs these miracles you are speaking about?" he suddenly heard someone ask. Pale with shock, he turned to find his daughter standing beside him, having left her place near the oven. Rabbi Eliyahu Moshe and his wife could scarcely believe their eyes: for the first time in six years, their daughter had uttered a few words, and—most importantly—she sounded completely normal!

Recovering from his surprise, Rabbi Eliyahu Moshe began relating all he knew about the Baal Shem Tov, telling many stories about his ability to perform miracles. "He sounds like an extraordinary *tzaddik*," his daughter interrupted excitedly, her eyes shining brightly. "I must first bathe, and then I will listen some more."

Rabbi Eliyahu Moshe and his wife quickly shuttered the windows and closed the doors so as not to prematurely publicize what had happened. Their daughter bathed and, for the first time in six years, sat down to eat a meal with her parents. Though she appeared to have made a full recovery, she still felt very weak and tired.

That night, Rabbi Eliyahu Moshe hardly slept. He had not breathed a word of this miraculous transformation to anyone, not even his closest neighbors. Instead, he sat down to compose a letter addressed to his son-in-law Rabbi Shlomo and his father Rabbi Uri Nosson Nota, detailing all that had occurred since his return from their meeting with the Baal Shem Tov.

Three days passed. Rabbi Eliyahu Moshe's daughter spoke and ate like a regular person, albeit weakly. On the third day she became ill with malaria. Hot and feverish, she rolled about listlessly in bed, mumbling about the Baal Shem Tov. "I want to see the *tzaddik*," she wept. "Show me the *tzaddik* who performs wonders."

Thunderstruck, Rabbi Eliyahu Moshe realized he had failed to transmit the Rebbe's message. "The Rebbe sent a message for you!" he whispered in her ear. "He is in Slutsk now, and he urgently wants to meet you." Immediately his daughter smiled. Her parents looked on in astonishment as her fever dissipated and she quickly returned to perfect health. The very next day, Rabbi Eliyahu Moshe, his wife and his daughter, traveled to meet the Baal Shem Tov in Slutsk.

* * *

Meanwhile, Rabbi Eliyahu Moshe's letter had caused considerable excitement in Rabbi Uri's home. Rabbi Shlomo could hardly contain his glee: his wife had recovered! Seizing the opportunity, Rabbi Shlomo used the prevailing atmosphere to impress some of the Baal Shem Tov's teachings on his father. Indeed, having just witnessed an obvious miracle performed by the Rebbe, Rabbi Uri was most receptive to his son's words, and listened attentively to the Rebbe's teachings.

Rabbi Shlomo spoke to his father at great length, elaborating on some fundamental topics of Chasidism—the concept of detailed Divine Providence; the inherent value and quality of even the simplest, most unlearned Jew; the importance of *Ahavat*

Yisrael, the absolute and unconditional love toward each and every Jew. The elderly scholar listened in amazement to these novel ideas, contemplating the veracity of each topic. After extended thought, he decided to join the other Chasidim and become a follower of the Baal Shem Tov.

Having made his decision, Rabbi Uri went immediately to the Baal Shem Tov and expressed his desire to become a Chasid. "I have heard many of your ideas from my son," he told the Rebbe. "I now wish to become a follower of the Rebbe. Moreover, I have joyous news to relay: due to the Rebbe's blessing, Rabbi Eliyahu Moshe's daughter has already recovered!"

"Things just changed today," responded the Baal Shem Tov. "Your daughter-in-law has just become ill again. She will be cured only when her father fulfills his mission and transmits my message."

The next day, Rabbi Eliyahu Moshe's family arrived in Slutsk and met with Rabbi Shlomo's family. Rejoined at last, the young couple went to meet the Baal Shem Tov, but the Rebbe merely repeated his stipulation that they agree to divorce. "But my husband is such a fine person!" protested the newly cured wife. She extolled her husband's virtues at length, and expressed her great regard for him. "However," she began crying bitterly, "the *tzaddik* knows best. If the *tzaddik* has decreed we must divorce, I am obviously unworthy to continue serving as Rabbi Shlomo's wife and I am forced to fulfill the decree."

Rabbi Shlomo, too, could not stop the tears cascading down his face. "My wife has all the virtues one expects to find," he said with heavy grief. "She is a true woman of valor. However, if the *tzaddik* decrees we must divorce, I will definitely comply." Having expressed his consent, Rabbi Shlomo burst into uncontrolled weeping.

The Baal Shem Tov looked at the devastated couple standing before him. "I give you three days," he said softly. "On the fourth, come back to me and I will arrange the particulars for the divorce."

Three excruciatingly tense days passed. The distraught couple and their parents spent the days in tears, prayer and fasting, hoping to reverse the grave decree. However, as the fourth day dawned, they strengthened themselves to carry out the Baal Shem Tov's stipulation, regardless of their inner suffering and anguish.

When the couple and their parents entered the Rebbe's room they found a rabbi, a scribe and witnesses already waiting, ready to perform the divorce according to the precise instructions required by Jewish law. The Baal Shem Tov turned to the couple and asked, "Are you both willing to divorce each other with wholehearted acceptance?"

The couple burst into bitter tears, crying over their unfortunate fate. "Yes," they finally responded. "We firmly believe that the Rebbe has our best interests at heart, and we also wish to ensure our ability to remarry unhindered in the future. Therefore, we have assented to divorce each other, and we do so willingly."

The Baal Shem Tov rose and went into an adjoining room. After what seemed like an eternity, the Rebbe returned to the room, his face suffused with joy. "Six years ago, you both faced a severe Heavenly accusation," he said to the young couple. "The Heavenly Court passed judgment on both of you, decreeing that the wife would be struck dumb and the husband, unable to remarry, would suffer the pain of becoming a live widower. Now, however, since you have accepted to divorce each other purely due to your uncompromising faith in *tzaddikim*, the decree has been annulled. Your self-sacrifice has abolished all punishment!"

The couple listened in stunned silence, hardly believing their ears. "Return home in peace," beamed the Baal Shem Tov. "May G-d grant you children and long life."

Rabbi Shlomo and his wife returned to their home in the village near Slutsk. After three years, they moved to Minsk, where Rabbi Shlomo became one of the foremost Chasidim in the town, influencing a great many students to join the Chasidic movement. After some time, the Baal Shem Tov instructed Rabbi Shlomo to move again—this time to the city of Bayev.

Rabbi Shlomo and his wife merited to raise a large family and, in 5556 (1796), they immigrated to Israel. Rabbi Shlomo passed away fifteen years later, having merited to live a long and fruitful life—just as the Baal Shem Tov had promised.

Dream Deliverance

IN MEZIBUSH THERE LIVED A GREAT TORAH SCHOLAR. His incredible erudition was well-known to many scholars throughout the land, and few could match his level of scholarship. Yet, despite his close proximity to the Baal Shem Tov, the scholar never visited the Rebbe, nor did he believe in his greatness. In fact, he refused to have any association with the Rebbe and his followers. The Baal Shem Tov greatly desired to meet this scholar and gain his acceptance, but the scholar always kept a careful distance from the Rebbe and his students.

One day, as the scholar sat immersed in his studies, he encountered a particularly complex *Tosfot*. Despite hours of concentrated effort, the scholar made no headway in his efforts to understand the *Tosfot*, causing him great anguish. The following day the scholar tackled the *Tosfot* again, but he could make no sense of the words. Days passed into weeks as the scholar toiled mightily, drawing on his vast knowledge to help explain the *Tosfot*, but he could claim no success. His frustration increased, and the scholar began doubting if he would ever merit to fully understand the issue.

One night, as the scholar slept, he saw himself ascending the Heavenly spheres, passing through countless supernal chambers. The light emanating from these spiritual chambers was so intense and blinding that the scholar shut his eyes tight, afraid to gaze at the dazzling brightness. Finally, after being led into a certain chamber, the scholar was commanded to open his eyes. The scholar opened his eyes and looked around. Dozens of *tzaddikim* and lesser disciples sat there studying Torah and, at their head, sat the Baal Shem Tov.

To his surprise, the Baal Shem Tov suddenly turned and addressed him directly. "Why are you having such a difficult time understanding the *Tosfot?*" he asked. The Baal Shem Tov then proceeded to explain the problematic *Tosfot*, clarifying the text in a lucid and clear manner.

As morning dawned and the scholar woke, he hurried to analyze the *Tosfot*. Delving once more into the complex problem, he soon agreed to the Baal Shem Tov's reasoning and explanation. "But it's just a dream!" the scholar thought pensively. "How can I judge the Baal Shem Tov's greatness based on a dream?"

Upon pondering the matter, the scholar decided to visit the Baal Shem Tov during the upcoming Shabbat. That week, on Shabbat afternoon, he entered the Baal Shem Tov's synagogue as the Rebbe presided over *Seudah Shlishit*. As the scholar crossed the doorway, the Baal Shem Tov turned and called out, "Welcome! Did you check my interpretation of the *Tosfot?* Isn't it truly the correct explanation?"

Shaken by the Divine spirit resting on the Baal Shem Tov, the scholar became a devout follower of the Rebbe, and joined his growing movement.

The Miracle Sefer Torah

THE COMMUNITY ELDERS STOOD QUIETLY in the Baal Shem
Tov's room, their faces drawn and grim. A devastating plague
had ravaged Mezibush, infecting countless people regardless of
age or strength. Some were critically ill, barely expected to live
another day. Not a single house was spared; affliction and despair
were everywhere. The community elders turned now to their
revered leader, their only hope in these trying times.

After explaining the gravity of the situation, the community
elders listened in disbelief as the Baal Shem Tov expressed his
inability to help. "But, Rebbe, how can this be?" they protested.
"You are able to assist anyone and everyone who comes to you for
help, but you can't help your own neighbors?"

"Our townspeople themselves are our only hope," explained
the Baal Shem Tov. "Only you can stem the plague. In our daily
prayers, we beseech G-d to 'always find favor with the service of
Your people Israel.' This means that our service is constantly present before G-d, effecting Divine kindness and negating evil
decrees. What, then, is our 'service'? This refers to two elements
of Torah: the recital of Torah and Tehillim, or the writing of a
Sefer Torah with the participation of the entire community.

"Therefore," concluded the Baal Shem Tov, "I advise you to
write a Sefer Torah."

Word of the Baal Shem Tov's suggestion spread quickly throughout the town and the Jewish residents immediately resolved to commence writing a *Sefer Torah*. Every single person participated in this holy project. The Baal Shem Tov summoned his personal scribe, the *tzaddik* Rabbi Tzvi, and instructed him to begin writing the first two folios of parchment.

To everyone's amazement, the sick immediately began to heal. The plague abated and not another person fell ill. Awed by the great miracle, the villagers dubbed the scroll "The Miracle *Sefer Torah*."

With His Touch Alone

DURING HIS MANY TRAVELS, the Baal Shem Tov once passed through the village of Shpola. Hundreds of people crowded the streets to greet the famed *tzaddik*, straining to get a glimpse of his holy countenance.

Among the crowd stood a young boy called Leib, later to become a renowned Chasidic leader known as the "Grandfather of Shpola." The child was brought before the Baal Shem Tov for a blessing, after which the Rebbe laid his saintly hands on the child's head and heart.

"From that moment," Rabbi Leib later recounted, "I felt that my mind was opened wide to Torah study and my heart become consumed with the burning desire to serve G-d, and to love each Jew dearly."

SUPPLEMENTS

- Glossary
- Sources
- Bibliography
- Related Works

Glossary

Ahavat Yisrael: Love of fellow Jew.

Aggadah: Lit., "Narrative." The sections of the Talmud which do not deal directly with the law (*halachah*), but contain ethical teachings and sayings, historical and other popular material. See *Ein Yaakov*.

Akeda: The binding of Isaac related in Genesis 22.

Al Chet: Confessional prayer recited on Yom Kippur and other times of repentance.

Alef-Beit: Hebrew alphabet.

Aliyah: To be called up to the *bimah* for the reading of the Torah.

Amen: Lit., "I believe." Communal response offered during the prayers.

Amidah: Central portion of the daily prayers comprised, on weekdays, of nineteen benedictions.

Anenu: Special prayer added to the *Amidah* on fast days.

Arba'ah Turim: Lit., "Four rows." Also abbreviated as *Tur*, it is an important work of Jewish law, composed by Rabbi Yaakov ben Asher of Spain (1270-c. 1340). Commentaries on *Arba'ah Turim* include *Beit Yosef* by Rabbi Yosef Caro and *Bayit Chadash* by Rabbi Yoel Sirkis. Rabbi Yosef Caro's Code of Jewish Law is a condensation of *Beit Yosef* and follows the basic structure of the *Arba'ah Turim*, including its division into chapters.

Arizal: Acronym for Rabbi Yitzchak Luria of blessed memory (1534-1572). Founder and leader of a Kabbalistic school in Safed that soon became the dominant school in Jewish Mysticism and exerted a profound influence on world Jewry. The intricate system of Lurianic Kabbalah, which forms the theoretical basis of Chasidic thought, is authoritatively recorded in the multi-volume writings of Arizal's principal disciple Rabbi Chaim Vital (1543-1620).

Avot: See *Pirkei Avot*.

Avraham: Abraham, the first of the three Patriarchs.

Ay!: Yiddish expression of regret or anguish—"Woe!"

Bachurim: Unmarried men, usually yeshivah students.

Bar Mitzvah: Status of a full-fledged Jew reached by a boy at the age of thirteen years.

Bava Batra: Talmudic tractate discussing certain monetary laws.

Bava Metzia: Talmudic tractate discussing certain monetary laws.

Bedikat Chametz: The search for leaven on the eve of Pesach.

Beit Din: Lit., "House of Law." Rabbinical Court. Also called *Beit Din Tzedek*, Rabbinical Court of Justice.

Beyadcha Afkid Ruchi: Lit., "In Your hand I entrust my soul," a bedtime prayer.

Bimah: Platform in the middle of a synagogue, primarily used for communal Torah reading.

Birkot Hashachar: The Morning Blessings, recited before the Morning Prayer.

Challah (pl. **challot**): Braided bread eaten on Shabbat and festivals.

Chametz: Leaven. Any fermented food or beverage which one is prohibited to consume, or possess, during Pesach.

Chasid: Lit., "pious man." Follower of Chasidism.

Chasidus: Philosophy and teaching of the Chasidic movement, as expounded by its leaders.

Chazzan: Reader or cantor in the synagogue.

Cheder: Lit., "room." School for junior boys, preparatory to the yeshivah.

Chevrah Kaddisha: (a) Burial society; (b) Elite circle of scholars and saints.

Chumash: Pentateuch.

Daven: To pray.

Davening: Prayers.

Ein Yaakov: Lit., "Fountain of Yaakov." A popular compilation of Aggadic passages from the Talmud, compiled by Rabbi Yaakov ben Shlomo ibn Chaviv (d. 1516).

Eliyahu Hanavi: Elijah the Prophet.

Eretz Yisrael: the Land of Israel.

Erev: Lit., "eve of." The day preceding a holy day, e.g. *Erev Shabbat* (Friday).

Farbrengen: informal get-together of the Chasidic brotherhood.

Galut: Exile.

Gan Eden: Garden of Eden.

Gaon: Lit., "genius." Title given to an exceptionally brilliant Talmudist.

Gehinom: Purgatory.

Hachnasat Orchim: Hospitality.

Haggadah: Lit., "Narrative." Book containing the service at the Passover *Seder*.

Hakafot (sing. **Hakafah**): Processions with the Torah around the *bimah* on Simchat Torah.

Halachic: According to the dictates of Jewish law.

Havdalah: Lit., "separation." Blessing over a cup of wine marking the conclusion of Shabbat.

Hekdesh: Communal boarding house offering free lodging to travelers and homeless paupers.

Kabbalah: Lit., "traditional or transmitted teachings." The teachings and doctrines dealing with the "secrets of the Torah" and mysteries of Creation, transmitted by Kabbalists through the generations. The *Zohar* is one of the basic books of Kabbalah.

Kaddish: Prayer for the souls of the departed.

Kashrut: Dietary laws.

Kedushah: Responsive prayer recited during the repetition of the *Amidah*, describing how the angels praise the Creator.

Kiddush: Blessing of sanctification marking the start of Shabbat and festivals.

Kuzari: Fundamental exposition of Jewish philosophy by R. Yehudah Halevi (c. 1080-1140), written in the form of debate between a rabbi and a heathen king.

Maariv: Evening prayer service.

Maftir: Final *aliyah* to the Torah on Shabbat, festivals and public fast days.

Maggid (pl. **Maggidim**): Preacher who arouses the audience to repentance and good deeds.

Maharal: Acronym for Rabbi Yehuda Loew (1512-1609), famed rabbi of Prague, Bohemia; celebrated Talmudist and philosopher.

Matan Torah: The giving of G-d's Law to the Jews at Mount Sinai.

Matzot (sing. **matzah**): Unleavened bread; the only kind of bread permitted on Pesach.

Mazal Tov: Lit., "Good luck." Popular greeting or blessing on a happy occasion.

Melava Malka: Festive meal eaten at the conclusion of Shabbat, escorting the Shabbat Queen.

Midrash: Homilectic explanations of Scripture by Sages of the Talmudic era.

Mikveh: Ritual immersion pool.

Minchah: Afternoon prayer service.

Minyan: Lit., "number" or "quorum." Congregation of at least ten male worshippers. (Colloq.: synagogue.)

Mishnah (pl. **Mishnayot**): The Oral Law, divided into six sections, compiled by Rabbi Yehudah Hanassi (c. 150 C.E.).

Mitzvah (pl. **Mitzvot**): Biblical commandments. There are 613 *mitzvot* in the Torah, of which 248 are positive commands, and 365 are prohibitions.

Modeh Ani: Lit., "I thank You." First prayer on arising in the morning.

Moshiach: Lit., "the anointed one." The Redeemer, who will usher in the final Redemption.

Mussar: "Ethics" or "admonition." The study of topics on admonition and self-improvement.

Nashim: Lit., "Women." Name of the third of the six orders of the *Mishnah*, dealing with the laws of marriage and other issues related to women.

Neilah: Concluding prayer of Yom Kippur, regarded as the spiritual climax of the entire year.

Nevelah: An animal that died without being ritually slaughtered, whose consumption is prohibited by Torah law.

Parush: Lit., "recluse." A scholar and pious man, devoting all his time to study and worship, and taking little or no interest in worldly matters.

Parsa: Talmudic measuring of distance, equivalent to approximately two and a half miles.

Pesachim: Talmudic tractate discussing the Passover laws.

Pidyon Nefesh: Lit., "redeeming the soul." Note presented to the Rebbe, wherein the Chasid asks for guidance and blessing.

Pidyon Shevuyim: Lit., "ransom of prisoners." The mitzvah of trying to obtain the release of captives.

Pilpul: Method of Talmudic study, consisting of exam-

ining all arguments pro and con of a given text, often involving reconciliation of apparent contradictory texts. The method is usually a means of sharpening the mind and erudition of the student.

Pirkei Avot: "Ethics of our Fathers." Mishnaic tractate devoted to moral and ethical refinement.

Rambam: Rabbi Moshe ben Maimon (Maimonides), famous Talmudist, codifier, philosopher and physician (1135-1204); author of *Mishneh Torah* or *Yad Hachazakah, Sefer Hamitzvot,* and *Moreh Nevuchim.*

Rashi: Rabbi Shlomo Yitzchaki, famous expounder of Scripture and Talmud (1040-1105).

Rav: Rabbi.

Rosh Chodesh: Beginning of a new Jewish month.

Ruach Hakodesh: Divine spirit.

Shliach Mitzvah: An emmisary sent to perform a good deed.

Seder: Lit., "order." The home service on the first two nights of Pesach.

Pardes: Anthological work of

Kabbalah by Rabbi Moshe Cordovero, 1522-1570, known by the acrostic *Ramak*. He was the leader of a prominent Kabbalistic school in Safed and is regarded as one of the most important and lucid expositors and systematists of Jewish mysticism.

Sefer Torah: Torah Scroll.

Seudah Shlishit: Lit., "the third meal." The third of the Shabbat meals, held in the afternoon.

Seudat Mitzvah: A meal celebrating the fulfillment of a particular mitzvah.

Shacharit: Morning prayer service.

Shamash: Caretaker of a synagogue.

Shema: First word of "Hear, O Israel, the L-rd is our G-d, the L-rd is One," by which this verse is referred to. Also, three-paragraph Biblical text recited at least twice daily.

Shofar: Ram's horn sounded on Rosh Hashanah.

Shavuot: Festival commemorating the giving of the Torah on Mount Sinai celebrated on the 6th of the Hebrew month of *Sivan*.

Shul: Synagogue.

Simchat Torah: The festival of Rejoicing with the Torah, celebrated on the 23rd of the Hebrew month of *Tishrei*.

Tachnun: Prayers of supplication recited after the *Amidah*.

Tallit: Prayer shawl with four fringes.

Tanya: Famous philosophical work by Rabbi Schneur Zalman of Liadi, in which the principles of Chabad Chasidus are expounded. The name is derived from the initial word of this work. Also called *Likkutei Amarim* (*Collection of Sayings*).

Tefillin: Phylacteries, made of leather boxes and straps, consisting of the *shel yad* (hand tefillin) and the *shel rosh* (head tefillin).

Tehillim: Book of Psalms.

Teshuvah: Lit., "return." Repentance.

Tikkun Chatzot: Midnight prayer lamenting the destruction of the Holy Temple in Jerusalem and the ensuing exile.

Torah Tziva: Biblical verse first taught to young children, stressing the share of all Jews in G-d's Torah.

Tosfot: Lit., "Additions." Comments and interpretations of the Talmud composed by the famous scholars, the *Baalei Hatosfot*, as "additions" to the commentary of Rashi.

Tosfot Yom Tov: Commentary on the *Mishnah* by Rabbi Yom Tov Lipmann Heller (1579-1654), a disciple of Maharal, and head of the *beit din* in Prague, Vienna, and Cracow.

Treifah: An animal that is not healthy enough to live for twelve months, whose consumption is prohibited by Torah law.

Tzaddik (pl. **Tzaddikim**): Lit., "righteous." A very pious man; leader of a Chasidic group.

Tzitzit: Fringes on each of the four corners of the *tallit*.

Yahrzeit: Anniversary of the day of passing.

Yetzirah: Lit, "Formation." Third of the four supernal worlds.

Yeshivah: Talmudic academy.

Yevamot: Talmudic tractate discussing the laws of a childless widow having to marry her deceased husband's brother.

Yom Kippur: Day of Atonement, the 10th day of the Hebrew month of *Tishrei*.

Yom Kippur Katan: "Minor" Yom Kippur, observed on the day preceding *Rosh Chodesh*; a day conducive to repentance.

Yoshon: Grain harvested before the grain sacrifice offered in the *Beit Hamikdash* on Shavuot. It is forbidden to eat "new" grain, harvested before this sacrifice. Even today, many observe this, as a custom.

Zohar: Lit., "Brightness." The principal work of Kabbalah, the author of which is Rabbi Shimon bar Yochai, a Talmudic Sage of the second century. It is arranged after the Torah portions, and is written in Hebrew and Aramaic; it contains commentaries and interpretations of the Torah, prayers and customs, and profound doctrines and teachings concerning the purpose of Creation, the human soul, and various spiritual aspects of life.

Sources

A LIFE OF RADIANCE

Blessed Beginnings: *Sefer Hasichot 5697* pp. 161-162.

In the Forest: At three months of age: *Keter Shem Tov, Hosafot* # 280. *Sefer Hasichot 5703* pp. 165-167.

Ingenious Concepts: *Igrot Kodesh* vol. 4, p. 292, *Sefer Hasichot 5703*, p. 152.

> **Concern, not Condemnation:** Rebuking G-d: *Sefer Hasichot 5696*, pp. 34-39. "May a blessing come upon him": *Igrot Kodesh* vol. 4, p. 292.

> **Encourage Tehillim and Divine Praise:** A Visit from Eliyahu Hanavi: *Sefer Hasichot 5703*, pp 167-8. The Porush: *Sefer Hamaamarim Yiddish*, p. 138 ff. (See also *Likkutei Sichot* vol. 7, pp. 135-8.)

> **Uplift the Sincere and the Simple:** *Sefer Hasichot 5701*, pp. 155-6. *Sefer Hasichot 5706-10*, p. 421.

> **Bolster Economic Stability:** *Igrot Kodesh* vol. 3, p. 74 (see also vol. 6, p. 253).

> **Educational Involvement:** Fundraising: *Sefer Hazichronot* vol. 2, pp. 200-1. *Sefer Hasichot 5701*, pp. 156-7. Vicious dogs: *Sichot Kodesh, Bereishit 5724* (Gathering II). Improving parent-child relationships: *Sefer Hazichronot* vol. 1, p. 101.

Rabbi Hirsh Leib: *Sefer Hazichronot* vol. 2, p. 181.
A Decade of Spiritual Gain: *Hatamim* pp. 19-21, p. 248.
End of an Era: Ibid. pp. 17-18.
The Two Stories: Ibid. pp. 14-15.
  Reluctant revelation: Ibid. pp. 16-19, p. 250, p. 251, p. 20, p. 23, p. 25, p. 24, p 348.
The Twofold Approach: Ibid. p. 349, p. 447, p. 347, p. 448, p. 451, p. 455.
The Inner Circle: *Sefer Hasichot 5696*, p. 20, *Hatamim* p. 340, p. 344, p. 451, p. 454, p. 455,
Winds of Opposition: Ibid. p. 125, pp. 24-5, p. 340, p. 444, p. 125, p. 124, p. 452-3, p. 560.
Final Days: *Likkutei Dibburim* vol. 4, p. 1054. *Sefer Hasichot 5703*, p. 169. *Torat Shalom*, p. 46. *Hatamim*, p. 562, p. 561, Testimonial of the *Maggid: Maamarei Admur Hazaken Haketzarim*, p. 531. (See also *Sefer Hachakirah*, 65a.)
Note: Though the Baal Shem Tov's passing occurred on Shavuot, the exact date—the first or second day of the festival—remained shrouded in doubt for many years. Much later, Rabbi Schneur Zalman of Liadi commented that the passing was on a Wednesday. Since the second day of Shavuot cannot occur on a Wednesday, it is evident that the passing occurred on the first day of Shavuot. (See *Torat Menachem 5711*, vol. 2 p. 148.)

THE FOUNDATIONS OF CHASIDUS

Innovative Teachings:
  Sanctity of the Words of Torah: *Sefer Hasichot 5697*, p. 197. "Enter the *teiva*"—*Igrot Kodesh* vol. 3, p. 199 ff. *Tehillim* saves a town—*Sefer Hasichot 5702*, p. 158. "Who can recount G-d's greatness?"—*Maamarei Admur Hazaken, Ketuvim* vol. 1 p. 95. *Likkutei Sichot* vol. 4, p. 1310. Hirshel the digger—*Sefer Hamaamarim 5709*, p. 87. The Tzemach Tzedek finds salvation—*Igrot Kodesh* vol. 4, p. 268.
  Divine Providence: When two Jews meet—*Igrot Kodesh* vol. 8, p. 100 ff. Everything is a lesson—ibid. vol. 3, p. 289. To move a leaf—*Sefer Hamaamarim Kuntresim* vol. 2, p. 557.

How the grass sways—*Sefer Hamaamarim 5696*, p. 120. To make His Name dwell there: *Sefer Hasichot 5697*, p. 191.

Within the Simplest Jew: The greatest scholar—*Sefer Hasichot 5705*, p. 92. (See also *Igrot Kodesh* vol. 6, p. 399; *Sefer Hasichot 5705*, p. 109.) Generating great delight— *Sefer Hasichot 5706*, p. 3. An only child—*Likkutei Sichot* vol. 3, p. 982. The Jewish body—*Sefer Hamaamarim Yiddish*, p. 212. The fiery bush—*Sefer Hasichot 5702*, pp. 46-7. The hand-*tefillin*—*Sefer Hasichot 5700*, p. 133. A guarded grapevine—*Sefer Hazichronot* vol. 1, p. 53. Sukkot joy—*Sefer Hasichot 5706*, p. 3. Had he only known—*Sefer Hasichot 5696*, p. 148. Avraham of Chasidus—*Likkutei Dibburim*, vol. 4, p. 1582.

LESSONS IN SINCERITY: Chasidus for the simple—*Sefer Hamaamarim Yiddish*, p. 15. "I love the simple"— *Igrot Kodesh*, vol. 3. p. 285. Pesach the water-carrier—*Sefer Hasichot 5700*, p. 133. Two interpretations—*Sefer Hamaamarim Yiddish*, p. 212. Stronger than a *shofar*—*Sefer Hasichot 5705*, p. 6. "Father! Save your children"—*Likkutei Dibburim* vol. 1, pp. 145-146. The Yom Kippur rooster—*Kuntres Torat Hachasidut* p. 5-6, *Sefer Hasichot 5701*, p. 158.

A LASTING VISION: *Igrot Kodesh* vol. 3, p. 451.

THE INTERNAL DIFFERENCE: *Sefer Hamaamarim Yiddish* p. 215.

Unconditional Love Toward Fellow Jews: G-d's courtyard— *Sefer Hasichot 5696*, p. 20. G-d's children—*Igrot Kodesh* vol. 3, p. 554. Empathy for all—ibid. vol. 5, p. 101. Mirroring ourselves—*Hatamim*, p. 740. Self-negation— *Igrot Kodesh* vol. 5, p. 88. Seventy, eighty years—ibid. vol. 3, pp. 174 ff; *Sefer Hasichot 5705*, p. 67. The limits of trust and faith—*Igrot Kodesh* vol. 3, p. 76. Rivaling the angel Michael—*Sefer Hasichot 5705*, p. 68. The power of a sigh—*Sefer Hasichot 5703*, p. 161.

INNER INTERPRETATIONS: Three Novel Interpretations —*Igrot Kodesh* vol. 4, p. 96. Rebuke your fellow—

ibid. vol. 3, p. 278. Torah without work—*Sefer Hasichot 5700*, p. 115. Who works In mighty waters—*Sefer Hazichronot* vol. 2, p. 427. Dividing a lost cloak—ibid. vol. 2, p. 426.

HIS ENDURING LESSON: Loving every Jew—*Sefer Hamaamarim 5710*, p. 86. With *cheder* children—ibid. and *Sefer Hamaamarim 5709*, p. 87. A worthy portion in *Gan Eden*—*Sefer Hamaamarim 5703*, p. 161. The Arizal and the Baal Shem Tov—*Igrot Kodesh* vol. 8, p. 110. Revolutionizing *ahavat yisrael*—*Sefer Hasichot 5705*, p. 117. Hearing every sigh—*Sefer Hasichot 5700*, p. 115. Rabbi Mordechai Bayever—*Igrot Kodesh* vol. 3, p. 269. His inestimable influence—ibid. vol. 9, p. 367-8.

Initiated Intervention: *Sefer Hatoldot Admur Harayatz*, vol. 1, p. 128.

Humbling the Angels: *Sefer Hasichot 5699*, pp. 317-8.

THE POWER OF SINCERITY

Sincere Blessings: *Sefer Hasichot 5704*, p. 4.

Sincere Words: The hide tanner—ibid, p. 98. The third Shabbat meal: *Keter Shem Tov*, # 386.

Sincere Interpretations: The horse dealers—*Sefer Hasichot 5702*, p. 3. Rain for Mezibush—*Keter Shem Tov*, # 385. The meaning of *Amen yehay shmay rabbah*—*Sefer Hasichot 5704*, p. 140.

Sincere Faith: *Sefer Hasichot 5701*, p.132.

Sincere Tears: *Igrot Kodesh* vol. 3, p. 262 ff.

Sincere Joy: Ibid. vol. 3, pp. 72-76

Sincere Charity: *Sefer Hasichot 5701*, p. 39.

Sincere Reaction: *Sefer Hasichot 5696*, p. 148; *Sichot Kodesh, B'haalotecha 5727.*

Sincere Kindness: *Sefer Hamaamarim 5711*, pp. 309-316.

The Sincere Porter: Hirshel Goat: *Sefer Hamaamarim 5709*, pp. 94-97.

SPREADING THE WELLSPRINGS

Denburg: *Sefer Hatoldot Admur Harayatz* vol. 1, p. 126
Kalisk: *Igrot Kodesh* vol. 3, p. 170 ff.
Slutsk: *Sefer Hazichronot* vol. 2, ch. 73 ff, with additional details from *Sefer Hasichot 5702*, pp. 33 & 127.

NEW REVELATIONS, NEW TEACHINGS

The *Maggid*: Meeting the Baal Shem Tov—*Keter Shem Tov*, # 424. The sinner's staff—*Hatamim*, p. 122-3. Explaining Divine punishment—*Igrot Kodesh* vol. 3, p. 557. The Baal Shem Tov's *pidyon*—*Igrot Kodesh Admur Hazaken*, p. 205.
The Great Mission: *Likkutei Dibburim*, vol. 4, p. 1167.
Illumination and Instruction: The warm icicles—*Sefer Hasichot 5700*, p. 174. Torn like a fish—*Igrot Kodesh* vol. 6, p. 112-3. The human ox—*Sefer Hamaamarim 5698*, p. 207.
Real Remembrance: *Sefer Hamaamarim 5711*, p. 304-9.
Rewarding the Righteous: Rabbi Shimon the water carrier—*Sefer Hasichot 5701*, p. 101. Rabbi Yaakov *Shamash*—ibid. 5701, p. 152. The ninetieth birthday—ibid, p. 96. Rabbi Yaakov Yosef—*Sefer Hasichot 5700*, p. 133.
The Sound of the *Shofar*: *V'Kacha, 5637*, ch. 70.
Spiritual Shoes: *Sefer Hasichot 5701*, p. 31. (See also *Sichot Kodesh, Simchat Torah & Bereshit 5731*.)
Relived Again: *Likkutei Sichot* vol. 6, p. 189.
Spiritual Murder: *Igrot Kodesh*, vol. 6, p. 112.
On Song and Joy: *Igrot Kodesh* vol. 3 p. 219. *Sefer Hasichot 5702*, p. 122.
Timeless Time: *Derech Mitzvotecha* p. 59a and further notes in the addendum.
The Scholarly Debate: *Igrot Kodesh*, vol. 3, p. 269 ff.
Validated By Heaven: *Igrot Kodesh*, vol. 4, pp. 96-97. See also *Sefer Hasichot 5696*, pp. 133-134.
Joy and Sorrow: *Sefer Hasichot 5696*, p. 132-133.

A Kosher *Sukkah*: *Sichot Kodesh*, second day of *Sukkot*, 5725.

WONDERS AND MIRACLES

Curing the Mute: *Sefer Hasichot* 5703, p. 158.
Dream Deliverance: *Keter Shem Tov*, # 361.
The Miracle *Sefer Torah*: *Igrot Kodesh* vol. 6, p. 281.
With His Touch Alone: *Igrot Kodesh* vol. 9, p. 98.

Bibliography

Derech Mitzvotecha: Chasidic explanations of the reasons for certain *mitzvot*, by Rabbi Menachem Mendel Schneersohn, the third Lubavitcher Rebbe, the "Tzemach Tzedek."

Hatamim: Quarterly journal issued in Warsaw, 1936-1939.

Igrot Kodesh: Letters by Rabbi Yosef Yitzchak Schneersohn, the sixth Lubavitcher Rebbe; fourteen volumes.

Keter Shem Tov: A collection of teachings of Rabbi Yisrael Baal Shem Tov, culled from the writings of his students.

Likkutei Dibburim: Anthology of talks and writings of Rabbi Yosef Yitzchak Schneersohn. References to this book refer to the four-volume Yiddish edition.

Likkutei Sichot: Edited talks by Rabbi Menachem M. Schneerson, the Lubavitcher Rebbe; thirty-nine volumes.

Maamarei Admur Hazaken: Discourses by Rabbi Schneur Zalman of Liadi; twenty-four volumes.

Sichot Kodesh: Unedited talks of Rabbi Menachem M. Schneerson, the Lubavitcher Rebbe, from the years 5710-5740; fifty volumes.

Sefer Hachakirah: A work containing proofs of the continual creation of the world, following the methods of Jewish philosophy, Kabbalah, and Chasidus. Authored by Rabbi Menachem Mendel Schneersohn, the "Tzemach Tzedek."

Sefer Hamaamarim: Chasidic discourses by Rabbi Yosef Yitzchak Schneersohn.

Sefer Hamaamarim Yiddish: Chasidic discourses in Yiddish by Rabbi Yosef Yitzchak Schneersohn; one volume.

Sefer Hasichot: Talks by Rabbi Yosef Yitzchak Schneersohn. References to this book refer to the Yiddish edition.

Sefer Hatoldot Admur Harayatz: Biography of Rabbi Yosef Yitzchak Schneersohn; four volumes.

Sefer Hazichronot: Memoirs of Rabbi Yosef Yitzchak Schneersohn; two volumes.

Torat Menachem: Unedited talks of Rabbi Menachem M. Schneerson, the Lubavitcher Rebbe, from the years 5710-5720; twenty-five volumes.

Torat Shalom—Sefer Hasichot: Talks by Rabbi Shalom DovBer Schneersohn, the fifth Lubavitcher Rebbe; one volume.

V'Kacha: Series of discourses delivered by Rabbi Shmuel Schneersohn during the year 5637 (1877), named for its opening word.

Related Works

published by Kehot Publication Society

Keter Shem Tov

A classic Chasidic work containing collected sayings, teachings, and directives from the founder of the Chasidic movement, first printed more than 200 years ago. A newly typeset, thoroughly researched edition (2004), entitled *Keter Shem Tov Hashalem*, features copious corrections, footnotes and cross-references.

Tzava'at Harivash

An anthology of wondrous teachings and instructions in serving the Creator through Torah study, prayer and other means, which are attributed to the Baal Shem Tov and his successor, R. Dov Ber, the Maggid of Mezritch.

The 1998 edition also contains a collection of explanations from the Lubavitcher Rebbe, annotations, an index and more.

Tzava'at Harivash;
The Testament of Rabbi Israel Baal Shem Tov

Translated and annotated by Jacob Immanuel Schochet.

This first complete English rendition, by a foremost authority on Chasidism and Jewish Mysticism, is enhanced by source-references, brief commentaries, notes on the passages that were perceived to be controversial, and a comprehensive introduction. (1998)

Lubavitcher Rabbi's Memoirs;
The memoirs of Rabbi Yosef Y. Schneersohn
Translated by Nissan Mindel
    Enter the magical world of mystics and scholars, and discover the fascinating history of the origins of the Chasidic movement. 2 volumes. (2004)